BLESSING OR CURSE:

YOU CAN CHOOSE!

FREEDOM FROM PRESSURES YOU
THOUGHT YOU HAD TO LIVE WITH

Books by Derek Prince

Biography
Appointment in Jerusalem
Pages from My Life's Book

Guides to the Life of Faith
Baptism in the Holy Spirit
Blessing or Curse: You Can Choose!
Chords from David's Harp
Does Your Tongue Need Healing?
Extravagant Love
Faith to Live By
Fasting
Fatherhood
God Is a Matchmaker
God's Medicine Bottle
God's Plan for Your Money
God's Remedy for Rejection
How to Fast Successfully
If You Want God's Best
Life's Bitter Pool
Objective for Living: To Do God's Will
Prayers and Proclamations
Protection from Deception
Shaping History Through Prayer & Fasting
Spiritual Warfare
Thanksgiving, Praise and Worship
The Divine Exchange
The Grace of Yielding
The Holy Spirit in You
The Marriage Covenant
They Shall Expel Demons
Uproar in the Church

Systematic Bible Exposition
Foundations for Righteous Living
Christian Foundations Bible Correspondence Course
In Search of Truth
Self-Study Bible Course
The Destiny of Israel and the Church
The Last Word on the Middle East

DEREK PRINCE

BLESSING OR CURSE:

YOU CAN CHOOSE!

Derek Prince Ministries – UK
Harpenden, Hertfordshire

BLESSING OR CURSE: YOU CAN CHOOSE!

Copyright © 1990 Derek Prince Ministries – International

Published by Derek Prince Ministries – UK 1998

First published in the UK by Word (UK) Ltd, 1990

All rights reserved.

No part of this book may be reproduced or transmitted in any form or by any means, electronic or mechanical, including photocopying, recording, or by means of any information storage and retrieval system, without permission in writing from the publisher.

ISBN 1 901144 02 X

To protect the privacy of some of the individuals referred to, names of persons and places, and some other details, have in a few cases been changed.

Unless otherwise noted, Scripture quotations in this publications are from The New King James Version (NKJ). Copyright © 1979, 1980, 1982 Thomas Nelson, Inc., Publishers. Other versions quoted are: the King James Version (KJV); the New American Standard (NASB); the New International Version (NIV); The Living Bible (TLB).

Front cover illustration: Saskia Vreede

Printed in the United Kingdom by
Redwood Books, Trowbridge, Wiltshire

Derek Prince Ministries
http://www.derekprince.com

This day I call heaven and earth
as witnesses against you that I have
set before you life and death,
blessings and curses.
Now choose life, so that you and
your children may live . . .
Deuteronomy 30:19, NIV

CONTENTS

FOREWORD

In 1978, shortly before our marriage, Derek and I were lying on the beach in Fort Lauderdale, Florida. I said to Derek, "Would you pray for my legs? They hurt so much." Immediately he knelt, placed his hands on the calves of my legs – and began to speak to them:

> "Thank you, legs. I want you to know I appreciate you. You have carried Ruth safely everywhere she needed to go – and now you have brought her to me. Thank you, legs!"

I thought that was an extraordinary way for a serious Bible teacher to pray for his fiancee! But the pain subsided.

Later Derek told me that he thought he had been "un-saying" something I might have said about my legs. I recalled a scene in the girls' room at my high school when I was 15 or 16. Another girl had come in and stood combing her hair. I looked at her shapely legs, and at my own heavy calves and ankles, and said, "I *hate* my legs!" In effect, I had placed a curse on my own legs!

Together Derek and I broke the curse I had pronounced on my own legs more than 30 years before. I thought that was the end of the story.

Nine years later I found myself being rushed by ambulance to the hospital in Jerusalem with thrombosis (blood clots) in both legs. A pulmonary embolism (blood clot which moved to the lungs) came near to taking my life. It seemed there was still a curse or curses on my legs – and perhaps on my very person.

Since then, now nearly three years, I have battled for my health – and my life. It was painfully obvious to both of us that supernatural forces were at work in my physical body. As we worked together on this book, we realised that every mark of a curse referred to in Chapter 5 applied to me and/or my family. Releasing myself from the self-imposed curse had been only the *beginning* of the process. The Holy Spirit revealed ancestral curses, curses resulting from involvement in the occult, curses resulting from specific sins, and much more.

Renouncing any and all curses has been a lengthy process, but the Holy Spirit has been wonderfully patient and thorough. Often He has given supernatural direction through words of knowledge and words of wisdom. We have enlisted the prayer support of thousands of Christians around the world. Our way of thinking about the power of Scripture – and about ourselves – has changed remarkably.

Many times I have asked God this question: "Why did You give Derek Prince a wife with so many physical problems, and so many curses over her life?" (Those who have read *God Is a Matchmaker* will recall that God specifically chose me to be

Derek's wife.) I have not received a direct answer to that question, but I am so grateful that God took me, *just as I was*, so He could receive the glory as He releases me and heals me.

Furthermore, Derek and I can affirm: We have proven the truths contained in this book in our own experience! My health is not yet perfect, but I know in reality that the blessing promised to Abraham is *mine*. As with Abraham, it has been a pilgrimage.

Our prayer is that *Blessing or Curse: You Can Choose!* will release you – and others whom you seek to help – into the full liberty which is your inheritance in Jesus Christ!

Ruth Prince

SECTION 1
BLESSING AND CURSES

INTRODUCTION

It could be you and your family. Or the family next door. Or the person who works with you. Whoever it may be, their life is a history of disappointments, frustrations, and even tragedies. Somehow the story never ends.

Conversely, we all know families who are similar in background and social position – and yet trouble never seems to touch them. They are almost "too good to be true."

In both cases, there are invisible forces at work which determine each person's destiny, whether for better or for worse. The Bible identifies these respectively as *blessings* and *curses*. Furthermore, it shows us how to relate to these forces in such a way that we can enjoy the beneficial effects of the one and protect ourselves from the harmful effects of the other.

A scriptural understanding of both blessings and curses, and how they work, will give you a totally new perspective on your own life, and an answer to problems that have hitherto perplexed and frustrated you.

1
WRESTLING WITH
SHADOWS

To the superficial observer, human life presents a confused mingling of light and shadow, arranged according to no recognisable pattern, governed by no discernable laws. Across this scene two men may start out walking side by side. Similar in background and ability, they are headed in the same direction. Yet one walks almost always in the light of success and fulfilment. The other, close by him, scarcely sees the light. He is continually overshadowed by failure and frustration, and his life is snuffed out at an untimely age.

Neither of these men understands the forces at work in their lives. The sources of light and shadow are hidden to them both. Probably they have never even considered the possibility that both light and shadow may have their source in previous generations.

The Bible speaks plainly about these forces. In fact, it has a great deal to say about them. It calls them respectively *blessings* and *curses*.

Let us look closer, for a moment, at the man under the shadows. He does all the right things: changes his job or place of residence; acquires further vocational skills; studies all the latest literature on positive thinking. Perhaps he even takes a course on how to release some mysterious "potential" within himself.

Yet success continually eludes him. His children are rebellious, his marriage under strain, accidents and illnesses are routine. His cherished goals slip through his fingers like water through the fingers of a drowning man. He is "haunted" by a sense of inevitable failure, which he can perhaps postpone, but never overcome.

All his life he has the sense of struggling against something he cannot identify – something amorphous and elusive. He feels at times as if he is wrestling with a shadow. No matter how hard he struggles, he cannot pinpoint the cause of his problem or get a grip on it. Often he feels like giving up.

"What's the use?" he exclaims. "Nothing ever goes right for me! My father had the same problems. He was a failure, too!"

The person under the shadows could just as well be a woman, of course. She has married young and started out with all sorts of plans for a successful marriage and a happy home. She finds herself, however, on an invisible "teeter-totter" – "up" one day and "down" the next. Physically, she goes from one problem to another, always on the verge of health, but never quite achieving it. Her son begins to abuse drugs and then her husband leaves her. One day she wakes up to the shocking realisation that she herself has become an alcoholic.

Like the man under the shadows, this woman, too, did all the right things. She studied books on nutrition and child psychology. In her pursuit of success, she goaded herself on from one effort to the next – each one demanding all the strength that she could muster. Yet she watched other women, with less motivation or qualifications, achieve the goals which she herself could never attain.

As you look closer at the person under the shadows, perhaps you see something that reminds you of yourself. You feel as if you are looking at your own life – but somehow from a point outside yourself. With a shock you begin to wonder if the cause of your problems could be the same: *a curse going back to preceding generations.*

Or again, it may not be yourself that you see, but someone close to you – a spouse or a family member or a dear friend. You have often agonised over this person and longed for some ray of hope, but always in vain. Now you are confronted with a possible explanation of the shadows, which is a new idea to you. Could the root of the problem really be a curse?

Your mind goes back to events and situations in your life or your family which never seemed to make sense. You tried many times to dismiss them from your thoughts, but never completely succeeded. You realise that you need to know more. *Suppose I am the one under a curse*, you may say to yourself. *What can I do? What could be its source?*

A curse could also be likened to a long, evil arm stretched out from the past. It rests upon you with a dark, oppressive force that inhibits the full expression of your personality. You never feel completely free to be yourself. You sense that you have potential within you that is never fully developed. You always expect more of yourself than you are able to achieve.

Or again, that long, evil arm may have the effect of tripping you up as you walk. Your way seems clear before you, but from time to time you stumble – yet you cannot see what it was you stumbled over. For some uncanny reason, the moments at which you stumble are those when you are within reach of attaining some long-sought goal. Yet your goal eludes you.

Actually, the word *uncanny* could be likened to a red warning light. You experience events or situations for which you can find no natural or logical reason. It seems that there is some force at work that is not completely subject to the usual laws of nature or of averages.

There is one word that sums up the effects of a curse: *frustration*. You reach a certain level of achievement in your life and everything looks set for a bright future. You have all the obvious qualifications – and yet something goes wrong! So you start all over again, and reach the same level as before, but once again things go wrong. After this happens several times, you realise that this is the pattern of your life. Yet you cannot see any obvious reason for it.

Many people have shared with me the story of a life that has a similar pattern. The individual details may differ, but the pattern is there. Often such people say something like, "The same thing always happened to my father. I feel as if I'm reliving his frustrations," or, "I can hear my grandfather saying again and again, 'Things never go right for me.'"

This pattern may occur in various areas of people's lives: business, career, health or finance. Nearly always it has some kind of negative effect on personal relationships – especially marriage and family. Frequently, too, it affects not just one isolated individual, but a larger social group. Most often this would be a family, but it can extend to a wider circle, such as a community or a nation.

It would be misleading, however, to suggest that a curse always causes a person to fail. A person may achieve what appears to be real success and yet be plagued by frustration, never enjoying the fruits of success.

On a ministry journey in Southeast Asia I met an intelligent, well-educated female judge, who was descended from royalty.

She knew Jesus personally as Saviour and was not conscious of any unconfessed sin in her life. Yet she told me that she was not truly satisfied. Her successful career and her high social position had not brought her personal fulfilment.

As I talked with her, I discovered that she was descended from many generations of idol worshipers. I explained to her that, according to Exodus 20:3-5, God had pronounced a curse on idol worshippers down to the third and fourth generations. Then I showed her how to receive release from this curse through Jesus her Saviour.

Sometimes curses may not have their origin in previous generations. They may be the result of deeds or events in your own lifetime. Or it may be that a curse from previous generations has been compounded by things you yourself have done. Whatever the source of your problem, however, one thing is certain: You are struggling with something that you can neither identify nor understand.

Like that judge, you, too, may have tasted success. You do indeed know the sweetness of it – but it never lasts! Suddenly, for no reason you can explain, you are dissatisfied. Depression settles over you like a cloud. All your achievements seem so insubstantial.

You look at others who appear content in similar circumstances, and you ask yourself, *What's wrong with me? Why don't I ever experience real fulfilment?*

Perhaps at this point your reaction is something like this: *Some of these descriptions really fit me. Does that mean there is no hope for me? Do I have to go on like this for the rest of my life?*

No, there is hope for you! Do not be discouraged. As you read on, you will discover that God has provided a remedy, and you will be given simple, practical instructions on how to apply the remedy in your own life.

Meanwhile, you will find encouragement in the following letters which I received from two people who listened to my radio Bible teaching programme on the theme "From Curse to Blessing." The first letter is from a man and the second from a woman.

> I listened to your messages on the curse and I found out that I had been under one for years and never knew it. I was never able to be successful in life, and constantly suffered from feelings of homosexuality, though I never fuelled the feelings into action. I have been a Christian for 10 years now but because of the curse was never able to get as close to God as I wanted to. I became very depressed.
>
> Since I have been freed from this curse I have felt so free in Jesus and alive in Him. I have never felt so close to God!

*   *   *

> Thank you for your recent broadcasts on curses and your booklet "From Curse to Blessing." My life has been greatly changed by them.
>
> For most of my life I have been troubled by recurring depression, and altogether for five years I have been under the care of a psychiatrist.
>
> This spring a lady prayed with me and for me and I renounced all involvement with the occult, such as tarot cards and tea leaves. Praise the Lord, the beginning of real freedom!
>
> Then I heard your broadcasts on being under a curse without really knowing it and prayed with you as you

prayed the prayer of release from curses. Now I am free!

It is as if a dam has broken and God can move in my spirit. The blockage is gone and I have grown so much spiritually in a few weeks that I can only praise Him for His blessing. Sometimes I weep when I think about all He has done and is doing for me, and it is such a relief to be able to relax.

Truly, we worship a wonderful God!

2
INVISIBLE BARRIERS

In previous years I spent much time counselling people like those described in the previous chapters. But it was often a frustrating task. Certain people would progress spiritually up to a point, and then they seemed to encounter an invisible barrier. It was not that they lacked sincerity or dedication. In fact, they often seemed more sincere and dedicated than others who made better progress. They would accept the counsel I gave them and try to put it into practice, but the results were – to say the least – disappointing, both for them and for me.

After dealing with such a case, I would find myself praying, "Lord, why is it that I cannot better help this person? Is there something I don't understand – something more that I need to know?" After a while, I realised that God was answering my prayer. He began to draw aside a veil and to reveal a world of powerful forces that do not operate according to natural laws. The revelation did not come all at once, but step by step as I discerned a single thread running through a series of apparently unconnected incidents.

One key incident occurred when I was a guest speaker in a Presbyterian church. I had come to the end of my prepared message, and was uncertain how to proceed. As I remained standing behind the pulpit, I noticed a family – father, mother and teenage daughter – on the front row to my left. The thought came to me, *There is a curse over that family.* This was not related to the theme of my message, or to anything I had in mind at that time. Yet the impression would not leave me: *There is a curse over that family.*

Finally, after some moments of hesitation, I stepped out from behind the pulpit and went over to the father. I explained to him what I was feeling and asked if he would like me to revoke the curse and release the family from it in the name of Jesus. He replied immediately that he would. It was the first time I had ever done anything like this, and I was quite surprised that the man so readily accepted my statement. Only later did I come to understand why.

I stepped back behind the pulpit and said a brief prayer out loud, breaking the curse over the family. I was not touching any member of the family as I prayed, but when I concluded with the words *In the name of Jesus,* there was a distinct, visible, physical reaction in the whole family. A momentary shudder seemed to pass through each of them in turn.

At this point that I noticed that the girl, who was about 18 years old, had her left leg in a cast from above the thigh to the bottom of her foot. I went over to the father again and asked if he would like me to pray for his daughter's leg to be healed. Again he responded very positively, then added, "But you need to know that she has broken the same leg three times in eighteen months, and the doctors say it will not heal."

Today, such a statement – that a person had broken the same leg three times in eighteen months – would set off an alarm bell inside me warning that a curse was at work. At the time, however, I did not see any connection between a curse and such an unnatural series of accidents. I merely picked up the leg in its cast, held it in my hands, and prayed a simple prayer for healing.

Some weeks later I received a letter from the father, thanking me for what had happened. He said that when they took their daughter back to the clinic, a new X-ray showed that her leg had healed. Shortly afterward the cast was removed.

He also mentioned briefly a series of strange, unhappy incidents that had affected the life of his family, and this explained his readiness to acknowledge the need for the whole family to be released from a curse.

In the months that followed, my mind kept returning to this incident. I felt that there was something significant about the order in which the Holy Spirit had led me. First, He had revealed the curse over the family and had prompted me to revoke it. Only then had He released me to pray for the healing of the daughter's leg. If I had prayed for healing without first revoking the curse, would the leg have been healed?

The more I pondered this, the more I was convinced that the revoking of the curse was an essential prelude to the healing of the girl's leg. It was an invisible barrier which would have prevented the healing that God wanted her to receive.

All this seemed to tie in somehow with an incident in my own life. In 1904 my maternal grandfather had commanded a British expeditionary force sent to suppress the Boxer Rebellion in China. He had returned with various specimens of Chinese art, which became family heirlooms. In 1970, at the death of my mother, some of them passed by inheritance to me.

One of the most interesting items was a set of four exquisitely embroidered dragons, which found a place of honour on the walls of our living room. Their blend of colours – mainly purple and scarlet – was typically Oriental. They had five claws on each foot, which – an expert informed me – indicated that they were "imperial" dragons. And, because my grandfather had been very close to me, they brought back memories of my early years in their home.

About this time, I began to sense some kind of opposition to the success of my ministry which I could not define or identify. It manifested itself in various kinds of frustrations which were apparently unrelated, but which produced a cumulative pressure against me. I encountered barriers of communication that had never been there before with people close to me. Others on whom I had been relying failed to keep their commitments. A substantial legacy from my mother's estate was delayed interminably by a lawyer's inefficiency.

Eventually I set aside a period for intensive prayer and fasting. Quite soon, I began to notice a change in my attitude toward the dragons. From time to time, as I looked at them, a question would form in my mind: Who in the Bible is represented as a dragon? I had no doubt about the answer: Satan.[1]

This question would be followed by another: Is it appropriate for you, as a servant of Christ, to display in your home objects that typify Christ's great adversary, Satan? Again, the answer was clear: No! My inner struggle continued for a while, but finally I got rid of the dragons. I did this as a simple act of obedience, without any ulterior motive.

At that period I was serving as a Bible teacher to the Church at large, speaking to groups of various kinds throughout the United

1. See Revelation 12:1-12

States. My income, which came from the honoraria I received, was just sufficient to cover the basic needs of my family. Shortly after I got rid of the dragons, however, my financial position underwent a dramatic improvement. Without any special planning on my part, or any significant change in the nature or scope of my ministry, my income more than doubled. Also my long-delayed legacy finally came through.

I began to wonder if there was some undiscovered principle which linked this unexpected improvement in my personal finances with the healing of the girl with the broken leg. In the case of the girl, a curse over her family had been an invisible barrier to healing. When the barrier had been removed, healing had followed. In my case, too, perhaps there had been an invisible barrier – not to physical healing, but to the financial prosperity which proved to be an important element in God's plan for my life.

The more I pondered this, the more certain I became that those embroidered dragons had brought a curse into my house. By disposing of them, I had released myself from the curse and opened myself up to the blessing God had planned for me.

These changes enabled me to buy a home, which was to play a decisive part in the subsequent extension of my ministry. Nine years later, I sold that house for more than three times as much as I had paid for it! This money came exactly at a time when God was challenging me to major new financial commitments.

That experience with the dragons gave me new insight into the passage in Deuteronomy 7:25-26 where Moses warned Israel against any association with the idolatrous nations of Canaan:

> *"You shall burn the carved images of their gods with fire; you shall not covet the silver or gold that is on them, nor take it for yourselves, lest you be snared by it;*

for it is an abomination to the Lord your God.

"Nor shall you bring an abomination into your house, lest you be doomed to destruction like it; but you shall utterly detest it and utterly abhor it, for it is an accursed thing."

My embroidered dragons were not carved images, but they certainly were images of a false god who had been worshipped for millennia in China. By bringing them into my home, I had unknowingly exposed myself – and my family with me – to a curse. How grateful I was to the Holy Spirit for opening my eyes to what was at stake!

This led me to make a systematic study of the Bible's teaching on both blessings and curses. I was surprised by how much the Bible has to say about them. Words for *bless* or *blessing* occur about 410 times – excluding instances where the word in the original text merely has the meaning of "happy" or "fortunate" (as, for instance, in the Beatitudes). The word *curse,* in various forms, occurs about 230 times. This caused me to reflect how little teaching I had ever heard on this theme in all the years of my Christian experience. In fact, I could not recall hearing even one message that dealt systematically with this whole subject.

As a result of my study, I began to teach about curses in my public ministry. Each time I did this, I was surprised both by the powerful impact this teaching produced and by the number of people who obviously needed to hear it. Tapes from some of these meetings were circulated to other groups, and astonishing reports came back to me. Often it seemed that the message had transformed not merely the lives of individuals, but even whole congregations. Eventually I released three cassettes entitled "Curses: Cause and Cure."

Subsequently, on a trip to South Africa, I met a Jewish lady who had come to acknowledge Jesus as her Messiah. This lady – whom we will call Miriam – personally described to my wife, Ruth, and me the miracle she had experienced through listening to those three tapes.

Miriam had been working as executive secretary for a businessman who was president of his own company. She had discovered that her employer and all the executives in the company were in some strange cult that was led by a female "guru."

One day Miriam's employer handed her a cassette and said, "Here are some blessings that our guru has pronounced over us. Please type them." As she began to type, Miriam realised that the "blessings" were actually fortune-telling, with strong occult overtones. She explained to her employer that such things were contrary to her faith in the Lord Jesus and the Bible, and asked to be excused. Her employer was gracious and apologised for having asked her to do something against her conscience.

Almost immediately after this, Miriam began to develop acute pain in both hands. Her fingers curled up and became absolutely rigid. She was no longer able to carry out her tasks as a secretary. The pain was so intense that she could not sleep in the same bed as her husband, because every time he turned over, the movement of the bed caused unbearable agony in her fingers. X-ray diagnosis revealed that her problem was rheumatoid arthritis.

A Christian friend of Miriam's heard of her distress and brought her my tapes on "Curses" to listen to. Miriam was a rather sophisticated lady, sceptical about such things as curses, which she associated with the Middle Ages. She had wondered, however, if there was any connection between her refusal to type the "blessings" and the subsequent problem with her hands. Could it be that the guru had pronounced a curse on her? So she consented to listen, feeling like the proverbial drowning man "clutching at a straw."

When they reached the point in the third tape where I led people in a prayer of release from any curse over their lives, the cassette jammed. It would not go forward or backward, neither would it eject!

"Obviously, then, I can't pray the prayer!" Miriam responded.

Miriam's friend had previously typed out the concluding prayer of release, however, and had a copy with her. She insisted that Miriam read the prayer out loud. Once again Miriam's scepticism asserted itself. She could not see how reading words from a typed sheet could have any effect on the condition of her hands.

Eventually, however, Miriam yielded to her friend's insistence, and began to read the prayer out loud. As she did so, her fingers uncurled and became free. The pain ceased, and by the time she had finished reading the prayer, she was completely healed. The whole experience had lasted only a few minutes.

Later Miriam returned to her doctor, who had taken the first X-rays. A second set of X-rays revealed no trace of arthritis.

One feature of this incident is particularly significant. The prayer of release which Miriam read *made no reference to physical healing*. Her hands were healed solely as a result of praying for release from a curse.

Here was further, dramatic evidence that a curse can be a barrier to keep people from receiving healing. The same had been true of the girl with the broken leg. In my own case, on the other hand, an unsuspected curse had been keeping me from the level of prosperity that God had intended for me.

If a curse could be a barrier to blessings such as healing or prosperity, was it not possible – or even probable – that many other kinds of blessing were likewise being withheld for the same reason? It was on this basis that I set myself to seek the answers to three related questions:

First, how can we recognise that there is a curse operating in our lives?

Second, what must we do to revoke a curse and release ourselves from its consequences?

Third, how can we enter into the blessing of God?

The results of my search are presented in the following pages.

3

HOW BLESSINGS AND CURSES OPERATE

The forces that determine history fall into two categories: visible and invisible. It is the interplay of these two realms that determines the course of history. As long as we confine our attention to things that are visible and material, we will find ourselves confronted from time to time by events and situations that we cannot fully explain or control.

To the visible realm belong all the normal objects and events of the material universe. We are all familiar with this realm and feel at home in it, even though events often do not follow the course we would wish. For many people, the limits of their awareness do not extend further. Yet the Bible opens a door to another, invisible realm, which is not material, but spiritual. The forces at work in this realm exercise a continuous and decisive influence on events in the visible realm.

In 2 Corinthians 4:17-18 Paul delineates these two realms:

For our light affliction, which is but for a moment, is working for us a far more exceeding and eternal weight of glory,
   while we do not look at the things which are seen, but at the things which are not seen. For the things which are seen are temporary, but the things which are not seen are eternal.

The things that belong to the visible realm are transitory and impermanent. It is only in the invisible realm that we can find true and abiding reality. It is in this realm, too, that we discover the forces which will ultimately shape our destiny, even in the visible realm. Paul makes it clear that success in life depends upon being able to apprehend and relate to that which is invisible and spiritual.

Both blessings and curses belong to the invisible, spiritual realm. They are vehicles of supernatural, spiritual power. Blessings produce good and beneficial results; curses produce bad and harmful results. Both are major themes of Scripture. As already pointed out, the two words are mentioned in the Bible more than 640 times.

Two important features are common to both. First, their effect is seldom limited to the individual. It may extend to families, tribes, communities or whole nations. Second, once they are released, they tend to continue from generation to generation until something happens to cancel their effects. A number of both blessings and curses mentioned in the Bible in connection with the patriarchs have continued to work for nearly four thousand years and are still at work today.

This second feature of blessings and curses has important practical implications. There may be forces at work in our lives that have their origin in previous generations. Consequently, we may be confronted with recurrent situations or patterns of behaviour that cannot be explained solely in terms of what has happened in our lifetimes or personal experiences. The root cause may go back a long way in time, even thousands of years.

The main vehicle of both blessings and curses is *words*. Such words may be spoken or written or merely uttered inwardly. Scripture has much to say about the power of words. The book of Proverbs, in particular, contains many warnings as to how words may be used either for good or for evil. Here are just a few examples:

The hypocrite with his mouth destroys his neighbour,
But through knowledge the righteous will be delivered.
                                        Proverbs 11:9

There is one who speaks like the piercings of a sword,
But the tongue of the wise promotes health.
                                        Proverbs 12:18

A wholesome tongue is a tree of life,
But perverseness in it breaks the spirit.
                                        Proverbs 15:4

Death and life are in the power of the tongue,
And those who love it will eat its fruit.
                                        Proverbs 18:21

The apostle James also has much to say about the use of words. He points out that the tongue is a small member of the body, but the hardest of all to control:

Even so the tongue is a little member and boasts

great things. See how great a forest a little fire kindles!
*And the tongue is a fire, a world of iniquity. The
tongue is so set among our members that it defiles the
whole body, and sets on fire the course of nature; and it
is set on fire by hell.*

*With it we bless our God and Father, and with it we
curse men, who have been made in the similitude
[likeness] of God.*

*Out of the same mouth proceed blessing and cursing.
My brethren, these things ought not to be so.*

James 3:5-6, 9-10

James uses vivid imagery to emphasise the tremendous power
that words have to affect people and situations, either for good or
for evil. It is significant that he singles out both blessings and
curses as words that can be charged with this kind of almost
measureless power.

Words are not, however, the only channels through which the
spiritual power of blessings or curses may be transmitted. There
are various ways in which, at times, physical objects may become
vehicles for this kind of power.

In Exodus 30:22-33 the Lord gave instructions to Moses for
making a special anointing oil, which was to be used solely and
exclusively for anointing the Tabernacle and its furniture, and also
the priests who were to minister in the Tabernacle. In Leviticus
8:1-12 we read how this oil was applied. In verses 10-12 the
account concludes:

*Then Moses took the anointing oil, and anointed the
tabernacle and all that was in it, and sanctified them.*
*He sprinkled some of it on the altar seven times,
anointed the altar and all its utensils, and the laver and*

its base, to sanctify them.
And he poured some of the anointing oil on Aaron's
head and anointed him, to sanctify him.

The word *sanctify* in this passage means to "set apart to God, make holy." Thus the anointing oil became a vehicle to impart the blessing of holiness both to the Tabernacle and its furniture and to the priests who ministered in it.

Later in Israel's history, olive oil was used to impart appropriate blessing to the kings who were to rule the people on God's behalf. First Samuel 16:13 records how the prophet Samuel set David apart as God's chosen king:

Then Samuel took the horn of oil and anointed him in
the midst of his brothers; and the Spirit of the Lord
came upon David from that day forward.

The oil poured on David's head by Samuel became a vehicle through which the blessing of the Holy Spirit was released in his life to equip him for his task as king.

In the New Testament, the emblems used in the Lord's Supper likewise become vehicles of God's blessing to those who partake of them. In 1 Corinthians 10:16 Paul says:

The cup of blessing which we bless, is it not the
communion of the blood of Christ? The bread which we
break, is it not the communion of the body of Christ?

For those who partake with scriptural faith, these emblems transmit the blessing of God. Paul speaks specifically of "the cup of blessing" – that is, the cup that transmits the blessings of the new covenant to those who drink from it.

It must be emphasised, however, that in all the ordinances described above there is no room for "magic." The blessings are not inherent in the physical objects as such. They are imparted only to those who apprehend the will of God as revealed in Scripture, and who then by personal faith and obedience receive what is offered to them through the physical objects. Without faith and obedience, no blessing results.

On the contrary, in 1 Corinthians 11:29, Paul says concerning the emblems of the Lords Supper: "He who eats and drinks in an unworthy manner eats and drinks judgement to himself." Such, then, are the alternatives. Faith and obedience receive God's blessing through the emblems; unbelief and disobedience provoke God's judgement. In both cases alike, it is the physical objects used in the Lord's Supper through which the spiritual power is transmitted, whether it be for blessing or for judgement.

Numbers 5:11-31 describes an ordinance used to determine whether a man's wife has been unfaithful to him or not. The appropriate prayers and sacrifices are required, but the focus of the ordinance is on a cup of water, into which the priest mixes dust from the floor of the Tabernacle and ink, which he scrapes from a written curse. The woman is then required to drink the water.

If she is guilty, the outworking of the written curse will be manifested in her physical body: "Her belly will swell, her thigh will rot, and the woman will become a curse among her people." That will be the punishment for her sin. In this case, the cup of water is the vehicle through which the curse is transmitted.

If the woman is innocent, on the other hand, she will not experience any harmful effects. In this way, God will have vindicated her righteousness, and her husband will not be free to bring any further accusation against her. Her innocence will have protected her from the curse.

The various instances given above establish one important scriptural truth: in certain circumstances, both blessings and curses can be transmitted through physical objects. On the other side, if we turn our attention from biblical practices to all the various forms of false religion and the occult, there is virtually no limit to the ways in which physical objects can become vehicles of curses.

In Exodus 20:4-5, in the second of the Ten Commandments, God explicitly forbids the making of any kind of idol or image for religious purposes, and He warns that those who break this commandment will bring judgement not only on themselves, but also on at least three following generations:

> *"You shall not make for yourself any carved image, or any likeness of anything that is in heaven above, or that is in the earth beneath, or that is in the water under the earth;*
>
> *you shall not bow down to them nor serve them. For I, the Lord your God, am a jealous God, visiting the iniquity of the fathers on the children to the third and fourth generations of those who hate Me."*

A wide range of objects comes under this ban. In my own case, which I have already described, the embroidered Chinese dragons exposed me to the invisible influence of a curse. It was true that I had no intention of worshipping them. Nevertheless, they represented something that had been an object of idolatrous worship for many centuries. They opened a channel into my home for the evil power of pagan worship that had been practised for millennia.

Looking back later, I noticed one particular effect that those dragons had on me. Not merely were they a barrier that kept me from moving forward into the blessing of prosperity. They even kept me from seeing that the blessing was actually there. Only after I was free from their influence could I discern by faith what God had prepared for me.

Since that time, I have observed the same effect in the lives of many people under a curse. The curse not only keeps them from receiving the blessing God is offering to them. It also keeps them from realising that the blessing is there to receive. Only when the Holy Spirit shines the light of Scripture into our lives do we begin to understand how the devil has been deceiving and cheating us.

4
MOSES' LIST OF BLESSINGS AND CURSES

Some people are happy to accept the fact that blessings are real, but are sceptical about curses, which they associate with superstitious practices from the Dark Ages. Such thinking is unrealistic. We cannot focus exclusively on one aspect of opposites because it is acceptable to us, and simply ignore the other because it is unacceptable. The opposite of hot is cold; both are real. The opposite of good is evil; both are real. In just the same way, blessings are real and so are curses.

My ministry brings me in touch with Christians from many different backgrounds in many different lands. I find that most of God's people do not know how to discern between blessings and curses. Many Christians who should be enjoying blessings are actually enduring curses. For this there are two main reasons: First, they simply do not know how to recognise what a blessing or a curse is, or how to discern between them; second, if they are under a curse, they do not understand the basis upon which they can be released.

God is the sole and supreme source of all blessings, although they may come to us through many channels. Curses, too, often proceed from God, but He is not the sole source. Later on, we shall deal with other sources of curses.

The curses which proceed from God are one of His main ways of bringing judgement on the rebellious, the unbelieving, and the ungodly. The history of the human race provides a long, sad record of the outworking of God's curses pronounced upon such people.

Over the years it has become fashionable to suggest that there is a dichotomy between the Old Testament and the New. According to this interpretation, the Old Testament depicts God as a God of wrath and judgement; the New depicts Him as a God of love and mercy. In fact, however, the two Testaments are consistent with each other. Each depicts God as being, at one and the same time, a God of mercy and of judgement.

The story of Jericho, related in Joshua 6, combines these two sides of God's dealings as vividly and dramatically as any passage in the New Testament. While the city of Jericho perished under one single, comprehensive judgement of God, the harlot Rahab, with her entire family, emerged unscathed. The record indicates, furthermore, that later Rahab became the wife of Salmon, one of the princes of Judah, and took her place in the genealogical line from which Israel's Messiah, Jesus, was to come! (See Matthew 1:5.)

In Romans 1:17-18 Paul explains that the Gospel contains the supreme revelation of these two aspects of God, His mercy and His judgement:

For in it [the Gospel] the righteousness of God is

revealed from faith to faith . . .
   For the wrath of God is revealed from heaven against
   all ungodliness and unrighteousness of men.

On the one hand, God's mercy offers His righteousness, which He imparts to those who receive by faith the substitutionary sacrifice of Jesus on their behalf. Yet, at the same time, this sacrifice is also the ultimate revelation of God's wrath, poured out upon Jesus when He became identified with man's sin. Christians who question the reality of God's judgement on sin should ponder afresh the significance of the crucifixion. Even Jesus could not make sin acceptable to God, but had to endure the full outpouring of His wrath.

Further on, in Romans 11:22, Paul again presents these two aspects of God's dealings side by side: "Therefore consider the goodness [or kindness] and severity of God." To obtain an accurate picture of God, we must always keep both aspects of His character before us. His blessings proceed out of His kindness, but His judgements proceed out of His severity. Both are equally real.

In Proverbs 26:2 Solomon makes it clear that there is always a reason for every curse:

> *Like a flitting sparrow, like a flying swallow,*
> *So a curse without cause shall not alight.*

This principle has a double application. On the one hand, a curse cannot take effect unless there is a cause for it. On the other hand, the converse is also true. Wherever there is a curse at work, there is a cause for it. In seeking to help people obtain release from a curse, I have learned by experience that it is often helpful first to discover the cause.

The 68 verses of Deuteronomy 28, which are devoted solely to the theme of blessings and curses, reveal the primary cause of each. In verses 1 and 2 Moses deals first with the cause of blessings: "If you diligently obey the voice of the Lord your God, to observe carefully all His commandments . . . all these blessings shall come upon you and overtake you, because you obey the voice of the Lord your God."

More literally, the first part could be translated: "If you will listen listening to the voice of the Lord your God . . ." The repetition of the verb *to listen* gives it added emphasis. Simply stated, the conditions for enjoying the blessings are: first, listening to God's voice; second, doing what He says.

Throughout all dispensations, these have been the unchanging requirements for living in a covenant relationship with God. In Exodus 19:5, when God prepared to enter into His first covenant with Israel at Sinai, He said: "Now therefore, if you will indeed obey My voice and keep My covenant, then you shall be a special treasure to Me above all people." The basic requirements were to listen to God's voice and obey the terms of His covenant.

Under the new covenant, in John 10:27, Jesus similarly described those whom He acknowledged as "His sheep" – that is, His true disciples: "My sheep hear My voice . . . and they follow Me." The basic requirements are still the same: hearing the Lord's voice and following Him in obedience.

Hearing the Lord's voice takes us beyond mere religious profession or formal observances. Nothing is more unique and distinctive than a person's voice. Hearing the Lord's voice implies an intimate relationship with Him in which He can speak to each one of us *personally*.

The Lord does not speak in this way to our physical ears or to our natural minds. His communication is Spirit-to-spirit – that is, by His Spirit to our spirit. Projected in this way, His voice penetrates to the innermost depths of our being. From there its vibrations are felt in every area of personality.

The Lord may speak in this way through the Bible, or He may impart a word of direct revelation. Merely reading the Bible, however, is not sufficient by itself, unless the words on its pages are transformed by the Holy Spirit into a living voice. It is only a relationship of this kind with God that truly qualifies us for the blessings He has promised to those *who hear and obey His voice*.

Further on, in Deuteronomy 28:15, Moses states the primary cause of all curses:

> *"But it shall come to pass, if you do not obey the voice of the Lord your God, to observe carefully all His commandments and His statutes which I command you today, that all these curses will come upon you and overtake you."*

The cause of curses is exactly opposite to that of blessings. Blessings result from hearing God's voice and doing what He says. Curses result from *not* hearing God's voice and *not* doing what He says. This refusal to hear and obey God's voice can be summed up in one word: *rebellion* – not against man, but against God.

In Deuteronomy 28 Moses also gives comprehensive lists of the various forms that both blessings and curses take. The blessings are listed in verses 3 through 13, the curses in verses 16 through 68. Anyone who seeks to understand this whole subject should carefully study this chapter in its entirety.

Out of my own studies, I have attempted to make two lists that sum up the blessings and the curses in the order in which they are mentioned. My suggested list of blessings is as follows:

Exaltation	Prosperity
Health	Victory
Reproductiveness	God's favour

Reproductiveness is not a common English word, but it is intended to describe a condition in which every area of a person's life is fruitful and reproductive. This would include family, livestock, crops, business, and the exercise of creative talents. All these should reflect God's blessing in appropriate ways.

In his list of curses in verses 16 through 68, Moses goes into much greater detail than with the blessings. Essentially, however, the curses are the opposite of the blessings. Here is my suggested summary:

Humiliation
Barrenness, unfruitfulness
Mental and physical sickness
Family breakdown
Poverty
Defeat
Oppression
Failure
God's disfavour

Earlier, in verse 13, Moses had concluded his list of blessings with two vivid verbal pictures. Each of us would do well to consider how these pictures might apply in our own lives.

First, Moses says: "The Lord will make you the head and not the tail . . ." I once asked the Lord to show me how this would apply in my life. I felt He gave me this answer: The head makes the decisions and the tail just gets dragged around.

It was left to me to decide which role I was playing. Was I

acting like a head, in control of each situation, making the appropriate decisions and seeing them successfully carried out? Or was I merely playing the part of a tail, being dragged around by forces and circumstances I did not understand and could not control?

To drive his meaning home, Moses uses a second phrase: "You shall be above only, and not be beneath." This might be illustrated by a meeting between two Christian acquaintances.

"How are you doing?" the first asks.

"Under the circumstances," the second replies, "I'm not doing badly."

"I'm glad for that," the first one responds." But whatever are you doing under the circumstances?"

These illustrations of Moses confront us with an opportunity for self-evaluation. Am I living like a head or a tail? Am I living under my circumstances, or above them? The answers we give will help us to see how much of God's blessing we are actually enjoying.

5
SEVEN INDICATIONS OF
A CURSE

Through personal observation and experience, I compiled the following list of seven problems indicating that a curse is at work. When I compared my list with that of Moses in Deuteronomy 28, I was impressed by the close correspondence between them.

1. Mental and/or emotional breakdown
2. Repeated or chronic sicknesses (especially if hereditary)
3. Barrenness, a tendency to miscarry, or related female problems
4. Breakdown of marriage and family alienation
5. Continuing financial insufficiency
6. Being "accident-prone"
7. A history of suicides and unnatural or untimely deaths

The presence of only one or two of these problems would not necessarily be sufficient, by itself, to establish conclusively the working of a curse. But when several of the problems are present, or when any one of them tends to recur repeatedly, the probability of a curse increases proportionately. In the last resort, however, it is only the Holy Spirit who can provide an absolutely accurate "diagnosis."

1.   Mental and/or emotional breakdown

The corresponding phrases from Deuteronomy 28 are: *madness, driven mad* (28, 34)[2]; *confusion of heart* or *confusion of mind* (20, 28); *a trembling heart* or *an anxious mind* (65); *anguish of soul* or *a despairing heart* (65).

The areas affected are described as the heart, the soul or the mind. In other words, the inner citadel of human personality has been breached by invading, hostile forces. Such people no longer have full control over their own thoughts and emotions and reactions. They may be "haunted" by an inner spectre continually taunting them: "You're losing control . . . There's no hope for you . . . Your mother ended up in a mental institution, and you'll be the next!"

I have been amazed to discover how many Christians are going through these inner struggles. Often they are reluctant to acknowledge their problem to others – or even to themselves – for fear that this would be a denial of their faith.

Two key words are *confusion* and *depression*. These almost invariably have their roots in some form of occult involvement. Often there is demonic activity. In most cases, however, it is

2.   The numbers in parentheses indicate verses in Deuteronomy 28 that speak of similar conditions. In some cases, the words used in the NIV are included beside those of the NKJ Version.

necessary to deal with the occult involvement and to revoke the resulting curse, before the demons can be driven out.

2. Repeated or chronic sicknesses (especially if hereditary)

The corresponding phrases from Deuteronomy 28 are numerous: *plague* or *plagued with diseases* (21); *consumption* or *wasting disease* (22); *severe burning fever* (22); *inflammation* (22); *incurable boils* (27, 35); *tumours* (27); *scabs* or *festering sores* (27); *incurable itch* (27); *blindness* (28); *extraordinary, fearful, prolonged plagues* (59); *serious and prolonged sicknesses* or *severe and lingering diseases* (59); *every other kind of sickness and plague* (61).

This list does not necessarily indicate that every form of sickness or disease is the direct result of a curse. There are, however, certain key words that occur: *plague, incurable, extraordinary, fearful, prolonged, lingering.* These serve as warning signals. They create what might be called "the atmosphere of a curse." They suggest evil, malevolent forces at work.

There is another common medical term which is not explicitly used in Deuteronomy 28, but has a similar connotation. It is *malignant* or *malignancy.* The primary definition of *malignant* in *Collins English Dictionary* is "having or showing desire to harm others." Obviously this describes a person, rather than a mere physical condition. Even more than the words in the previous paragraph, it suggests an evil, malevolent intelligence at work. Our use of such a term indicates an unconscious recognition that we are dealing with factors that are not purely physical.

Another very significant term used in reference to certain types of sickness is *hereditary.* It describes a condition that passes down from generation to generation. This is one of the commonest and most typical marks of a curse at work. For this reason, whenever

I am asked to pray for someone who has a hereditary physical problem, I am always open to the possibility that I am confronting the effects of a curse.

At about the age of sixty, a friend of mine, who is a pastor, developed a condition diagnosed as hemochromatosis, a disease which causes the patient to produce too much iron in the blood, especially storing it in the vital organs, namely the liver and heart. His father had died of the same disease at age 67. The doctor pronounced it hereditary, incurable and life-threatening. Every week he had to have phlebotomy (old-fashioned blood-letting).

After much prayer, especially by one of the prayer groups, my friend stood before his congregation in a Sunday morning service and made a simple, unemotional affirmation: "In the name of Jesus, I release myself from every evil inheritance from my father."

He was immediately and completely cured. Five years have passed since then. He has received no further treatment and there has been no recurrence of his problem.

In the foregoing comments, I have deliberately refrained from suggesting that any specific sickness is always, or necessarily, attributable to a curse. In many of the sicknesses mentioned, it would be highly probable that there is a curse at work, but, without further evidence, it would be wrong to assert that this is necessarily so. There is only one "expert" whose diagnosis is final, and that is the Holy Spirit. We always need to be conscious of our dependence on Him.

3. *Barrenness, a tendency to miscarry or related female problems*

The key phrase here from Deuteronomy 28 is: "Cursed shall be the fruit of your body" or your womb" (18). This curse may affect any of the various organs or functions involved in procreation. Ruth and I have ministered to hundreds of women whose infirmities came under the heading of "female problems." These included: inability to conceive; a tendency to miscarry; failure to menstruate; irregular menstruation; debilitating menstrual cramps; frigidity; cysts, tumours or other growths or structural defects affecting any of the various organs connected with the reproductive process. Quite often this kind of curse affects whole families, with the result that all, or almost all, the females in a family may be afflicted with problems of this kind.

Ruth and I make it a principle not to minister to such people without first instructing them on the nature and causes of curses, and then praying with them for release. In many cases this has produced healing and wholeness in the affected areas or functions. Sometimes it proves sufficient merely to revoke the curse, without any specific prayer for healing.

The following letter illustrates the results that can follow when the curse of barrenness is revoked.

> My husband and I had been married for twelve years and had not been able to have children. Medical tests revealed that there was nothing physically wrong with us.
>
> On July 7, 1985, we attended a meeting in Amsterdam at which you were speaking. You taught on healing, and also reasons why people are not healed. As you began speaking on curses over families, the Lord spoke to my heart that this was a problem in my family. As you led everyone in a prayer for deliverance from any curse over their lives, I felt a definite sense of release from bondage.
>
> When I came to the platform, you asked me to fetch

my husband for prayer also. Then as you prayed over us, you pronounced that the curse over my life had been broken, and as Ruth laid hands on my womb, she spoke that I would be "neither barren nor unfruitful." The whole congregation was asked to stand and join in prayer for us. Following that meeting, my husband and I both felt strongly that the Lord had heard our prayers.

About two and a half years later, in another public meeting in England, this couple came up to show us the beautiful baby boy who was the manifestation of the blessing that had replaced the curse of barrenness over their lives.

The connection between menstrual problems and a curse is brought out in another letter, dated December 22, 1987, from a Christian lady in her thirties serving the Lord in Southeast Asia:

In 1985 I borrowed a set of tapes that had been recorded in Singapore, among which was the message by Derek Prince on "Blessings and Cursings." After listening to this message one night in my room I stood in the darkness to say the prayer on the end of the tape even though I was not aware of anything in particular. I just thought, If there is something, I want to be free from it.

I didn't immediately become aware of any change, although something did happen, the significance of which didn't strike me until later. The Lord prompted me shortly after this to make a note in my diary when I had my period. This was something I had never done before as I'd not had regular periods since the time they first began at age thirteen. Therefore there had been little point in keeping a record. My periods in fact had been so irregular that I'd even gone six or eight or ten months at a time without having one at all.

I'd been to doctors about this in my twenties and had been given medication (without result) and much unwise and ungodly advice.

I had prayed about my condition but not too seriously – possibly because I was single – but I had been told that I would experience a certain amount of discomfort and irregularity in my metabolism due to hormonal imbalance until this condition was corrected.

On listening to the tape again a few months later, I was struck by Derek Prince's statement that "almost all, if not all, menstrual disorders are a result of a curse." I realised as I reached for my diary and checked the dates that I'd been perfectly regular (28-day cycles) since praying the prayer in August 1985. I was amazed to realise I was healed and that it had been the Lord who had prompted me to write down the dates of my periods.

As I reflected on my life, questioning where "the curse" could have come in, since no curse can alight without a cause, I remembered how throughout my high school years (ages 13-17) menstruation was generally referred to as "the curse" by me and my peers. Surely that confirms that "death and life are in the power of the tongue" (Proverbs 18:21).

Since that time in August '85 I have regularly kept a record and found my cycle to be consistently 27-29 days. Also, my weight which previously fluctuated has remained stable.

It is important to notice that – like Miriam in chapter 2 – this lady did not pray for physical healing. She simply released herself from a curse, and healing followed as a consequence.

In this area of the procreative functions there is another common indication of a curse at work: an infant born with the umbilical cord wrapped around its neck – sometimes more than once. Quite often, of course, this can result in a stillbirth – thus causing death where there should be a new life.

4.   Breakdown of marriage and family alienation

One effect of the curse in this area is described in Deuteronomy 28:41: "You shall beget sons and daughters, but they shall not be yours; for they shall go into captivity." Countless parents in the present generation have experienced this curse. They have seen their sons and daughters taken captive by a rebellious subculture devoted to drugs, sex, satanic music, and every form of the occult.

In Malachi 4:5-6 the prophet paints a grim picture of conditions in the world just before this age closes:

> *"Behold, I will send you Elijah the prophet*
> *Before the coming of the great and dreadful day of the*
>   *Lord.*
> *And he will turn*
> *The hearts of the fathers to the children,*
> *And the hearts of the children to their fathers,*
> *Lest I come and strike the earth with a curse."*

Malachi depicts an evil force at work, alienating parents from children and producing a breakdown of family relationships. Unless God intervenes, he warns, this curse that is destroying family life will be extended to the whole earth, bringing disaster in its train.

Malachi has put his finger on the most urgent social problem of our contemporary culture. We need to see it as the outworking of a curse, which is responsible for the agonies of strife-torn homes, broken marriages and disintegrated families. Perhaps the most accurate word to describe the force responsible for these results is *alienation.* It comes between husbands and wives, parents and children, brothers and sisters, and all others who should be united by the bonds of family. Its goal is the destruction of the family.

Nevertheless for those who will accept God's counsel, the situation is not hopeless. There is a remedy. First we must face the fact that there is a curse at work. Then we must take the steps indicated by Scripture to revoke the curse and release its captives. I have seen families transformed and restored by these means.

5. *Continuing financial insufficiency*

Two related phrases from Deuteronomy 28 are: "Cursed shall be your basket and your kneading bowl" or trough (17); "You shall not prosper in your ways" or you will be unsuccessful in everything you do (29).

The full outworking of this curse, however, is most graphically presented in verses 47-48:

> *"Because you did not serve the Lord your God with joy and gladness of heart, for the abundance of all things,*
> *"therefore you shall serve your enemies, whom the Lord will send against you, in hunger, in thirst, in nakedness, and in need of all things."*

Moses here presents two opposite alternatives. Verse 47 describes God's will for His obedient people: to "serve the Lord your God with joy and gladness of heart for the abundance of all things." The NIV renders this: to "serve the Lord your God joyfully and gladly in the time of prosperity."

Verse 48 describes the curse that will come on God's people if they are disobedient: to "serve your enemies, whom the Lord will send against you, in hunger, in thirst, in nakedness, and in need of all things." Consider what is depicted in this verse: hunger, thirst, nakedness and need of all things. Combine all four elements into one situation, and the result can be defined in a single phrase: *absolute poverty*.

Taken together, verses 47 and 48 point to a simple conclusion: prosperity is a blessing and poverty is a curse.

Over the centuries, however, a tradition has developed within the Christian Church that poverty is a blessing. Certainly God has great compassion on the poor, and Christians should have the same attitude and be willing to make great personal sacrifices on their behalf. But Scripture never suggests that God *inflicts* poverty as a blessing upon His believing people.

In this respect, the revelation of the New Testament harmonises with that of the Old. In 2 Corinthians 9:8 Paul sums up the abundance of God's provision for Christians:

> *And God is able to make all grace abound toward you, that you, always having all sufficiency in all things, have an abundance for every good work.*

In this one terse sentence Paul doubles and redoubles his words to emphasise the generosity of God's provision for His people. The word *abound* or *abundance* occurs twice. The word *all* – or its equivalent – occurs five times: *all* grace . . . *always* . . . *all* sufficiency in *all* things . . . *every* good work. Such is the measure of God's provision. It transcends mere sufficiency and lifts us to

a level of abundance, where we have something over and above
our own needs to minister to the needs of others.

It would be unscriptural, however, to interpret poverty and
abundance by the materialistic standards of contemporary
Western civilisation. In John 6:38 Jesus revealed the motivation of
His life on earth: "For I have come down from heaven, not to do
My own will, but the will of Him who sent Me." The motivation
of the disciple must be the same as that of the Master: *to do God's
will.*

It is from this perspective that "poverty" and "abundance" must
be defined. Poverty is having less than all you need to do God's
will in your life. The greater the gap between what you need and
what you have, the greater the degree of poverty. Abundance, on
the other hand, is having all you need to do God's will – and
something over to give to others. God's abundance is not provided
for us to squander on carnal self-indulgence, but *for every good
work,* that is, sharing with others the blessings of grace that have
enriched our own lives.

When poverty and abundance are interpreted in this way, it
follows that there is no absolute standard that can be applied to all
Christians. The standard for each believer must be determined in
relation to *the will of God for his or her life.*

These conclusions about poverty and abundance need to be
further qualified in two ways. First, we must recognise that faith
to appropriate God's abundance is certain to be tested. There may
be periods when we have to content ourselves with the barest
sufficiency. Such periods, however, should be temporary. Once
our motives have been purified and our faith has stood the test,
God will release His abundance in the measure that He can trust
us to use for His glory.

Second, we must recognise also that there is a higher level of
wealth than just the material. When Moses turned his back on the

wealth and luxury of Egypt and settled in a remote corner of a desert, the writer of Hebrews says that he esteemed "the reproach of Christ *greater riches* than the treasure in Egypt" (Hebrews 11:26). Moses did not settle for poverty. He exchanged material riches for riches of a higher order.

In the same way today, there is the kind of Christian who renounces material wealth deliberately in order to serve God in a situation where wealth would be an encumbrance. Often this is a prerequisite for identifying with the poor and oppressed of the earth. In Proverbs 13:7 Solomon contrasts such a person with one whose only wealth is material.

> *There is one who makes himself rich,*
> *yet has nothing;*
> *And one who makes himself poor,*
> *yet has great riches.*

There are also many Christians in our day who are enduring affliction and persecution for Christ's sake. They may be deprived of everything that could be described as material wealth, but in its place they are heirs to wealth of a higher order.

Nevertheless, this does not alter the basic nature of persistent material poverty. Where this is not the direct outcome of commitment to Christ, it is normally a mark of a curse, whether it affects an individual, a family or a larger social group.

6. Being "accident-prone"

This phrase describes a person who is unnaturally prone to personal accidents. Deuteronomy 28 contains no specific mention of this, although it is hinted at in the phrase "you shall grope . . . as a blind man gropes in darkness" (29).

One characteristic effect of this curse might be seen in what are called "freak" accidents. The girl described in chapter 2, who had broken the same leg three times in eighteen months, would be an obvious example.

To take another example, some people are good drivers, yet they have an abnormally high number of automobile accidents. In most cases, perhaps, it may be the fault of "the other driver." Nevertheless, the accidents still happen. A typical comment that identifies this kind of person would be: "Why does it always happen to me?"

Here are further examples, chosen more or less at random, of types of accidents that might indicate a curse at work: breaking an ankle through stepping off a curb; breaking a tooth on a soft piece of fruit; shutting a car door on a finger (here again, it may be "the other person"); slipping on a stair and falling headlong down a whole flight, with multiple injuries; swallowing a fish bone and choking on it; an insect in the eye causing some rare infection; being struck in the face by a stone thrown up by a passing car; a surgeon's error on the operating table resulting in permanent disability . . . the list could be endless.

It almost seems that there is an invisible, malicious force working against such people. At critical moments, it trips them, or causes them to stumble, or impels them to make a rash, unpremeditated move. Typically, such a person will exclaim, "I don't know what made me do that!" A remark of this kind is very revealing. It indicates that the person is aware that his actions are not entirely under his own control, but are affected by a nameless influence he cannot identify and against which he has no way of protecting himself.

The recognition of this type of problem is not purely subjective. It can be determined by statistical analysis. Some insurance companies use this kind of analysis to identify people who would be unusually high risks for insurance. They set their premiums accordingly.

7. *A history of suicides and unnatural or untimely deaths*

The references to unnatural or untimely death in Deuteronomy 28 are too numerous to itemise. A curse that takes this form affects not just a single individual but a larger social unit, such as a family or tribe. Normally, too, it continues from one generation to another. Many different cultures have recognised a force at work in human history that pursues the members of a family or a clan relentlessly until it finally destroys them. The ancient Greeks gave it the status of a "goddess," whom they named Nemesis. Other cultures have used different terminologies. Beneath the pagan overtones is an objective reality.

Quite often people who are affected by this type of curse experience a strong foreboding. They sense something dark and evil in the road ahead, but they do not know how to avoid it. A typical comment might be: "Well, it happened to my father, and I suppose I'm next on the list."

One common symptom of a curse of this kind is that people set dates for their own deaths. "I know I'll never live to see forty-five," they may say. Or, "All the men in my family die young." They imply, if they do not actually say, that this will be their fate, too. They have a kind of negative faith that embraces death, but refuses life.

The above list of seven indications of a curse is by no means exhaustive. Others could be added. You have probably read far enough by now, however, to take stock of your situation.

Various reactions are possible. You may, for example, no longer have any doubt about the nature of your problem. You have clearly identified one or more indications of a curse that apply to your life or to that of your family.

Alternatively, you may have an uneasy sense that a curse is at
work, but you cannot pinpoint the precise form that it takes. You
feel like the kind of person described in chapter 1. You have
sensed the dark shadow from the past, but you do not know its
source. Or you have seen that long, evil arm at work in various
situations, but it operates behind a veil that you have not been able
to tear aside.

In either case, you will be asking yourself: How could such a
thing happen to me? What is the source of my problem?

This means that it is time for you to move on to Section 2: "No
Curse without a Cause." This section explains many of the most
common sources of a curse. If you can once discover the cause of
your particular problem, you will be in a much better position to
deal with it effectively.

SECTION 2
NO CURSE WITHOUT A CAUSE

INTRODUCTION

The operation of blessings and curses in our lives is not haphazard or unpredictable. On the contrary, both of them operate according to eternal, unchanging laws. It is to the Bible, once again, that we must look for a correct understanding of these laws.

In Proverbs 26:2 Solomon establishes this principle with respect to curses: "A curse without cause shall not alight." Behind every curse that comes upon us, there is a cause. If it seems that we are under a curse, we should seek to determine its cause. Then we shall be in a position to take appropriate action against it. This will also silence that nagging question: "Why do things like this always happen to me?"

This section lays bare the causes of the main curses that commonly afflict our lives. After reading it, you will be better able to understand and apply God's remedy, which is unfolded in the following section.

6
FALSE GODS

In the preceding chapters we have established two important facts concerning curses that proceed from God. First, they are one of the main ways in which He brings judgement on the rebellious and the ungodly. Second, the basic cause of such curses is the failure to hear God's voice and do what He says – or, in one simple word, *disobedience.*

Disobedience can take many forms. It is natural, therefore, to ask: What are some of the main forms of disobedience that particularly provoke God's curse?

The Bible leaves no doubt about the answer. The form of disobedience which most surely and inevitably provokes God's curse is the breaking of the first two of the Ten Commandments, which are stated in Exodus 20:1-5:

And God spoke all these words, saying:

"I am the Lord your God, who brought you out of the land of Egypt, out of the house of bondage.

"You shall have no other gods before Me.

"You shall not make for yourself any carved image, or any likeness of anything that is in heaven above, or that is in the earth beneath, or that is in the water under the earth;

you shall not bow down to them nor serve them. For I, the Lord your God, am a jealous God, visiting the iniquity of the fathers on the children to the third and fourth generations of those who hate Me."

What are the two sins God specifies here? The first is acknowledging any other god before – or besides – the Lord. It is not enough to acknowledge the Lord as the first or greatest of all gods. We must acknowledge that He is *the only true God.* There is no other besides Him.

In Isaiah 45:21 the Lord declares with great emphasis:

> *"There is no other God besides Me,*
> *A just God and a Saviour;*
> *There is none besides Me."*

The second sin, described in the next commandment, is the making of any artificial representation of God and offering worship to it. In Romans 1:20-23 Paul analyses what is involved in the breaking of these two commandments:

> *For since the creation of the world God's invisible qualities – his eternal power and divine nature – have been clearly seen, being understood from what has been made, so that men are without excuse.*

For although they knew God, they neither glorified him as God nor gave thanks to him, but their thinking became futile and their foolish hearts were darkened. Although they claimed to be wise, they became fools and exchanged the glory of the immortal God for images made to look like mortal man and birds and animals and reptiles.

NIV

Those who acknowledge false gods and practice idol worship have deliberately rejected the clear revelation of God available to them through creation. Instead, they have chosen to worship idols that become progressively debased. First, they take human form, but from there they descend to birds, then to animals and finally to reptiles. This exactly describes the practices of ancient Egypt. Three of their main gods were the vulture, the jackal and the cobra.

Our human minds are slow to understand the awful wickedness of idol worship. The true God, revealed first in creation and then more fully in Scripture, is holy, awesome, glorious, omnipotent. To represent Him in the likeness of any created being – whether human or animal – is to offer Him a deliberate insult. It is a calculated provocation of His wrath.

Let me illustrate this by a crude example. Suppose someone were to find a cockroach crawling on the floor, photograph it, and then display the photograph over the title *Derek Prince*. I would surely interpret this as an insult deliberately aimed at me. How immeasurably worse is the insult offered to God by those who give His name not merely to the noblest of His creatures, but even to the most debased!

God's judgement on the breaking of these first two commandments bears the characteristic mark of a curse: It continues from generation to generation, at least as far as the fourth generation.

In some nations and some cultures, the practice of worshipping false gods goes back over hundreds and even thousands of years, compounding the effect many times over.

A person who comes from such a background is heir to a curse that may be compared to a weed planted in his life, linking him to satanic forces outside himself. This weed has two kinds of roots: one long tap root going straight downward, and the other less powerful lateral roots stretching out in various directions. The tap root represents the influence of ancestors who worshipped false gods. The lateral roots represent other influences to which the person has been exposed in his own lifetime, either through various sins he has committed or through his own attachment to false gods or in various other ways.

Before he can enjoy true liberty and the fullness of the new creation in Christ, this weed must be completely pulled out, with all its roots. The most important root, and the one hardest to deal with, is the tap root that links him to many generations who have worshipped false gods. Nothing but the supernatural grace and power of God can effectively remove all these roots. But thank God, there is hope in the promise of Jesus in Matthew 15:13: "Every plant which My heavenly Father has not planted will be uprooted."

The sins which bring this generational curse, however, do not stop short at the more obvious forms of idolatry. They include a second, wider range of practices which are not necessarily openly idolatrous, or even religious. Because their true nature is concealed by deceptive terminology, they are appropriately described as *occult* (derived from a Latin word meaning "hidden" or "covered over"). These occult practices have always held a powerful fascination[3] for fallen man, never more so than in the

3. It is significant that the word fascination is derived from a Latin verb that means "to bewitch."

present generation.

Two of the strongest cravings of human nature are the desire for knowledge and the desire for power. Up to a certain point, man is able to satisfy these cravings from natural sources and by natural means. If he is not fully satisfied by what he obtains in this way, he will turn inevitably to supernatural sources. It is at this point that he easily becomes entrapped in the occult.

The reason for this is that there are actually only two available sources of supernatural knowledge and power in the universe: either God or Satan. Every form of supernatural knowledge or power that does not proceed from God, therefore, necessarily proceeds from Satan. If derived from God, it is legitimate; if derived from Satan, it is illegitimate.

Since God's kingdom is the kingdom of light, His servants know whom they are serving and what they are doing. On the other hand, since Satan's kingdom is a kingdom of darkness, most of those in his kingdom do not know the true identity of the one whom they are serving, or the true nature of what they are doing.

It was this craving for illegitimate knowledge that prompted man's first transgression in the Garden of Eden. God had set an invisible boundary between him and the tree of knowledge of good and evil. When man crossed this boundary, he found himself in Satan's territory and became a captive of Satan. Ever since then, the same kind of craving for illegitimate knowledge or power has continually lured men into an area where Satan is able to take them captive at his will (see 2 Timothy 2:26). As already stated, the generic name for this area is the occult.

Those who trespass in this area are seeking from Satan the supernatural knowledge or power which God does not permit man to seek from any other source but Himself. In so doing, they are, in fact, acknowledging Satan as a god besides the one true God, and are thus breaking the first of the Ten Commandments. In this way they are exposing themselves to the curse God has pronounced on all who break this commandment – a curse that extends as far as the fourth generation.

This conclusion is so important that it needs to be re-emphasised: *All who become involved in the occult are exposing themselves to the curse pronounced on those who break the first commandment.*

In various passages the Bible describes the act of turning to false gods as "spiritual adultery," and condemns it as an even greater sin than physical adultery. Understood in this way, the warnings given in the book of Proverbs against involvement with an "immoral woman" – or an adulteress – apply to involvement in the occult. In Proverbs 5:3-6 this immoral woman is depicted as alluring and fascinating in her initial approaches, yet causing final ruin to those whom she seduces:

> *For the lips of an immoral woman drip honey,*
> *And her mouth is smoother than oil;*
> *But in the end she is bitter as wormwood,*
> *Sharp as a two-edged sword.*
> *Her feet go down to death,*
> *Her steps lay hold of hell.*
> *Lest you ponder her path of life –*
> *Her ways are unstable;*
> *You do not know them.*

The final statement is particularly illuminating: "Her ways are unstable; you do not know them." No limit can be set to the forms of deception practised in the occult. As soon as one is exposed, another emerges in its place. It is, therefore, impossible to give a complete or definitive list of the various types of occult practices. It is, however, possible to identify and briefly describe the following three main branches: witchcraft, divination, and sorcery.

Witchcraft is the *power* branch of the occult. Its root is exposed by a brief statement in 1 Samuel 15:23: "For *rebellion* is as the sin of witchcraft." Witchcraft is an expression of man's rebellion against God. It is man's attempt to gain his own ends without submitting to God's Law. Its driving force is a desire to control people and circumstances. To gain this end it may use either psychological pressures or psychic techniques, or a combination of both.

There are three key words that expose the activity of witchcraft: manipulate, intimidate, dominate. Domination is its ultimate purpose. Manipulation and intimidation are alternative ways of achieving this purpose. Wherever people use verbal or non-verbal tactics to manipulate, intimidate and dominate those around them, witchcraft is at work.

In its simplest form, witchcraft is merely an expression of the corrupt, rebellious nature of fallen humanity. In Galatians 5:20, in the King James Version, it is listed – with idolatry – among "the works of the flesh." There are probably few people who have not resorted at some time or other to witchcraft in this form.

This is only "the tip of the iceberg," however. It is characteristic of Satan that he exploits this "work of the flesh" as an opening for supernatural, demonic power that emanates from the kingdom of darkness. Through this opening, he moves in and takes control of men and women, making them tools of his evil purposes and slaves of his kingdom. The result is witchcraft practised as an occult art, operating primarily through spells and curses.

The other two forms of the occult – divination and sorcery – are motivated by the same basic desire: to control people and circumstances.

Divination is the *knowledge* branch of the occult, offering many different forms of knowledge which cannot be obtained by purely natural means. In its commonest form, as *fortune-telling,* it offers supernatural knowledge of the future. It also includes all false forms of religious revelation that claim a supernatural source.

Sorcery operates through *material objects* or through other ways of impacting the physical senses, such as *drugs or music.* In Revelation 9:21 the word for *sorceries* is directly derived from the Greek word for *drugs.* In 2 Timothy 3:13 Paul warns that at the close of this age "evil men and impostors will grow worse and worse, deceiving and being deceived." The word translated *impostors* means literally "enchanters." Chanting – or incantation – has always been a technique of sorcery. The contemporary drug culture, with its accompaniment of "heavy metal" rock music, is a vivid example of two forms of sorcery working together.

The following is a brief list of various categories under which the "tools" of sorcery may be classified:

Any objects associated with idolatrous worship, whether pagan or professing to be Christian.

Any objects representing any kind of false religion or cult or satanic practice.

Any objects upon which a practitioner of the occult has invoked supernatural power. (Even if this power is ostensibly directed toward a "good" purpose, such as healing, its source makes it the channel of a curse.)

Any objects that are the expression of superstition, such as horseshoes, "lucky" coins, figures of "saints" and so on.

The following are some specific forms of the occult prevalent in our contemporary culture:

1. The power branch of the occult

Acupressure, acupuncture, astral projection, hypnosis, levitation, martial arts (those that invoke supernatural spiritual power), mind control, mind dynamics, parakinesis, table-tipping, telekinesis, "touch" healing, witchcraft.

2. The knowledge branch of the occult

Astrology, automatic writing, "channelling," clairaudience (hearing "voices"), clairvoyance, crystal balls, diagnosing by colour therapy or a pendulum, divining, ESP, handwriting analysis, horoscopes, iridology, kabbala, mediums, mindreading, numerology, omens, palmreading, phrenology, seances, tarot cards, tea leaf reading, telepathy, "witching." Also all books that teach occult practices.

Also included under this heading are all false religions or cults which claim supernatural revelation but contradict the Bible. Distinguishing between true and false in this realm is like distinguishing between straight and crooked in the natural realm. Once we have established a standard of what is straight, we know that anything departing from that standard is crooked. It makes no difference whether it varies by one degree or by ninety degrees. It is crooked.

In the spiritual realm, the Bible is the standard of that which is *straight* – that is, *true*. Anything that departs from the Bible is *false*. Whether it departs by little or much is relatively unimportant. Some of the subtlest deceptions are those that appear to differ only a little from the Bible.

Particularly dangerous are religions that misrepresent the Person, the nature or the redemptive work of Jesus Christ. The New Testament, for example, presents Jesus as "God manifest in the flesh," but Jehovah's Witnesses teach that He was a created being. Again, Islam rejects the claim of Jesus to be the Son of God, and denies that He ever actually died on the cross. Yet the atoning death of Jesus is the only basis on which man can claim forgiveness of sins.

The following are some of the many false religions or cults that are active today: Anthroposophy, Black Mass, Children of God, Christadelphians, Christian Science, Freemasonry, Inner Peace Movement, Jehovah's Witnesses (Dawn Bible Students), Mormons (Church of Jesus Christ of Latter-day Saints), New Age movement, Religious Science, Rosicrucianism, Scientology, Spiritual Frontiers Fellowship, Spiritualism, Theosophy, Unification Church (Moonies, One World Crusade), Unitarian Church, Worldwide Church of God (founded by Herbert W. Armstrong).

Also, Eastern religions or cults, such as Bahai, Buddhism, Confucianism, Divine Light Mission, gurus, Hare Krishna, Hinduism, Islam, Shintoism, Transcendental Meditation, yoga.

3.   The branch of the occult operating through physical objects, etc.

Amulets, ankhs (an ankh is a cross with a ring at the top), birth-stones, charms (e.g., for wart removal), crystals used for healing, hallucinogenic drugs, "heavy metal" rock records or cassettes, hex signs, "lucky" symbols (e.g., inverted horseshoes), ouija boards, pagan fetishes or religious artifacts, planchettes, talismans, zodiac charms.

God's estimate of those who are involved in the kinds of practices listed above is stated plainly in Deuteronomy 18:10-13:

> *Let no one be found among you who sacrifices his son or daughter in the fire, who practices divination or*

*sorcery, interprets omens, engages in witchcraft, or
casts spells, or who is a medium or spiritist or who
consults the dead. Anyone who does these things is
detestable to the Lord, and because of these detestable
practices the Lord your God will drive out those nations
before you. You must be blameless before the Lord your
God.*

NIV

Notice that those who engage in these occult practices are
classed in the same category with those who sacrifice their
children in the fire to pagan gods. Under the law of Moses, the
mandatory penalty for all such practices was death.

It is important to recognise that *books* can be channels of occult
power. When the professing Christians in Ephesus were
confronted through the ministry of Paul with the reality of Satan's
power, their reaction was dramatic:

*Many of those who believed now came and openly
confessed their evil deeds. A number who had practised
sorcery brought their scrolls together and burned them
publicly. When they calculated the value of the scrolls,
the total came to fifty thousand drachmas.[4]*

Acts 19:18-19, NIV

The only appropriate way to deal with such occult material is
to destroy it completely – by fire or by whatever means may be
most suitable – even though the value of the material destroyed
may be very great.

It has already been pointed out that the occult, like the

---

4. A drachma was about a day's wage. At today's rates in the United States, the total
amount could be as much as $200,000.

"immoral woman," is constantly changing its ways. Therefore, no final or exhaustive list of occult practices can ever be offered.

Over many years I have sought to help people with problems that had not been resolved by the type of counselling or ministry normally offered by the majority of churches today. So far as I could tell, these people's problems were not due to lack of sincerity or earnestness. In fact, they often seemed to be more earnest and sincere than many regular churchgoers who manifested no obvious problems.

In the cases where I did succeed in helping such people, I almost invariably discovered some root of involvement with the occult in their backgrounds. Often they themselves did not see this as a potential cause of their problems. Yet once the occult root was exposed and dealt with, it was usually comparatively easy to resolve the other, more obvious problems.

A simple but vivid example comes to my mind. In a home prayer meeting, I found myself next to a young man in his early twenties. We had not met before, but I felt led to ask him, "Have you received the Holy Spirit?"

"Yes," he replied, but then added rather wistfully, "but I don't speak in tongues." Clearly he felt there was something lacking in his experience.

Without discussing any further the issue of tongues, I asked him, "Did you ever visit a fortune-teller?"

He reflected for a moment, and then said, "Yes, once, when I was about fifteen. But I only did it as a joke. I didn't really believe in it."

"But still," I pressed him, "you did actually have your fortune told?"

"Yes," he acknowledged rather reluctantly, and then added defensively, "but I didn't mean anything by it."

Would you be willing to confess that as a sin," I said, "and ask

God to forgive you and release you from its consequences?"

When he agreed to this, I led him in a simple prayer, in which he confessed his visit to the fortune-teller as a sin, and asked God to forgive him and release him from its consequences. Then, without a further word of explanation, I put my hand on his shoulder and asked God to release the Holy Spirit within him. Instantly, without hesitation or stammering, he began to speak clearly and fluently in an unknown tongue. In a few moments he was lost in the presence of God, oblivious to all that was going on around him. The invisible barrier in his life had been removed!

Since then, I have reflected many times on my brief encounter with that young man. His problem was not lack of earnestness or sincerity. It was a failure to recognise the nature of his act in visiting the fortune-teller. He did not understand that in God's sight he had been guilty of spiritual adultery.

Suppose I had asked him, "Did you ever commit adultery with a married woman?" He would never have replied, "Yes, but I only did it as a joke . . . I didn't mean anything by it."

Countless multitudes of people today are in a similar situation. Many of them are churchgoers. Yet, through ignorance, they have trespassed in the area of the occult and have become involved in a sin which is worse than physical adultery. Until they recognise the true nature of what they have done, they must continue under the shadow of the curse which God has pronounced on all who turn away from Him to false gods. Furthermore, the same shadow may continue to rest over the lives of the next four generations of their descendants.

When confronted with these issues, Christians sometimes respond, "But I didn't know that I was doing anything wrong." My reply is to point out that in 1 Timothy 1:13-15 Paul describes himself as "the chief of sinners" for sins which he committed "ignorantly in unbelief." Ignorance does not absolve us from the guilt of our sins, but it may dispose God to show us mercy if we repent and turn to Him.

All of us, without exception, need to consider carefully how these principles may apply in our lives. In the first two of the Ten Commandments God has pronounced His judgement on two specific sins: turning to any false god besides the one true God; and making and worshipping any artificial representation of God. These two sins include the whole area of the occult. God's judgement on those who commit them, as we have seen, extends to the four generations following.

Conversely, any one of the four generations preceding us, by having committed these sins, could be the cause of a curse over us in our generation. Each of us has two parents, four grandparents, eight great-grandparents and sixteen great-great-grandparents. This makes a total of thirty persons, any one of whom might be the cause of a curse over our life. How many of us would be in a position to guarantee that none of our thirty immediate ancestors was ever involved in any form of idolatry or the occult?

Thank God He has provided a way of release from any curse that might have come from this source! Thank God we can avail ourselves of His provision! In the final day of reckoning, God will not hold against us the fact that our ancestors brought a curse upon us, but He will hold us guilty if we refuse to avail ourselves of the provision He has made for us to be released from such a curse.

7
VARIOUS MORAL AND ETHICAL SINS

The primary form of disobedience that provokes God's curse is stated in Exodus 20:3-5: acknowledging and worshipping false gods. In addition, the Old Testament also reveals a large number of secondary forms of disobedience upon which God has pronounced a curse. In this category, in Deuteronomy 27:15-26, Moses lists twelve moral and ethical sins, all of which provoke God's curse.

Earlier in this chapter Moses had instructed Israel to carry out a solemn ceremony after they had entered the land of Canaan. On the two adjoining mountains of Ebal and Gerizim they were to offer sacrifices and set up large stones with all the words of the Law written on them. With these words in plain view, half of the tribes would first invoke a blessing on all Israelites who were obedient. Then the other six tribes would invoke a curse on all who were disobedient. To both the blessing and the curse, all the people were required to respond "Amen!"[5]

In this way, God ordained that Israel's occupation of Canaan would confront them with two diametrically opposite alternatives: a blessing for obedience or a curse for disobedience. Between these two was no middle ground. No other option was open to them. From then onward, every Israelite who entered Canaan would either enjoy God's blessing, or endure His curse.

These two alternatives are here presented with stark clarity in the history of Israel, and subsequent records confirm their outworking. Nevertheless, these alternatives are not confined to Israel. They apply equally to all who would enter into a covenant relationship with God. Under the New Covenant, just as under the Old, God offers the same two alternatives: either blessing for obedience or curse for disobedience. One great delusion among Christians, which Satan carefully fosters, is that there is some third possibility, which is neither obedience, with its blessings, nor disobedience, with its curses. Neither the Old Testament nor the New offers any such option.

The twelve curses pronounced on the Israelites from Mount Gerizim were detailed and specific. The following is a suggested summary of the main kinds of conduct covered by them:

Acknowledging and worshipping false gods.
Disrespect for parents.
All forms of oppressions and injustice, especially when
    directed against the weak and the helpless.
All forms of illicit or unnatural sex.

The final curse covered all forms of disobedience to the Law.
As always, the primary cause of God's curse is any form of

5. Joshua 8:32-35 records how this ceremony was actually carried out after Israel had entered the land of Canaan.

involvement with false gods. This is followed by disrespect for parents. The requirement to respect our parents is restated and re-emphasised in the New Testament. In Ephesians 6:1-3 Paul reaffirms the fifth of the Ten Commandments:

> *Children, obey your parents in the Lord, for this is right.*
> *"Honour your father and mother," which is the first commandment with promise:*
> *"that it may be well with you and you may live long on the earth."*

Countless people today – including many Christians – are unaware that disrespect for parents brings God's curse. I could not estimate the number of people I have dealt with personally on this issue. Thank God that I have seen a wonderful change for the better in the lives of those who have recognised this sin, repented of it, and changed their attitude to their parents!

On this theme, it is appropriate to quote a passage from my book on marriage, *God Is a Matchmaker.*

> Paul points out that the preceding four command-ments had no promise attached to the keeping of them. But to this fifth commandment, relating to parents, God added a special promise: "That it may go well with you." At the same time, the promise implies a condition: If you want it to go well with you, you must be careful to honour your parents. Conversely, if you do not honour your parents, you cannot expect it to go well with you.
>
> Bear in mind that it is possible to honour your parents without agreeing with them on all points or endorsing

everything they do. You may disagree strongly with them in some matters, yet maintain a respectful attitude toward them. To honour your parents in this way is also to honour God Himself, who gave this commandment.

I am convinced that a proper attitude toward parents is an essential requirement for God's blessing on any person's life. In all the years I have dealt with Christians in teaching, pastoring, counselling, and other relationships, I have never met one who had a wrong attitude toward his parents and enjoyed the blessing of God. Such a person may be zealous in many areas of the Christian life, active in the church, energetic in ministry. He may have a place in heaven waiting for him. Yet there is always something lacking in his life: the blessing and favour of God.

I have seen many Christians, on the other hand, whose lives were revolutionised when they acknowledged a wrong attitude toward parents, repented of it and made the necessary changes. I remember one man who was convicted of a lifetime of bitterness and hatred toward his father. Although his father was already dead, this man journeyed hundreds of miles to the cemetery where his father was buried. Kneeling beside the grave, he poured out his heart to God in deep contrition and repentance. He did not rise from his knees until he knew his sin was forgiven and he was released from its evil effects. From that point on, the whole course of his life changed from frustration and defeat to victory and fulfilment.

The next form of conduct in the list in Deuteronomy 27 is oppression and injustice, especially against the weak and the helpless. There are certainly many examples of such behaviour in our contemporary culture, but none is more likely to provoke God's curse than the deliberate aborting of an unborn infant. Who is more helpless and incapable of self-defence than a baby in its mother's womb, if its own parents do not protect it?

How strange that people who are active in the fight against racial prejudice and injustice – and rightly so – actually condone and promote the practice of abortion! Strange, too, that people who would never think of raising a hand in violence against a small child feel no compassion toward an even smaller child in its mother's womb. Somehow the substitution of the word *fetus* for *infant* dulls people's consciences. Yet the change in terminology in no way affects the real nature of such an act.

Someone has asked, "What hope is left for a society in which mothers kill their own babies?" God's attitude toward abortion is not affected by a change in terminology. He classifies it quite simply as "murder" – and deals with it accordingly. In nation after nation around the world today, millions of lives are being blighted by the curse that follows this act.

The final form of curse-provoking conduct in the list taken from Deuteronomy 27 is the abuse and perversion of the sexual relationship. Some – Christians, unfortunately, have formed the impression that sex is somehow unclean, something that cannot be avoided but nevertheless needs an apology. Yet the biblical picture is just the opposite. Sex is part of the Creator's original plan for man, something sacred and beautiful. For this reason God has set stringent boundaries around the sexual act, to protect it from abuse and perversion. These boundaries are marked out by the curses pronounced in verses 20 through 23 of Deuteronomy 27.

The forbidden acts here listed cover sex with various persons related either by blood or marriage, and any form of sex with animals. The acts forbidden in the Bible also include all expressions of homosexuality. In Leviticus 18:22 God declares: "You shall not lie with a male as with a woman. It is an abomination" – also translated "detestable." This is the same word used in Deuteronomy 18:12 to describe various forms of occult practice.

Today many of these boundaries designed to protect the sanctity of sex are being deliberately set aside – sometimes even in the name of Christianity. Yet no arguments based on "situation ethics" or "the new morality" (which is by no means new) can affect or change the laws of God that govern human behaviour. All who indulge in sexual perversion expose themselves to the curse of God.

It is significant that this list of acts that provoke God's curse in Deuteronomy 27 is followed immediately in Deuteronomy 28 by the complete list of blessings for obedience and curses for disobedience. It is as if God says: "Before you decide whether to obey or not, you had better give careful consideration to the consequences. So here they are!"

8
ANTI-SEMITISM

About 4,000 years ago God made a choice that has affected all subsequent history. He was looking for a man who would meet His conditions so that he might ultimately become a channel of God's blessing to all nations. The man He chose was called Abram (later renamed Abraham).

God's purpose in choosing Abraham is unfolded in Genesis 12:2-3. Characteristically, blessing and curse are closely connected. God pronounces four promises of blessing upon Abraham:

> *"I will bless you."*
> *"You shall be a blessing."*
> *"I will bless those who bless you."*
> *"In you all the families of the earth shall be blessed."*

Interposed in the midst of these blessings, however, is a curse:

"I will curse him who curses[6] you."

The addition of this curse serves a very important practical purpose. Any person on whom God pronounces His blessing is thereby automatically exposed to the hatred and opposition of the great enemy of God and His people: Satan. Paradoxical as it may seem, the blessing of God provokes the curse of Satan, channelled through the lips of those whom Satan controls. For this reason, when God blessed Abraham, He added His curse on all who would curse Abraham. This meant that no one could curse Abraham without incurring the curse of God in return.

In Genesis 27:29, when Isaac blessed his son Jacob, he also extended to him the same protection that God originally provided for Abraham: "Cursed be everyone who curses you." Later, under divine compulsion, Balaam uttered a prophetic revelation of Israel's destiny, which was exactly opposite to his original intention to curse Israel. Part of this revelation, recorded in Numbers 24:9, echoed the words already spoken concerning Abraham and Jacob:

> *"Blessed is he who blesses you,*
> *And cursed is he who curses you."*

Taken together, these Scriptures make it clear that both the blessing and the curse originally pronounced on Abraham were extended to his descendants, Isaac and Jacob, and then on to their succeeding generations, who are today known collectively as the Jewish people.

---

6. This second verb here translated "to curse" also means "to revile," "to speak evil of."

God did not make it impossible for His enemies to curse Abraham, Isaac, Jacob and their descendants, but He did ensure that no one could do it with impunity. From that time onward, no one has ever cursed the Jewish people without bringing upon himself a far more fearful curse: that of almighty God. In contemporary speech, the attitude that provokes this curse of God is summed up in a single word: *anti-Semitism.*

It would take a full-length book to trace the outworking of this curse in the history of individuals and nations from the time of the patriarchs until our day. Suffice it to say that in nearly 4,000 years, no individual and no nation has ever cursed the Jewish people without bringing upon themselves in return the blighting curse of God.

The story of Nabil Haddad provides a vivid contemporary illustration of both aspects of God's promise to Abraham: on the one hand, the curse on those who revile the Jewish people; and on the other hand, the blessing that results from blessing them. Nabil is a Palestinian Arab, born in Haifa into a well-known Arab family. Subsequently, he emigrated to the United States, where he became a successful businessman. He also had a powerful personal encounter with the Lord Jesus Christ. Here is his story in his own words:

My name is Nabil Haddad. I am a Palestinian Arab born in Haifa in 1938 to Christian Arab parents.

I remember that from my earliest childhood, I would always go to bed depressed. I became determined to find a way to be happy. I knew my parents loved me, but that didn't change my unhappiness. I became convinced that if I could become rich and successful, then I would be happy. That became my goal.

In 1948, the fighting between the Arabs and the Jews

began. Our whole family moved to Lebanon. In the late 1950s I came to the United States for college.

So, in America, I set out to achieve my goal of becoming rich and successful through education and business. Over the next few years, I married, became an American citizen, started a family and became a franchisee of McDonald's restaurants. By the age of thirty I was a millionaire. However, the depression had not left me. I started seeking material things – cars, trips, recreation, anything that money can buy – to make me happy. Nothing worked.

Finally, I began to ask questions: Who is this Man Jesus? Who is this One that people still talk about 2,000 years after His death? Who is this One that some people even worship?

I opened the Bible, wanting to see what this Jesus had said about Himself, and a Presence filled the room. Somehow I knew that Jesus is the Son of God. I spent most of the next year reading the Bible and talking to my friends about Jesus. But still I was depressed. During this time, I sold my nine McDonald's restaurants for a few million and started a new business. Things started to go sour. I became more depressed. I began to question God again.

"Why, Lord? Before I knew that Jesus is Your Son, I was doing fine. Now everything is going wrong!"

God replied, What have you done with the revelation that Jesus is My Son? Nothing in your life has changed. Even Satan knows that Jesus is My Son.

"What do You want me to do, Lord?"

Repent, and receive Him into your life.

I found someone who could show me how to pray. I

repented and asked Jesus into my heart. A few months later, I was baptised in the Holy Spirit. Now I had the answer. I no longer went to bed depressed. But my life was still not right. My business continued to go downhill. Again I confronted the Lord.

"Lord!" I said. "You tricked me. Before I knew anything about Your Son Jesus, I was doing all right. Then you showed me He is Your Son, and things started going wrong. Then I received Him into my life, and now I'm losing everything!"

I'm a jealous God, He replied. Your business is your god, your Rolls Royce is your god, your position is your god. I'm going to take all these false gods away from you to show you who the true living God is. But – I will restore you.

Within ten months, I was bankrupt.

A little later I went to Fort Lauderdale for a seminar called "Curses: Cause and Cure" taught by Derek Prince. I learned that many areas of my life were under a curse – financial, physical, not enjoying my children, etc. I remembered the same kinds of problems in my father's life and in the lives of other family members.

On the third day, when Derek led the few hundred people in a prayer to be set free from curses, I stood up. People in front of me, next to me, and behind me had physical manifestations of release. But my release did not occur at the meeting. The next day, for eight straight hours, I was being released from curses with painful vomiting of things that were attached deep inside my body. When I asked the Lord what I was being delivered from, He showed me witchcraft and many other specific problems.

For months the Lord continued to show me additional areas of curses. Each time I repented and claimed my release on the basis of Jesus becoming a curse for me.

One day as I was worshipping, I said, "How great You are! You created the universe and everything in it!" The Lord asked me if I really believed that. I said, "Yes, Lord."

He said, What about the Jewish people? You still hold resentment in your heart against them.

I remembered how my whole family had always cursed the Jews. I was trained to hate them from my earliest years. Now, in the presence of the Lord, I said, "I renounce any resentment in my heart toward the Jewish people. I forgive them!" Immediately something changed inside of me.

Shortly after this I saw that God in His Word had told Abraham, the father of the Jews, "I'll bless those who bless you and curse those who curse you" (Genesis 12:3). Then I realised that my finances had not been under a blessing, but under a curse – a curse of insufficiency. I had never been able to make enough money to meet my needs. Even if I made $250,000, I would need $300,000. Later, when I made $500,000, I would need $700,000 to cover my expenses.

Since 1982, when I was released from the curse of anti-Semitism and the curse of insufficiency that went with it, my income has always exceeded my expenses and my needs. And I am able to give liberally to the work of the Kingdom of God.

God has also healed my body and my emotions. I am totally free from depression. I can truly say I am walking in victory. My testimony has helped many others to be delivered from the curse and to live under God's blessing.

The lesson of Nabil's life is clear: *No one can afford to hate or curse the Jewish people.* This lesson was never more needed than it is today. Both socially and politically, anti-Semitism is one of the most powerful forces at work in our contemporary world. Yet ultimately it spells disaster for all who allow themselves to be controlled by it.

Unfortunately, throughout many centuries, the professing Christian Church has often been guilty of propagating flagrant anti-Semitism. Yet the Church owes every spiritual blessing she claims to those who have been her victims: the Jewish people. Without the Jews, the Church would have had no apostles, no Bible, and no Saviour.

Here is one main reason for the present lukewarm, powerless condition of so much of Christendom – especially in Europe and the Middle East, where anti-Semitism is most deeply entrenched. The story of Nabil Haddad points to the solution: open acknowledgement of anti-Semitism as a sin, followed by repentance and renunciation. This would result in a deep, inner change of heart toward the Jewish people, and a recognition of the measureless spiritual blessings the Christian Church has received through them.

On this basis, we can then entreat God to remove the dark shadow of the curse, which at present rests upon major sections of the Church, and to replace it by His blessing.

9
LEGALISM, CARNALITY, APOSTASY

In Jeremiah 17:5 God pronounces His curse on another kind of sin which, like anti-Semitism, is at work in many sections of the Church:

> *Thus says the Lord:*
> *"Cursed is the man who trusts in man*
> *And makes flesh his strength,*
> *Whose heart departs from the Lord."*

In this context – as in many other passages of Scripture – the word *flesh* does not denote the physical body. Rather, it denotes the nature each of us has received by inheritance from our common ancestor, Adam. Adam did not beget any children until he himself had transgressed God's commandment. The essential motivation of his transgression was not so much the desire to do evil as the desire to be independent of God.

This desire is at work in every one of Adam's descendants. It is the distinctive mark of the "flesh." In the field of religion, it seeks to perform righteous acts without depending on the supernatural grace of God. No matter how good its intentions, the final product will always be an "Ishmael," not an "Isaac."

The adjective which Scripture applies regularly to the flesh is *corrupt*. Although it can produce much that is designed to impress the mind and the senses, it is all tainted by corruption. The outcome of all its efforts is described in Hebrews 6:1 as "dead works," from which God requires us to repent.

The kind of person described in Jeremiah 17:5 is not a stranger to God's grace. This is indicated by the closing phrase: "whose heart departs from the Lord." If he had never known the Lord, he could not be said to "depart" from Him. A person of this kind has experienced God's supernatural grace and power, but then turns back to relying on his own natural ability. His conduct reveals that he has more confidence in what he can do for himself than in what God can do for him. He has, in fact, "snubbed" God. It is this attitude which calls forth God's curse.

The next verse describes the outworking of the curse that such a person brings upon himself:

> *"For he shall be like a shrub in the desert,*
> *And shall not see when good comes,*
> *But shall inhabit the parched places in the wilderness,*
> *In a salt land which is not inhabited."*

What a vivid picture of a person under God's curse! He finds himself living in "parched places" and "a salt land." All that surrounds him is barren and dreary. Refreshing may come to others all around him, but in some mysterious way it always passes him by. He is doomed to barrenness and frustration.

The curse of Jeremiah 17:5-6 is at work in the lives of many individuals, but it also applies to a much wider area. It is one real but invisible cause of the barrenness and ineffectiveness of many sections of the contemporary Christian Church. Almost every movement of any significance in Christendom can trace its origin to a powerful, supernatural work of God's grace and God's Spirit. It is to this, above all else, that they owe the impact they have made on history.

Yet, today, many – perhaps most – of these movements no longer place much emphasis on the grace of God and the power of the Holy Spirit. They have turned back to relying on the best that they can accomplish by their own efforts. They are "trusting in man" – that is, in themselves – and "making flesh their strength." Surely, but imperceptibly, "their heart has departed from the Lord." They have, perhaps, achieved religious and intellectual "respectability," but in so doing they have forfeited God's favour. In its place, they have brought upon themselves the dark shadow of the curse pronounced in Jeremiah 17:5.

To put human ability in the place of divine grace is to exalt the carnal above the spiritual. The effect will be manifested in many different areas. For example:

> *Theology* will be exalted above *revelation;*
> *intellectual education* above *character building;*
> *psychology* above *discernment;*
> *programme* above the *leading of the Holy Spirit;*
> *eloquence* above *supernatural power;*
> *reasoning* above the *walk of faith;*
> *laws* above *love.*

All these errors are different manifestations of one great, basic error: putting man in a place God has reserved solely for the Lord Jesus Christ.

This was the kind of situation Paul sought to deal with in the churches of Galatia. In Galatians 3:1-10 he traces the problem from its source to its culmination. The following is a brief outline.

In verse 1 Paul identifies the source as a deceiving satanic influence he calls *witchcraft:*

> *O foolish Galatians! Who has bewitched you . . . before whose eyes Jesus Christ was clearly portrayed . . . as crucified?*

An alternative version renders Paul's question, "Who has put you under *a spell?"*

This satanic influence had obscured the only source of God's all-sufficient grace: *Jesus Christ crucified.* Cut off in this way from God's grace, His people inevitably turn back to the only alternative: a system of religious laws. This leads to Paul's next question in verse 2: "Did you receive the Spirit *by the works of the law,* or by the hearing of faith?" The word normally used to describe this is *legalism.* Since this word is often used in an imprecise way, however, it is important to define it more exactly.

Legalism may be defined in two related ways. First, it is the attempt to achieve righteousness with God by observing a set of rules.

In Romans 3:20 Paul has ruled this out with absolute finality: "Therefore by the deeds of the law no flesh will be justified in His sight, for by the law is the knowledge of sin." The word *the* in front of *law* is put in by the translator. What Paul actually says is, *"By the deeds of law* no flesh will be justified." The primary reference is to the Law of Moses, but the statement applies no less to any other set of religious rules. Law can show us that we are sinners, but it does not have the power to change us.

Alternatively, *legalism* could be defined as the attempt to impose any extra condition for achieving righteousness beyond what God Himself has laid down. God's requirement is stated in Romans 4:24-25:

> It *[righteousness] shall be imputed to us who believe in Him who raised up Jesus our Lord from the dead, who was delivered up because of our offences, and was raised because of our justification [in order that we may be reckoned righteous by God].*

This is God's simple but all-sufficient requirement to attain righteousness: that we trust ourselves to Him, believing that He did two things on our behalf. First, He delivered Jesus to death for our sins. Second, He raised Jesus from the dead that we might be reckoned righteous. God asks no more than this, and no one has ever been authorised to add anything to God's requirements.

After that, once we have received righteousness in this way by faith, the righteous acts that are appropriate will flow out of our faith. But if we add any extra requirement for attaining righteousness, God will not meet us on this basis, and the righteous acts will not follow. We will never be able to go beyond the best that we can achieve by our own fleshly efforts.

This explains Paul's next question in Galatians 3:3: "Having begun in the Spirit, are you now being made perfect *by the flesh?*" The normal term for this is *carnality* – that is, relying on our own fleshly nature. Further on, in Galatians 5:19-21, Paul lists at least 15 "works of the flesh." Not one of them is good or acceptable to God, because the flesh is not capable of producing anything that God will accept. In Romans 8:8 Paul sums this up: "So then, those who are in the flesh cannot please God."

Finally, in Galatians 3:10, Paul states the culmination of this descending process: *a curse.* "For as many as are of the works of the law are under the curse."

Thus, by the logic of the Holy Spirit, Paul analyses the problem of the Galatian churches, which is also the problem of many contemporary churches. It stems from a deceiving, satanic influence that infiltrates the church and diverts the attention of God's people from the only source of His grace: *Jesus Christ crucified.* Paul categorises this influence as *witchcraft* or *a spell.*

Cut off in this way from the source of grace, Christians inevitably degenerate into carnality and legalism. The final outcome of this downward drift is a *curse.* It has already been pointed out – in chapter 6 – that spells and curses are the main tools of witchcraft.

In this way, the truth of Jeremiah 17:5-6 is carried over into the New Testament, and finds its expression in Galatians 3:1-10. "Trusting in the works of the law [legalism]" and "making flesh our strength [carnality]" culminate in a curse. As a result, God's people find themselves living in "parched places" and "a salt land."

Carnality can take many forms. Often these are obvious and unappealing to people with a religious outlook. Some typical examples would be: sexual uncleanness or immorality; vulgar language; overindulgence in food or drink; driving personal ambition; uncontrolled anger or other evil passions. What makes legalism especially dangerous is that it appeals to earnest, dedicated men and women who would not easily be entrapped by these more obvious sins of the flesh. Yet in its final consequences, legalism is just as deadly as other, less "respectable" sins. It is Satan's favourite tool to divert Christians who could otherwise become a serious threat to his kingdom.

For me personally, the analysis of the Galatian problem is no mere exercise in abstract theology. On the contrary, it is very real, and also painful. In 1970, in Fort Lauderdale, I found myself sovereignly and supernaturally "joined" to a small group of ministers from various backgrounds. None of us had anticipated what happened to us, and none of us understood what God had in mind for us. Doubtless, if we had continued to rely on the Holy Spirit who had initiated our relationship, He would have gradually unfolded His purpose to us, but that was not the path we followed.

All too soon, and without our discerning what was happening, the various features of the Galatians 3 "syndrome" began to manifest themselves. Our decisions and actions were no longer initiated by the Holy Spirit, but were based on an elaborate system of rules and concepts which had been devised. We continued to acknowledge the Holy Spirit, but in the way that guests in a restaurant might acknowledge a waiter. If we felt we needed something, we would summon Him briefly. But for the most part we relied on methods and plans of our own devising.

Looking back, I realise now that the work the Holy Spirit had initiated among us posed a serious threat to Satan. He resorted, consequently, to the tactics that had been so successful in Galatia, and in countless other situations throughout subsequent Church history. There were two decisive steps. First, he displaced the cross from the centre of our lives and ministries. Second, he displaced Jesus as "Head over all things" in our practices and relationships[7]. By an inevitable process, we degenerated into the normal type of religious organisation, operating on the plane of our natural reason and ability.

Paradoxically, one main cause of our problems was the very fact that we had had a supernatural beginning. Like the Galatians,

7. See Ephesians 1:22 - 23.

we had "begun in the Spirit." From that beginning, there was no easy or painless route by which we could simply become just another religious organisation, functioning on the natural plane and taking our place alongside countless similar groups throughout Christendom. As Paul pointed out to the Galatians, that which has been initiated by the Holy Spirit can never be brought to completion by human flesh.

It was not long before we were confronted by the outworking of the curse which we had thus brought on ourselves. Its manifestations were characteristic of other similar developments throughout Church history. Personal relationships were ruptured; congregations were split and scattered; promising ministries were cut short or else diverted from God's purpose; once-enthusiastic Christians were blighted by frustration and disillusionment. Many abandoned their faith. If we had been obliged to give a name to it all, we would have had to call it "Ichabod, saying, 'The glory has departed' " (1 Samuel 4:21).

The product of all religious activity that is not initiated and directed by the Holy Spirit is summed up, in Hebrews 6:1, by the phrase *dead works.* For this, the remedy is stated in the same verse: *repentance.* This was made real to me personally. I could not blame others. I had to accept responsibility for what I had been involved in. More than anything else, I realised that I had grieved and slighted the Holy Spirit.

I saw that I had to confess my sins to God and trust Him for forgiveness and restoration. This was a personal decision that only I could make. I could not make it on behalf of others, but if I could find a path that led to restoration, then those who saw their need could follow the same path. In 1983 I repented and made the break.

In His mercy, God showed me, step by step, the path I was seeking. I discovered that there is a way to pass out from under the curse and enter once more into the blessing. If I had not made this discovery, this book would never have been written. For those who may find themselves in a similar situation, I offer a full explanation of the steps they need to take in Section 3: "From Curse to Blessing."

In Galatians 1:6-9 Paul exposes another way a curse may come upon the people of God: *apostasy.*

> *I marvel that you are turning away so soon from Him who called you in the grace of Christ, to a different gospel,*
>
> *which is not another; but there are some who trouble you and want to pervert the gospel of Christ.*
>
> *But even if we, or an angel from heaven, preach any other gospel to you than what we have preached to you, let him be accursed.*
>
> *As we have said before, so now I say again, if anyone preaches any other gospel to you than what you have received, let him be accursed.*

The kind of person here described is one who represents himself as a minister of Christ, but perverts the central truth of the Gospel. Paul declares that such a person brings a curse upon himself. The Greek word translated "accursed" is *anathema.* It denotes something that provokes God's wrath and is subject to His irrevocable condemnation and rejection.

The Gospel contains a central core of revealed truth which has been accepted and upheld by the general Church throughout all generations. It may be summed up as follows:

> Jesus Christ is the divine, eternal Son of God, who became a member of the human race by virgin birth. He

led a sinless life, died on the cross as a propitiatory
sacrifice for the sins of humanity, was buried and rose
again in bodily form from the grave on the third day. He
ascended into heaven, whence He will return to earth in
person, to judge the living and the dead.

Everyone who repents of sin and trusts in the
sacrifice of Jesus receives forgiveness of sins and the
gift of eternal life.

It is important to emphasise that the Gospel centres in the death
and resurrection of Jesus. In 1 Corinthians 15:3-4 Paul sums up its
message in three historical facts: "Christ died for our sins
according to the Scriptures . . . He was buried . . . He rose again
the third day according to the Scriptures."

The first authority that Paul cites in support of these facts is
"the Scriptures" – at that time meaning the Scriptures of the Old
Testament. As further confirmation of the resurrection, Paul goes
on to list various eyewitnesses who saw Jesus after He rose from
the dead. Their testimony is secondary, however, to that of the Old
Testament Scriptures.

In two successive statements, Paul then stresses that faith in the
bodily resurrection of Jesus is essential to salvation:

> *And if Christ is not risen, then our preaching is vain and
> your faith is also vain . . . And if Christ is not risen, your
> faith is futile; you are still in your sins!*
> 1 Corinthians 15:14, 17

In 2 Thessalonians 2:3 Paul warns that at the close of this age
there will be widespread apostasy from the Christian faith. There
are strong reasons for believing that we are now in the predicted
period of apostasy. In some major Christian denominations, many

recognised leaders have publicly renounced faith in the Scriptures and – in particular – in the bodily resurrection of Christ. Probably they do not realise that their declaration of unbelief is in itself a fulfilment of the Scriptures which they are rejecting!

One fact, however, they cannot change: unless they repent, those who in this way pervert the Gospel bring upon themselves the wrath and the curse of God.

10
THEFT, PERJURY, ROBBING GOD

The last three prophets of the Old Testament – Haggai, Zechariah and Malachi – all deal with various areas in which Israel experienced the outworking of God's curse. It is as though these prophets were given the task of summarising the history of the Israelites since they had come under the Law of Moses, and of confronting them with the reasons why specific curses of the Law had come upon them.

In Zechariah 5:1-4 the prophet describes a vision he had of God's curse coming upon the homes of His people:

> *I looked again – and there before me was a flying scroll!*
> *He asked me, "What do you see?"*
> *I answered, "I see a flying scroll, thirty feet long and fifteen feet wide."*

And he said to me, "This is the curse that is going out over the whole land; for according to what it says on one side, every thief will be banished, and according to what it says on the other, everyone who swears falsely will be banished. The Lord Almighty declares, 'I will send it out, and it will enter the house of the thief and the house of him who swears falsely by my name. It will remain in his house and destroy it, both its timbers and its stones.'"

NIV

The curse that Zechariah depicts enters the house of all who have committed two specific sins: theft and swearing falsely. (The contemporary term for the latter is *perjury*.) Having once entered, the curse remains until it has destroyed the entire house – timbers and stones and all.

This is a vivid picture of the way a curse works, if we once admit it into our lives. We cannot set limits of our own choosing to the areas that will be affected by it. Unless we repent and seek God's mercy to deliver us, it will ultimately destroy the whole house.

The prevalence of these two sins of theft and perjury in our contemporary culture may be measured by some simple statistics. Theft is so pervasive today in the United States that nearly ten percent of the price of goods displayed in retail stores is due to the cost of insurance against theft. Here is a little-publicised cause of inflation! On the other side, perjury defrauds the U.S. Internal Revenue Service of billions of dollars each year through dishonest tax returns. Complete honesty in this area could perhaps wipe out the entire budget deficit!

According to Zechariah's vision, the curse that follows these two sins of theft and perjury affects not merely the individual, but also his entire house. In biblical Hebrew, the word *house* applies not simply to a material structure, but also to the people who live in it – that is, a family. Much more than would at first appear, these two sins, and the curse that follows them, have contributed to the breakdown of family life, which is a unique feature of our present age. Their ultimate effect will be similar to that of the scroll Zechariah saw in his vision: the erosion of whole nations, and even an entire civilisation.

Earlier, Haggai had given an equally vivid picture of the blight that was affecting the lives of his people:

> *"Is it time for you yourselves to dwell in your panelled houses, and this temple to lie in ruins?"*
> *Now therefore, thus says the Lord of hosts: "Consider your ways!*
> *You have sown much, and bring in little;*
> *You eat, but do not have enough;*
> *You drink, but you are not filled with drink;*
> *You clothe yourselves, but no one is warm;*
> *And he who earns wages,*
> *Earns wages to put into a bag with holes."*
>
> Haggai 1:4-6

The curse which Haggai describes can be summed up in one word: *insufficiency.* To all outward appearances, the Israelites had everything they required to satisfy their main material needs. Yet for some reason they could not understand, there was always a deficiency. God had to send them a prophet to show them that the invisible force eroding their provisions was a curse they had brought upon themselves by putting their own selfish concerns before the needs of God's house.

Many of the affluent nations of the world today face a similar situation. Most people are earning far more than their parents or grandparents ever earned. Yet while the previous generations enjoyed a sense of contentment and security, the present generation is plagued with a restless craving which is never satisfied. In some of these nations, the level of personal indebtedness is higher than it has ever been.

Malachi, the last of the three prophets, combines the charges already brought against Israel by his two predecessors. He accuses his people not only of a wrong attitude toward God, but also of theft in its most serious form: robbing not merely men, but even God Himself.

> *"Will a man rob God?*
> *Yet you have robbed Me!*
> *But you say,*
> *'In what way have we robbed You?'*
> *In tithes and offerings.*
> *You are cursed with a curse,*
> *For you have robbed Me,*
> *Even this whole nation."*
>
> Malachi 3:8-9

This passage reveals a principle that governs God's dealings in every age and dispensation: He keeps a record of what His people offer to Him. More than a thousand years earlier, God had ordained that Israel should set aside for Him the first tenth of their total income, in cash or in kind. This was one important mark of their covenant relationship with God. Disobedience in this was a breach of their covenant.

Now, through Malachi, God presents His account. In respect of all that His people have unlawfully withheld, He charges them with "robbery." He points out that this has brought a blighting curse on the whole nation and on every area of their lives.

But God does not end on this negative note. In the next verse He instructs His people how to pass out from under the curse and enter into His blessing:

> *"Bring all the tithes into the storehouse,*
> *That there may be food in My house,*
> *And prove Me now in this,"*
> *Says the Lord of hosts,*
> *"If I will not open for you the windows of heaven*
> *And pour out for you such blessing*
> *That there will not be room enough to receive it."*
> Malachi 3:10

To pass from the curse to the blessing, God requires from His people two things: repentance and restitution. In every case of robbery, these requirements never vary, whether it is God or man who has been robbed.

In the New Testament, God never establishes a specific law, like that of the Old Testament, requiring Christians to set aside for Him a tenth of their total income. The covenant of grace does not operate through laws enforced from without, but through laws written by the Holy Spirit in the hearts of believers. In 2 Corinthians 9:7 Paul instructs Christians, "So let each one give *as he purposes in his heart,* not grudgingly or of necessity."

One thing, however, is certain: The Holy Spirit will never cause a believer to be stingy. In Psalm 51:12 David prays to the Lord, "Uphold me with Your *generous* Spirit." One distinctive characteristic of the Holy Spirit is generosity. God Himself is the greatest of all givers. When His Spirit moves on the hearts of His people, He will make them like Himself: generous givers.

In Hebrews 8:6 the writer contrasts the Old and the New

Covenants, and reminds Christians that they have entered into "a better covenant, which was established on better promises." It is inconceivable that people who enjoy this better covenant should be less generous in giving to God than those who were under an inferior covenant. If God's people under the Law gave Him their tithes – and much more – how could Christians under grace possibly justify doing less? The standards of grace are higher, not lower, than those of law.

Throughout all dispensations, one basic principle continues unchanged: stinginess toward God provokes His curse, but liberality releases His blessing.

11
AUTHORITY FIGURES

B oth blessings and curses are part of a vast, invisible spiritual
realm, which affects the lives of every one of us. One central
and decisive factor in this realm is *authority*. Without a grasp of
the principles of authority, it is impossible to understand the realm
of the spirit or to function effectively in it.

The twentieth century has witnessed an almost worldwide
revolt against forms of authority that have been generally recognised by the human race for millennia. Major areas of social
structure that have been affected include the family, the church
and the various branches of secular government.

People often assume that this revolt has changed or abolished
these forms of authority, but *this is not so*. The principles that
govern the exercise of authority are as objective and universal as
the law of gravity.

A person in an attitude of revolt may decide to reject the law of gravity and to jump out of a window on the tenth floor. But his rejection of that law in no way changes or invalidates it. He will still fall to his death on the sidewalk below. The same applies to the laws that govern the exercise of authority. People may ignore them or reject them, but the course of their lives will still be determined by them, whether they recognise it or not.

Throughout the universe there is one, and only one, supreme source of authority: God the Creator. However, God does not normally exercise His authority directly, however, but delegates it to others of His choice. After Jesus rose from the dead, He told His disciples, "All authority has been given to Me in heaven and on earth" (Matthew 28:18). Since that time, God has placed all authority in the hand of Jesus. But Jesus, in His turn, delegates to others the authority He has received from the Father.

Thus authority throughout the universe may be pictured as an extremely strong cable, descending from God the Father to Jesus. In the hand of Jesus, the cable is separated into countless smaller cables that reach to persons whom He has appointed – both angelic and human – in various parts of the universe.

One term used in the Bible to denote a person who exercises authority is *head*. In 1 Corinthians 11:3, for instance, Paul writes:

> *But I want you to know that the head of every man is Christ, the head of woman is man, and the head of Christ is God.*

By this analogy of headship, Paul depicts a "cable" of authority which originates with God the Father, descends to Christ and from Christ to the man who fills the role of husband and father in a family. By virtue of this relationship, the man is the appointed authority in his home.

In human social relationships, the husband/father is the primary example of a person appointed to exercise authority. However, there are many other commonly recognised authority figures: a ruler over his people; a military commander over his soldiers; a teacher over his pupils; a pastor over the members of his congregation.

God alone has *absolute* authority. All other forms of authority are subject to limitations of various kinds. Delegated authority is valid only *within a given sphere.* A ruler's authority, for instance, is normally limited by the laws of his nation and does not extend to "private" areas in the lives of his subjects. A father's authority over his family does not permit him to infringe the laws of the secular government. A teacher has authority over his pupils only within the limits of school life. A pastor has authority over his congregation only in matters that are governed by the form of religion which the congregation has accepted.

All the above examples are generalities. For complete accuracy, it would be necessary to add many other qualifications and restrictions. Also, there could be cases where two forms of authority overlap, giving rise to conflicts. The examples given are sufficient, however, to establish the basic principles that govern the exercise of authority.

It is commonly assumed that whenever authority is abused, it is automatically cancelled. This may happen in extreme cases, but normally it is not so. Authority in some form is a basic necessity for any kind of social life. Authority that is abused may inflict many hardships, but even so it is better than the alternative, which is anarchy[8].

In many population centres today, the air that people breathe has become so polluted that it is dangerous to health. God does not for this reason, however, remove all air from that area of the

8. Webster's Dictionary defines anarchy as: (i) The complete absence of government (ii) political disorder and violence; lawlessness (iii) disorder in any sphere of activity.

earth's surface. Even polluted air is preferable to no air at all. Similarly, even abused authority is better than anarchy.

One important way a person may exercise authority is by blessing those under his authority. Genesis 27 records the tremendous importance that both Jacob and Esau attached to the blessing of their father Isaac. And with good reason, since the history of their descendants has been determined ever since by the words Isaac spoke over each of them at that time. Nor is Isaac an isolated exception. On the contrary, all through the Bible, the blessing of a father is considered second in importance only to that of God Himself.

Implicit in the authority to bless, however, is the authority also to curse. Blessing and cursing can never be separated from one another, any more than heat from cold or day from night. This means that persons with authority may exercise it in one of two ways: to bless or to curse. The same authority that makes a blessing effective makes a curse equally effective.

One dramatic example is provided by the family life of Jacob. Genesis 31 records how Jacob, with his two wives, two concubines and eleven children, departed by stealth from his Uncle Laban in Mesopotamia and set out to return to the land of Canaan. Laban, however, with a company of his relatives, set out in pursuit of Jacob and overtook him in the mountains of Gilead. There followed a confrontation between them, in which Laban accused Jacob of stealing his *teraphim* (household images, or "gods," used for divination and supposed to "protect" a home from evil forces).

What Jacob did not know was that Rachel, the wife he loved most dearly, had secretly taken the images. Consequently, Jacob reacted indignantly to Laban's accusation. He challenged Laban to search all his family's belongings, and then – to protest his innocence – he added what was in effect a curse: "If you find anyone who has your gods, he shall not live" (Genesis 31:32, NIV).

Laban did proceed to search all the belongings of Jacob's household, but Rachel succeeded in keeping the *teraphim* hidden. Nevertheless, the words of Jacob's curse were charged with a husband's authority. They were equivalent to a sentence of death on the person who had stolen the images. The fact that Jacob did not realise that his words were directed against Rachel did not prevent the curse from taking effect. Shortly afterward, in giving birth to her second son, Rachel died in labour. (See Genesis 35:16-19.) Such is the authority of a husband, either to bless or to curse!

It should be added that, by taking possession of false "gods," Rachel had trespassed in the area of idolatry and of the occult. Thus, by her own action she had already forfeited God's protection and exposed herself to the curse that inevitably follows occult involvement. Here is a clear example that the laws governing blessings and curses are – in their own sphere – as real and as objective as the law of gravity. They work, whether people recognise them or not.

In God's plan for marriage, husband and wife become "one flesh," thus merging their separate identities in a new unity. On this basis, a husband naturally includes his wife in the authority they share jointly over their children. Failing to do this, the husband may become arbitrary or despotic.

Today, however, it is more common for a husband to go to the opposite extreme by reneging on his responsibilities to his wife and children, and even abandoning them completely. In such circumstances, the wife is left to carry on her own a burden that should have been shared by the two of them together. The result is frequently a complete breakdown of the whole family structure. All credit should be given to Christian wives who find themselves in this situation, but by faith, prayer and the grace of God success- fully carry the extra burden that has been thrust upon them.

In the case of Jacob, he did not realise that the words he had uttered were directed against Rachel. In our contemporary culture, however, it often happens that a husband knowingly and deliberately directs bitter and crushing words against his wife. Here is a typical example:

Mary, who never received any domestic training from her mother at home, marries Jack, a business executive with a quick temper. Mary never succeeds in serving meals that are tasty or attractive. For a while, Jack exercises self-control and contains his impatience. Finally, he blurts out his frustration: "I'm sick of the way you serve our meals. You'll never learn to cook!" He repeats this – with variations – on many subsequent occasions.

From then on, Mary's hands tremble whenever she brings food to the table. Meals become an ordeal from which she longs to escape. After some years, the marriage breaks up. But the curse pronounced by Jack follows Mary through the rest of her life. Although talented and successful in other areas, she never does learn to cook. Whenever she finds herself in a kitchen, something dark comes over her that inhibits her natural ability. There is only one solution for her: to recognise the fact that her husband put a curse on her and to seek the release God has provided.

It also transpires, however, that Jack has pronounced a curse on himself, without knowing it. From the time he says, "I'm *sick* of the way you serve our meals," he begins to develop chronic indigestion, for which physicians can find no natural cause or cure. Just like Mary's inability to cook, Jack's indigestion follows him to the end of his days.

(Chapter 12 will cover this important area of *self-imposed* curses.)

Obviously there could be many variations to the story of Jack and Mary. Mary's problem might be overweight. Jack's comment would take this form: "You just don't have the willpower that it takes to lose weight. You'll be fat for the rest of your life."

Or again, Mary might be one of those women who do not know how to handle money. Her budgeted amount runs out before the week is up. She never succeeds in balancing her chequebook. Jack might give vent to his frustration by saying: "A fourth-grader could handle money better than you do. You don't deserve to prosper. You'll be struggling for the rest of your life."

Picture another couple: Jim and Jane. Jim's language is more brutal than Jack's. He frequently closes bitter arguments by saying, "I hate your guts!" In the years that follow the inevitable divorce, Jane requires surgery in the area of the abdomen for three successive conditions, none of them directly related to the others.

The correct diagnosis for all three of Jane's problems is stated in Proverbs 12:18: "There is one who speaks like the piercings of a sword." It required the surgeon's scalpel to deal with the invisible wounds that Jim had inflicted by his bitter words.

Words such as Jack uses against Mary – or Jim against Jane – proceed out of moods that may range from impatience to anger to rage. Usually there is demonic pressure behind them. They are like barbed arrows, tipped with poison. Once they penetrate the flesh, the barbs make it difficult to pull them out. Yet if they are left in, the poison spreads on the inside.

Greater even than the authority of a man over his wife is that of a father over his children. This is the most basic of all authority relationships. It is actually an extension of the eternal relationship of Father to Son within the Godhead.

Just as a father's blessing has measureless potential for good, so a father's curse has a corresponding potential for evil. Sometimes such a curse may be uttered deliberately. More often, perhaps – as in the relationship of a husband to his wife – a father may speak words to a child that are not deliberately intended as a curse, but nevertheless have exactly the same effect. Each of the following examples is a composite of elements I have encountered in real-life situations.

A father has three sons. The firstborn is welcome just because he is that – the firstborn. The youngest has unusual talent and an outgoing personality. But the middle son has neither of these factors in his favour. He broods over misunderstandings, but tends to keep his feelings to himself. Furthermore, the father sees in this middle son aspects of his own character which he does not like, but has never been willing to deal with in his own life. He finds it less painful to condemn them in his son than in himself.

As a result, the middle son never has a sense of his father's approval. In the end, he no longer tries to win it. His father interprets this as stubbornness. More and more frequently, he vents his disapproval in words such as: "You don't even try! You're lazy! You'll never make good!" Little does he realise that he is pronouncing an evil destiny which may easily follow his son through the rest of his life.

I could not count the men I have encountered personally whose lives have been blighted by negative, critical, destructive words spoken by a father. Out of these encounters I have learned that such words are, in reality, a *curse*. The passage of time does not diminish their effect. Men past middle age may still find their lives blighted by words a father spoke to them in childhood. The only effective solution is to deal with them specifically as a curse, and to apply the remedy which God has provided.

As with the case of Jack and Mary, or Jim and Jane, there are many different variations to such a situation. A father who is skilful with his hands, for example, may have a son who is unusually late in developing manual dexterity. After the son has bungled various practical tasks assigned to him, the father exclaims, "Your fingers are all thumbs!" or, "You have two left hands!"

The father may speak these words jokingly, not in anger. Nevertheless, they make a permanent impact on the son. Thirty years later he is still embarrassed or diffident every time he is confronted with even a simple practical task. This continues to be an area of his life in which he never succeeds. Yet his root problem may not be so much lack of skill as lack of confidence. He has never rebuilt the confidence which his father unintentionally destroyed in childhood.

Daughters, too, like sons, may suffer from the effects of a father's negative words. A teenage daughter, for instance, acutely conscious of her acne, spends hours each morning in front of her mirror, struggling to cover the blotches with various types of skin cream. Her father, waiting to drive her to school, is increasingly irritated by her failure to be ready on time. One day, when the daughter is later than usual, his irritation explodes. "You're wasting your time in front of that mirror," he barks. "You'll never get rid of your pimples!" Twenty years later the daughter – now a married woman with children of her own – is still struggling vainly to cover up her acne.

Bitter, angry words – whether spoken by a husband to his wife or a father to his child – are usually the outcome of a period of growing inner tension. It is like a whistling kettle placed on a stove to boil. At first, the tension builds up inwardly, without any outward indication. But when the water inside reaches the boiling point, the steam is expelled and the whistle is blown. After that, there is no way to recall that whistle. The only remedy is to take the kettle off and cool the water down.

For a Christian, this means turning to God with an urgent, inward prayer: "Lord, I'm beginning to lose control, but I yield my spirit to You. Will *You* please take control?"

Otherwise, when irritation and anger continually build up inside a person, they will ultimately be expelled, like steam, in hurtful, wounding words. The curse that accompanies them is like the whistle. Once it has been uttered, there is no way to recall it. Then the only solution is to recognise that a curse has been uttered, and seek God's help to revoke it.

A mother, too, has authority over her children, which is either shared with her husband or delegated by him. Sometimes, however, a mother is not content with the exercise of her legitimate authority. Instead, she exploits her children's affection and loyalty to gain illegitimate control over them and to direct the course of their lives. Another example of "witchcraft"! This becomes particularly evident when her children come to choose their mates. If the mother approves of their choice, she is all sweetness. But if she disapproves, a totally different side of her character appears.

In the section that follows, a husband and wife each relate their experiences resulting from a curse pronounced by the wife's mother at the time of their marriage. They describe, first of all, the effects that the curse had on each of them; then how they became aware of the curse and took the scriptural steps to be released from it.

Husband

Living under a curse is like living in a vapour. The effects can be seen, yet it is without clear form and substance. Even though you may experience success, you feel only frustration and hopelessness.

For me, the blessings of God always seemed somewhat remote and unattainable. I often knew the Lord's presence and moved in the spiritual gifts, yet satisfaction in ministry and life always seemed just out of reach. My wife and children had nagging health problems, and finances were continually short (even though we tithed, gave regularly and lived frugally).

Though I knew clearly the ministry to which God had called me, I could not move into it. Most of my work seemed to end with just a measure of fruitfulness. I could start things, but couldn't complete them. I seemed to be facing some kind of invisible resistance.

This struggle went on for years. Then one day I found myself explaining the situation to a group of fellow ministers, including Derek Prince. They discerned a curse coming on my family from my mother-in-law. I will let my wife explain:

Wife

Early in my marriage I spent two days in prayer and fasting. I felt the Lord showed me that there was a curse in my family. My husband and I were newly baptised in the Holy Spirit and had never even heard of such a thing as a curse. Our experience, as we have sought to become free, could be compared to peeling layers off an onion.

This curse revolves around a spirit of witchcraft that has operated through the women in my family, especially my mother. My family was churchgoing, moral and quite "normal," but the witchcraft worked subtly to undermine the authority of the men in our family, while manipulating the other family members.

I was not aware of the extent of my mother's control until I became engaged. As my loyalty began to switch to my future husband, I could sense her growing resentment. That was when my mother said, "He'll

never make any money and you'll have to work the rest
of your life." All through the years of our marriage I
have laboured against that "curse." I was determined to
"show her" by not working in an outside job, but I was,
in fact, controlled by it because I wasn't free to have a
job! Also, my husband and I could never visualise
ourselves as prosperous, and we have had continual
financial problems.

Then, shortly after I married, my mother said, "You
know you're not a strong person physically." I felt as if
someone had hit me on the head! What she said was
such a shock to me because I had never perceived
myself as a weak or sickly person. On the contrary, I
had always been healthy and athletic. So I began to
think that perhaps I had been wrong, and really wasn't
strong physically . . . Subsequently I have battled a lot
of physical ailments, some of long duration.

I also struggled because I was responding to my own
husband and children in some of the same ways my
mother did. This left me with a sense of hopelessness.
How could I get completely free from this curse?
Witchcraft had exercised control in several generations
of my family. It seemed the spirit associated with it
truly believed it had the right to dominate me and, in
fact, it believed it owned me!

Whenever I would be ministered to for deliverance
this spirit would whisper to me that I couldn't really be
completely free. I blamed my mother . . . Through a
slow, "layer-by-layer" process of revelation and deliverance I came to see that my enemy is not my mother. I
have forgiven her, and acknowledged the curse of
witchcraft that had been influencing both of us.

Since having ministry specifically to break these curses, I have had to learn to battle old thought and habit patterns. Now I daily confess with confidence: "Through the sacrificial offering of Christ on the cross I have been purchased out from under the curse and have entered into the blessings of Abraham, whom God blessed in all things" (Galatians 3:13-14). Christ has redeemed me from the curse!

Husband

After prayer for breaking of curses, there was a distinct "clearing of the air." The changes have been neither dramatic nor immediate, but they have been real. There is a sense of direction in my life.

There is progress. I feel that I have a scriptural degree of control over my life and that I can take my rightful place in my family. I can also see productivity and fruitfulness as a result of my labours.

Most important to me, there is hope. The nebulous darkness of the future has been replaced by excitement and joy at what God is doing. The "fog" is clearing!

*   *   *

It is important to see that the wife's mother was not aware of all the effects that her words had on her daughter and son-in-law. She herself was the prisoner of a spiritual force that came from her own family background. Quite possibly it had affected that family for many generations. The mercy of God provided a way of release from its control.

School life is another area in which authority relationships are important, although the authority of a teacher over pupils is not so clear-cut as that of a parent. Negative words spoken by a teacher to a pupil may have the same blighting effect as if they had been spoken by a parent. For instance, a teacher may become exasperated by a pupil who is inattentive and slow to learn, and blurt out words such as: "You'll never be able to read properly!" or "You always get things the wrong way 'round; you'll never succeed!"

In all probability, the teacher is unaware of the danger of such words and will never see the result they produce on the pupils in later life. Yet I have met grown men and women who have been struggling for the rest of their lives against the effect of words spoken by a teacher in grade school. I recall one dedicated Christian lady who had been haunted for forty years by a sense of inferiority going back to a remark by a teacher who had told her, "You're shallow!" In fact, it would have been difficult to find anyone to whom these words were less applicable.

Examples have been given above of the potentially blighting effect of words spoken by people who have authority proceeding out of a relationship. The specific relationships – chosen merely as examples – were those of a husband, a father, a mother and a schoolteacher. There is one characteristic thread that runs through the various ways in which these authority figures expressed themselves. It can be summed up in one brief phrase: "You'll never prosper – or succeed!"

Surely it is significant that Moses, in describing to Israel the outworking of "the curse of the law," used precisely the same words: "You shall not prosper in your ways" (Deuteronomy 28:29). For my part, whenever I hear a person using such words, I am always on my guard against the possibility that a curse is being uttered.

Religion is another main area in which authority is vested in people who hold certain offices. Consequently, their words have a potential for good or evil which corresponds to the authority of their office. For many centuries in Europe, one main weapon used by the popes of the Roman Catholic Church was their papal "ban" (that is, *curse*), which they would proclaim on all whom they deemed to be heretics. It would be impossible to write an accurate history of Europe without taking into account the effects of this papal ban. Even rulers of nations feared it more than an actual declaration of war.

In the Protestant section of the Church, no person has ever achieved an authority equal to that of the pope. Nevertheless, wherever there is ecclesiastical authority, there is always the possibility of its misuse. Even the pastor of a small "independent" church, with a mere handful of members, can speak words that are, in effect, a curse.

I am reminded of a man with excellent business qualifications – let's call him Frank – who came for counselling. He had spent ten frustrating years in which nothing went right for him and he was barely able to support his wife and family. I asked Frank if anything had happened in his life at the point when things began to go wrong for him. His mind went back to a period when he and his family had been attending a small independent church. After various disagreements with the pastor, they had withdrawn their membership.

Since the family was one main source of the church's income, the pastor reacted out of fear and insecurity. The final exchange between Frank and the pastor was acrimonious – on both sides. Finally the pastor closed by saying: "God put you in this church. If you leave, you'll be out of His will. Nothing will ever go right for you!"

Sure enough, from that time on, nothing did go right for Frank. Fortunately, when he understood the cause of his frustrations, he was able to release himself from that pastoral curse. But first he had to forgive the pastor and put things right between them. After that, the course of Frank's life changed for the better.

Frank's case is not exceptional. I have met an astonishing number of people who have been through similar experiences. Almost invariably, the pastor has taken the same line: "God put you in this congregation. If you leave, you'll never prosper!" (Note those familiar words!) But thank God, He has provided a solution – for both parties to the dispute.

In 1985, while ministering in Australia, I was confronted by the effects of an ecclesiastical curse that had persisted for more than three centuries. A lady – whom we will call Margaret – heard me teach on the theme of blessings and curses. At the end of my message, recognising clear evidence of a curse at work in her family, Margaret stood – with many others – and repeated the prayer of release. Later, she sent me a letter giving the background of her case.

Her ancestors were from Scotland, from a clan called Nyxon. In the 1600s this clan had been involved in border wars between the Scots and the English. As a result, the Bishop of Scotland (who was appointed by the English) had pronounced a curse on the entire Nyxon clan. Margaret enclosed a copy of the curse, which decreed – among other things – that the members of the clan should be hung, drawn and quartered[9], and their entrails fed to the dogs and the swine. After the clan had been defeated in battle, this sentence was duly carried out on those members who were captured alive.

Two years later, on my return to Australia, I met Margaret briefly. Later she wrote this letter:

9. They were first hanged, then their corpses were dragged through the street by a horse or some other animal, and finally cut up into four pieces.

Thank you so very much for praying for me and my
family, and for delivering God's prophetic word to us
while here in Melbourne. You asked if our family had
changed since the release from the curse. I did not have
time to tell you when we spoke, but, yes, my whole
family – my husband, my two daughters, ages 24 and
23, and my son, age 21 – have all come to know the
Lord over the last two years and now we have joined a
full Gospel church here in Melbourne.

What astonishing testimony to the power of a curse! It had
followed Margaret's clan through three centuries, and Margaret's
branch of the clan right across the world, from Britain to
Australia. Once the curse had been identified and revoked, the
invisible barrier that kept God's blessing from Margaret's family
was removed, and her entire household entered into salvation.

This naturally raises the question, *How many other families are
being kept from salvation because of an unrecognised curse?*

12
SELF-IMPOSED CURSES

In one of the examples from the previous chapter, Jack said to his wife, *"I'm sick* of the way you serve our meals." By these words he unwittingly brought upon himself a curse of indigestion that continued to afflict him for the rest of his life.

With this example in mind, it is time now to examine more thoroughly this whole area of *self-imposed curses.* It is of vital importance for all who are concerned about their own personal welfare. It uniquely exposes the frightening power of the words we speak about ourselves. They are frequently like boomerangs, which come flying back to strike the one who spoke them.

In Matthew 12:36-37 Jesus gives a solemn warning about the danger of words carelessly spoken:

> *"But I say to you that for every idle word men may speak, they will give account of it in the day of*

judgement.
  *"For by your words you will be justified, and by your
  words you will be condemned."*

Jesus here focuses on "idle words" – that is, words spoken carelessly, without premeditation. Often when a person says something foolish or negative about himself, he then excuses himself by saying, "But I didn't really mean it." Yet it is precisely against words of this kind, which people "don't really mean," that Jesus warns us. The fact that the speaker "doesn't really mean them" does not in any way minimise or cancel the effect of his words. Nor does it release him from his accountability.

In Proverbs 6:2 Solomon warns a person who has unwisely put up security for a neighbour: "You have been trapped by what you said, ensnared by the words of your mouth" (NIV). This is only one of countless ways in which people are "ensnared by the words of their mouths." We may easily be caught in a snare of this kind without realising it, but to get free demands the conscious application of biblical principles. We need to remember that God takes our words seriously, even when we ourselves do not.

Mark 14:66-72 records how, in the court of the high priest, Peter three times denied that he was a disciple of Jesus. To enforce his third denial, he actually "began to curse and swear." In other words, he invoked a curse on himself.

Peter was quickly stricken with remorse, but it is doubtful even so that he understood the full implication of his own words. Three days later, at the empty tomb, the angels told the women, "Go and tell His disciples – *and Peter* – that He is going before you into Galilee" (Mark 16:7). Peter was no longer reckoned as being one of the disciples. By his own words he had forfeited his standing as a disciple of Jesus.

Later, John 21:15-17 records how, by the Sea of Galilee, Jesus graciously opened the way for Peter to regain his standing as a disciple. He asked Peter three times, "Do you love Me?" Peter answered each time in the affirmative, but he was grieved that Jesus put the question three times. He did not realise that Jesus was leading him in this way to revoke his previous denials. For each time that he had made a wrong confession, he now made the right confession. On this basis, he was reinstated as a disciple.

The way Jesus dealt with Peter establishes a pattern for all who need to be released from the snare of a bad confession. There are three successive steps: Repent – Revoke – Replace. First, we must acknowledge that we have made a wrong confession and *repent* of it. Second, we must *revoke* it – that is, we must unsay, or cancel, whatever we said that was wrong. Third, we must *replace* our previous wrong confession with the right one. These three steps, taken in faith, can release us from the snare.

Genesis 27:12-13 provides another example of a self-imposed curse. Rebecca was persuading her son Jacob to deceive Isaac, his father, in order to obtain his blessing (which Isaac intended to pronounce on his other son, Esau). Jacob was eager for the blessing, but fearful of the consequences if Isaac should discover his deception.

"Perhaps my father will feel me," he said, "and I shall seem to be a deceiver to him; and I shall bring a curse on myself and not a blessing."

Rebecca responded immediately, "Let your curse be on me, my son."

Rebecca's plan to obtain the blessing for Jacob succeeded, but her own words exposed her to a curse which kept her from enjoying the fruits of her success. Her mood quickly became one of pessimism and cynicism. Soon afterward we find her saying to Isaac, "I am weary of my life because of the daughters of Heth; if Jacob takes a wife of the daughters of Heth . . . what good will my life be to me?" (Genesis 27:46).

Almost immediately, too, Jacob had to leave home to escape the vengeance of his brother, Esau, and he was gone for about twenty years. The Bible tells us nothing about the rest of Rebecca's life or about the time and manner of her death. It would seem, however, that she never had the satisfaction of seeing Jacob enjoying the blessing that her deceptive scheme had obtained for him.

Over the years I have heard many people speak about themselves in the same way as Rebecca: "I'm tired of living . . . Nothing ever goes right . . . What's the use? . . . I give up! . . . I might as well be dead . . ." I have learned by experience that expressions such as these almost always indicate a self-imposed curse at work in the life of the one who utters them.

A much more tragic and far-reaching example of a self-imposed curse is depicted in Matthew 27:20-26. Against his own judgement, the Roman governor, Pilate, consents to release to the crowd a murderer named Barabbas and to impose the death sentence on Jesus instead. In order to disassociate himself from this act, however, he washes his hands in front of the crowd and says, "I am innocent of the blood of this just person."

To this the crowd responds, "His blood be on us and on our children."

These words combined two forms of curse: a *self-imposed* curse on themselves; a *relational* curse on their descendants. The objective record of history confirms the outworking of both. Within one generation the Roman armies had destroyed Jerusalem, and either killed or sold into slavery the entire population.

Since that time, for nineteen centuries, a dark strand of bloodshed and tragedy has been interwoven in the destiny of the Jewish people. Time after time, in pogrom after pogrom, Gentile rulers have turned loose against defenceless Jews violent, depraved men of the calibre of Barabbas – the one whom they had chosen.

But thank God, that is not the end! God has provided a way of reconciliation and restoration. Through His unsearchable wisdom and His marvellous mercy, the death of the One who was executed as a criminal has provided a way of escape from the consequences of the curse. Chapter 17 will explain this in detail.

Earlier, in chapter 8, we saw that when God originally called Abraham and blessed him, He also pronounced a curse on all who would curse him. Later, this curse was reaffirmed when Isaac blessed Jacob, and once more when Balaam pronounced a prophetic blessing on Israel as a nation. In this way God provided protection for Jacob and his descendants – the Jewish people – from all who would seek to put a curse on them. Subsequent history revealed, however, that there was one kind of curse from which even God could not protect His people: *the curse they pronounced on themselves.*

The same applies to Gentile Christians who have become heirs to Abraham's blessing through the New Covenant initiated by Jesus. Included in the provisions of the Covenant is the right to invoke God's protection against curses that proceed from any external source. But there is one kind of curse against which even God cannot provide protection: *the curses that Christians pronounce upon themselves.*

This is one way in which Christians frequently bring upon themselves various kinds of trouble of which they do not understand the source. By speaking negative words about themselves, they shut themselves off from blessings and expose themselves to curses.

In this, too, the history of Israel provides a vivid example. Chapters 13 and 14 of Numbers record how Moses sent twelve tribal leaders to spy out the land of Canaan which God had promised to Israel as an inheritance. Two of them – Joshua and – Caleb – returned with a positive report: "Let us go up at once and take possession, for we are well able to overcome it." The other ten gave a negative report that focused on giants and walled cities. Their conclusion was: "We are not able to go up against the people, for they are stronger than we."

In due course, the Lord pronounced His judgement. To all those Israelites who gave credence to the negative report He said: "Just as you have spoken in My hearing, so I will do to you: The carcasses of you who have murmured against Me shall fall in this wilderness." The carcasses of the unbelieving spies were the first to fall. To Joshua and Caleb, on the other hand, the Lord promised that they would take possession of the land concerning which they had given a positive report.

All those spies – both the believing and the unbelieving – determined their own destiny by the words they spoke concerning themselves. Those who said, "We are able to enter the land," did enter it. Those who said, "We are not able," did not enter. God took them at their own word. He has not changed! To Christians, just as much as to Israelites, God still says, "Just as you have spoken in My hearing, so I will do to you."

Earlier, in chapter 5, we listed seven characteristic conditions that may be marks of a curse. Often it is the way in which people speak about themselves that exposes them to these conditions. Without recognising it, such people are actually pronouncing curses upon themselves. To guard against this, they need to recognise the wrong forms of speech that they have been using and to cultivate new, positive speech patterns in their place.

The list below repeats the seven conditions that may indicate a curse, but adds under each heading typical forms of speech that commonly open people up to the condition described. These few examples should be sufficient to indicate the kinds of expressions that are dangerous and the areas in which it may be necessary to change. For our part, Ruth and I have learned to exercise continual vigilance and self-control in the way we speak about ourselves.

1.   *Mental and/or emotional breakdown*

"It's driving me crazy!"
"I just can't take any more."
"It makes me mad to think . . ."

2.   *Repeated or chronic sicknesses (especially if hereditary)*

"Whenever there's a bug, I catch it."
"I'm sick and tired . . ."
"It runs in the family, so I guess I'm the next."

3.   *Barrenness, a tendency to miscarry or related female problems*

"I don't think I'll ever get pregnant!"
"I've got the 'curse' again."
"I just know I'm going to lose this one – I always do!"

4.   *Breakdown of marriage and family alienation*

"The palmreader said my husband would leave me."
"Somehow I always knew my husband would find another woman."
"In our family we have always fought like cats and dogs."

5. *Continuing financial insufficiency*

"I never can make ends meet – my father was the same."

"I can't afford to tithe."

"I hate those 'fat cats' who get all they ever want – it never happens to me!"

6. *Being "accident prone"*

"It always happens to me!"

"I knew there was trouble ahead . . ."

"I'm just a clumsy kind of person."

7. *A history of suicides and unnatural or untimely deaths*

"What's the use of living?"

"Over my dead body!"

"I'd rather die than go on the way I am."

People who use this negative kind of language are unconsciously inviting evil spirits to take them over. The type of evil spirit that responds is determined by the language used. There are classes of spirits that correspond to each of the seven categories listed above.

One kind of spirit that is particularly common is the spirit of "death." This responds to the kind of language listed under the category of "Suicides and unnatural or untimely deaths." It produces a sense that life is meaningless and hopeless, and a morbid tendency to focus on thoughts of death. It is often manifested also in a never-ending series of physical infirmities, for many of which there is no obvious medical cause.

Ultimately, this spirit of death will either drive a person to suicide or cause untimely death in some other way. In John 8:44 Jesus warned us that Satan is a murderer. One of the agents that he uses to murder people is the spirit of death, which causes people to die before their time. When I shared this with a physician friend, he confirmed that he often saw people die when there was not sufficient medical cause to explain it.

It may be that in one or another of the categories listed above you have recognised things that you yourself have said. If so, don't be discouraged! There is a way out! Earlier in this chapter the apostle Peter provided an example of the three steps that are necessary to escape from a self-imposed curse: Repent – Revoke – Replace.

First, we must recognise that we have made a negative confession about ourselves and we must *repent* of it. Second, we must *revoke it* – that is, unsay or cancel it. Third, we must *replace* our previous wrong confession with the right one. All this will be explained more fully in chapter 21.

Another way in which people can bring a curse upon themselves is by pledges or oaths that are required for admission to a closed fraternity or sorority, or to a secret society. I recall a situation in which my first wife, Lydia, and I were seeking to help a Christian young woman be set free from demonic bondage. In spite of many prayers and struggles, there was no deliverance. Suddenly Lydia was prompted to tell the young woman to take off a ring she was wearing. As soon as she did so, she was set free without further struggles.

Lydia acted solely on the prompting of the Holy Spirit. She knew nothing about the ring, which was actually a college sorority ring. To join the sorority the young woman had been required to make certain pledges that were inconsistent with her Christian faith. By discarding the ring, she effectively cancelled those pledges and regained her liberty as a child of God.

On another occasion, Lydia and I were part of a group ministering to a young woman who confessed that she had been a priestess of Satan. She was wearing a ring that symbolised her "marriage" to Satan. When we told her she would have to take the ring off, she did so – but then, under the compulsion of Satan, she swallowed it. A young man present received a special anointing of faith, and commanded the woman to regurgitate the ring, which she promptly did! We then threw the ring into a nearby lake. The final stage in the woman's deliverance followed when she publicly burned all the clothes which she had worn while worshipping Satan.

Incidents such as these have made very real for me the directions given in Jude 23: "Save others, snatching them out of the fire; and on some have mercy with fear, hating even the garment polluted by the flesh" (NASB).

In both the above instances, satanic bondage was associated with a ring. The significance of a ring is that it often symbolises a covenant relationship. In our Western culture, for example, it is normal for a man and his wife each to wear a ring, symbolising the covenant relationship of marriage. By biblical standards, a covenant is the most solemn and powerful form of relationship into which a person can enter, whether the covenant is between God and man, or between man and his fellow men. Satan is well aware of this, and he therefore exploits covenant relationships of his own making in order to gain the strongest possible control over people.

For this reason, in Exodus 23:32, God instructed the Israelites concerning the idolatrous nations of Canaan: "You shall make no covenant with them, nor with their gods." God was warning His people that if they entered into a covenant with the Canaanites who worshipped false gods, that covenant would bind them not merely to the Canaanites, but also to their gods. They would thus be bringing themselves into bondage to those gods.

One section of contemporary society to which this warning particularly applies is Freemasonry. Masons claim that the nature of their association is a secret, but this is not correct. All the major rites and formulas of Freemasonry have been publicised at various times, both by people who were formerly Masons (including some who had advanced to the highest degree), and by others who have carefully examined the material that is available to any competent researcher.

For present purposes, it is sufficient to point out two facts about Freemasonry. First, in order to be initiated, a person has to bind himself by the most cruel and barbarous oaths never to reveal any of Masonry's secrets. It would be impossible to find anywhere a more frightening example of self-imposed curses than these oaths.

Second, Masonry is a false religion. Some Masons would deny that it is a religion, but here are some of the main features that clearly mark it as such: Masonry has its own *revelation;* its own *temples;* its own *altars;* its own religious *symbols* and *emblems* (which include a *ring*); its own *confession of faith;* its own *priests;* its own *rituals.* Finally, it has its own deity, a false god, whom it calls a "Creative Principle," or "the Great Architect of the Universe."

Masonry is a *false religion,* because it acknowledges a *false god.* Many of the objects and symbols associated with Christianity – including the Bible – are used in Masonry, but this is a deliberate deception. The god whom Masonry acknowledges is *not* the God of the Bible. Although the sacred, biblical name of four letters – JHVH (commonly spelled out as "Jehovah") – is used in Masonic literature, it is interpreted as referring to a divine entity that combines in itself both male and female principles. Again, the Royal Arch degree uses an abbreviated form of the name Jehovah in combination with abbreviated forms of two heathen deities, Baal and Osiris, and acknowledges this "combined" being as god. This is nothing short of a deliberate insult to the one true God revealed in the Bible as Jehovah[10].

For my part, I had no interest at all in Freemasonry until I began to discover the harmful effects it had produced in the lives of people who came for prayer. Some of the most frightening examples that I have encountered of curses at work in people's lives were associated with Freemasonry. The effects manifested in the second and third generations of those who had a Mason in their family background.

One case made a special impression on me. At the close of a Sunday morning worship service in Australia, Ruth and I were praying for people who needed healing. One of those who came forward was a young woman whose dull eyes, unkempt hair and slurred voice suggested a background in the subculture. In her arms she carried a tiny baby.

"She just won't take anything to eat," the mother mumbled with her eyes averted. "Just an ounce or two at a time."

"How old is she?" we asked.

"Six weeks," the mother replied, but the baby looked more like six days than six weeks old.

When Ruth and I placed our hands on the mother to pray for her, she fell backward under the power of the Holy Spirit. As she fell, Ruth caught the baby from her and held it in her own arms. Two church workers began to pray for the mother on the floor.

Ruth then received a word of knowledge by the Holy Spirit. "Her father is a Freemason," she said to the two workers. "Tell her to renounce that spirit."

The mother on the floor struggled to get out the words, "I

10. Anyone interested in a comprehensive study of this subject is referred to the book *Freemasonry: An Interpretation* by Martin L. Wagner (obtainable from HRT Ministries, Box 12, Newtonville, N.Y. 12128-0012).

renounce . . . that spirit . . . of Freemasonry." As soon as she uttered those words, the evil spirit came out of her with a prolonged scream. At the same moment, the baby in Ruth's arms emitted a precisely similar scream, and then became limp. The workers helped the mother onto her feet, and Ruth placed the baby back in her arms.

About six hours later we were back again in the same church for an evening service. At the close, the same young woman came up once more with her baby.

"How's she doing?" we asked.

"She's completely different," the mother replied. "She's taken three full bottles since the morning!" I could not help thinking that the mother, too, had undergone a dramatic change, which shone out of her eyes and sounded in the clarity of her voice.

I reflected later that in one brief encounter we had seen visible evidence of a curse due to Freemasonry that had carried over to at least two generations: from the father himself who was a Mason, to his daughter and then to his granddaughter, a baby just six weeks old. I determined from then on that I would be diligent to warn people of the harm that Masons bring not only on themselves, but on the members of their families, even those who have no direct involvement in Freemasonry.

To all who have made a pledge or a vow binding them to an evil association, such as those mentioned above, Solomon offers an urgent word of counsel in Proverbs 6:4-5:

> *Give no sleep to your eyes,*
> *Nor slumber to your eyelids.*
> *Deliver yourself like a gazelle from the hand of the*
> *   hunter,*
> *And like a bird from the hand of the fowler.*

There are two minimum requirements for deliverance. First, you must make a verbal renunciation of your association. *What you have said with your lips, only you can unsay.* It is best to do this in the presence of sympathetic witnesses who will support you with their faith.

Second, you must get rid of, and destroy, all the emblems, books and other materials that were marks of your association. In all the three types of situations mentioned above a ring was of special significance. In the case of a Freemason, there would also be various other objects – particularly the apron. Remember the words of Jude 23: "Hating even the garment defiled by the flesh."

13
SERVANTS OF SATAN

In this chapter we will uncover a completely different source of curses: servants of Satan.

Attitudes towards Satan among Christians vary between two extremes. Some ignore Satan totally, and try to act as if he is not real. Others are afraid of him and give him far more attention than he deserves. Between those two extremes there is a scriptural balance.

Satan is a created being, a rebellious angel, who was cast out of God's heaven. He rules over a spiritual kingdom of evil, rebellious angels, together with lesser evil spirits, who are called "demons."

The name *Satan* means "Adversary" or "Opposer." He is the unchanging, implacable enemy of God Himself and of the people and the purposes of God. His aim is to bring the whole human race under his control. His primary tactic is deception, of which he is a master. In Revelation 12:9 he is described as "the great dragon . . . that serpent of old, called the Devil and Satan, *who deceives the whole world.*"

Satan already exercises dominion over the great majority of mankind – all those who are in an attitude of rebellion against God. In Ephesians 2:2 he is described as "the spirit who now works in the sons of disobedience." Most of these have no clear picture of their real condition. They are simply driven to and fro by forces which they do not understand and cannot control.

There are those among them, however, who have deliberately opened themselves up to Satan, even though they may not be aware of his true identity. In pursuit of power and material gain, they systematically cultivate the exercise of the supernatural forces Satan has released to them. Such servants of Satan are recognised in almost all cultures and have been given a variety of different titles: witch doctor, medicine man, mchawi, shaman, tohanga, wizard, witch, priest or priestess of Satan, and so on. In almost all tribal cultures throughout the world there is a special name for this kind of person.

Jesus Himself is our main source of information concerning Satan. When He sent out seventy disciples to prepare the way before Him, they returned with joy, saying, "Lord, even the demons are subject to us in Your name." To this Jesus responded, "Behold, I give you the authority to trample on serpents and scorpions, and over all the power of the enemy, and nothing shall by any means hurt you" (Luke 10:17-19).

Jesus did not deny that Satan was real, or that he had power. But He promised His disciples that the authority He conferred upon them would make them victorious over Satan's power and would protect them against all his attempts to harm them. It is important for all of the Lord's servants to recognise the authority He has given them, and to learn to exercise it effectively.

Curses are one of the main weapons that servants of Satan use against the people of God. This is vividly illustrated by the story of Balak and Balaam in Numbers 22-24.

Balak was king of the territory of Moab, on the east of the Jordan. On their journey from Egypt to Canaan, Israel had encamped on the border of Moab. Balak felt his kingdom was threatened, but he lacked the strength or the courage to launch an open attack on Israel. Instead, he hired Balaam to pronounce curses on them, in the hope that Israel would thus be weakened to the point where Moab could defeat them. Balaam was a "witch doctor," famous throughout the whole region, who commanded a high fee for his services.

Many Christians today would dismiss all this as superstitious "nonsense," devoid of any real power. God's reaction, however, was entirely different. He viewed the curses that Balaam might pronounce as a serious threat to Israel. Consequently, He intervened supernaturally and warned Balaam not to accept the assignment. But Balaam was eager for the wealth which Balak had promised him, and so went ahead with the intention of doing what Balak had asked. In due course, however, each time Balaam tried to pronounce curses on Israel, God again intervened and changed the proposed curses into blessings!

Subsequently, in Deuteronomy 23:5, Moses reminded Israel of this incident as evidence of God's love for them: "Nevertheless the Lord your God would not listen to Balaam, but the Lord your God turned the curse into a blessing for you, because the Lord your God loves you."

One important fact needs to be emphasised: God did not view Balaam's proposed curses against Israel as empty words that had no power. He regarded them as a serious threat to Israel, and for this reason He intervened personally to frustrate Balaam's intention.

Time has not changed God's viewpoint. He does not ignore or belittle curses directed against His people by servants of Satan. On the contrary, as Jesus said, God recognises the power of Satan, but equips His own servants with superior power.

The Bible presents various pictures of the activities of Satan's servants. These serve to warn God's servants, against whom these satanic activities are often directed. In Ezekiel 13:17-20, for example, God condemns certain false prophetesses, or sorceresses:

> *"Likewise, son of man, set your face against the daughters of your people, who prophesy out of their own heart; prophesy against them,*
>
> *"and say, 'Thus says the Lord God: "Woe to the women who sew magic charms on their sleeves and make veils for the heads of people of every height to hunt souls! Will you hunt the souls of My people, and keep yourselves alive?*
>
> *"And will you profane Me among My people for handfuls of barley and for pieces of bread, killing people who should not die, and keeping people alive who should not live, by your lying to My people who listen to lies?"*
>
> *'Therefore thus says the Lord God: "Behold, I am against your magic charms by which you hunt souls there like birds."'"*

Some of the details are not clear, but it seems that these women played the typical role of a witch doctor. Anyone who had a quarrel with some other person would hire them to use their magic arts against that person. One of their methods was to attach magic charms to people's clothing. In this way, they "hunted souls" and actually killed innocent persons. In return, they were paid in handfuls of barley or pieces of bread.

This is not some farfetched accusation reminiscent of the Middle Ages. It is a charge brought against these women by God Himself. Furthermore, servants of Satan have used similar methods for the same purposes all through the centuries and still continue to use them today.

In 1979-80, in the city of Bath in the West of England, archaeologists uncovered the remains of a temple of the goddess Minerva dating back to the Roman period. The priests in this temple had a similar ministry to that of the sorceresses in Ezekiel's day. People seeking revenge on someone would employ the priests to write out an appropriate curse against that person. The writing of the curse required special skills possessed only by the priests. Once the curse had been written, some kind of magic ceremony was used to direct it against the person who was its target. For all this, of course, the priests received appropriate payment. Also, the worshipers would cast their votive offerings for the goddess into the spring associated with the temple.

This way of using curses and magical arts is still a familiar part of daily life among the majority of the world's peoples, particularly in Asia, Africa, Oceania and Central and South America. The following account comes from a missionary friend of mine who has lived his whole life in Zambia, in central Africa, and is intimately acquainted with the languages and the customs of the people there.

At a General Conference of Christians in our rural district of Zambia, the Holy Spirit had spoken a strong prophetic word calling for holiness in the Church. Many Christians were convicted of sin in their lives and had truly repented, confessing their sin and pleading for

God's forgiveness.

After the service, an elder from one of our remote village churches came to the preacher in tears, trembling all over, confessing to the terrible sin of murder through witchcraft.

The elder told him that for some years he had been fighting with his fellow elder in the church who was senior to him. The situation had gotten so bad that he had decided to punish him by going to a local witch doctor and paying him to curse this other elder. The witch doctor had been happy to do so, especially as he knew that these men were supposed to be Christians. He asked for a large down payment, and then told the man to come back the following day.

When he returned, the elder found the witch doctor sitting under a tree with a mirror in his hand and a bowl of witchcraft medicine on the ground before him. The witch doctor then proceeded to sponge the medicine all over the mirror, and asked the elder to look carefully at the mirror and tell him what he could see.

Startled, the elder saw the face of his fellow elder quite clearly. Whereupon the witch doctor took a razor blade and cut across the throat of the face reflected in the mirror. Immediately the mirror was covered in blood.

The elder cried out, "You have killed him! I only asked you to curse him." The witch doctor replied with a chuckle, "I thought I would do the job properly whilst I was at it!"

The elder hurried home. To his horror he learned that his fellow elder was indeed dead, having died mysteriously of a sudden haemorrhage. The elder was terrified

of the consequences of his action, so he had kept quiet
about it. Now the Holy Spirit had powerfully convicted
him of his sin.

Fortunately for him, "where sin abounded, grace did
much more abound." Through confession, repentance
and faith in Jesus Christ, the man was not only brought
to forgiveness and peace with God, but to the reality of
the new birth.

Some Western readers might be disposed to dismiss all of this
as primitive, superstitious practices from "darkest Africa." But the
truth is that even in the more highly civilised nations (so-called),
occult practices, which had been on the decline, are once again
making tremendous inroads. In West Germany, for example,
many businessmen, who would never seek counsel from a
Christian minister, make a regular practice of consulting a
fortune-teller concerning their business deals.

In the mid-1980s a leader of the Satanic Church in America
was interviewed on television. He was asked if it is true that
Satanists practice human sacrifice. He replied: "We perform
human sacrifices by proxy, you might say – the destruction of
human beings who would, let's say, create an antagonistic
situation towards us – in the form of curses and hexes[11]." This was
not a charge brought against him by some hostile critic; it was an
admission he made freely of his own accord.

In Israel, under the law of Moses, this would have been
punishable by death. In our contemporary culture, however,
occult practices are not a crime, and there is no penalty attached
to them, even if they are used to kill people.

---

11. Quoted from *America: The Sorcerer's New Apprentice* by Dave Hunt and T.A. Mc
Mahon (Harvest House Publishers, 1988).

The statement of the Satanist quoted above reveals their use of curses and hexes to kill people, but it by no means absolves them from the charge of performing human sacrifices. Gruesome evidence to the contrary is contained in the following report from the New York *Times,* which ran April 12, 1989, dateline Matamoros, Mexico:

> On Tuesday . . . officials [Mexican and U.S.] found the bodies of 12 people, including a 21-year-old University of Texas student who had vanished here a month ago, in eight crude graves on [a remote ranch near the U.S. border]. Today, at news conferences here and in Brownsville, Tex., the officials said that a drug gang, seeing human sacrifice as "a magical shield" that would protect it from the police, was responsible for the murders . . .
>
> Among the suspects still at large is an accused drug smuggler identified as Adolfo de Jesus Constanzo, a native of Cuba, whom the others call El Padrino – the godfather. The police said he ordered the ritual murders, pointing out young men at random on city streets for his followers to abduct, then murder and mutilate on the ranch.
>
> The officials described the murders as a twisted blend of sacrificial and black magic practices from Haiti, Cuba and Jamaica . . .

There have also been reports from various places in the United States of the sacrifice of infants and small children, carried out by Satanists as part of their rituals.

The primary targets of satanic curses and other occult weapons are the servants of God and Jesus Christ. Satanists rightly recognise who their main enemies are, and direct their attacks against them accordingly. This is illustrated vividly by an incident related to me by a minister friend.

A Christian lady known to my friend was eating with her family in a restaurant in New Orleans – which is reported to be the spiritual centre for witchcraft in the U.S.A. While at the table, they were approached by Satanists who had entered the restaurant to "witness" in the same way some Christians might do, going from table to table. They were actively recruiting people for Satanism and showed the lady a printed prospectus for the year 1988, outlining the following six-point, worldwide programme, which was to be accompanied by fasting and prayer (!):

1. That the antichrist would manifest himself soon.
2. That ministers, leaders, and missionaries would fall.
3. That ministries and works of God would be destroyed.
4. That Christians would become complacent; want peace over and above all; and seek churches that do not preach a full gospel with pastors that keep peace no matter what the sin.
5. That Christians cease their fasting and prayer.
6. That the gifts of the Holy Spirit be ignored.

This is but one of many evidences that the Church of Jesus Christ is currently under intense, systematic attack by the forces of Satan. What can the Church do? Christ defeated Satan on the cross. How can we, first of all, defend ourselves; and secondly, make Christ's victory a daily reality in our personal lives and in our churches?

Some illuminating answers are provided by the story of Balaam's attempt to bring a curse on Israel. God intervened on behalf of Israel and turned the proposed curse into a blessing.

What did God see in the conduct of Israel at that time that moved Him to take His stand against Satan on their behalf?

Here are some important factors that combined to draw God's favour down upon His people:

1. The people of Israel were moving in fulfilment of God's plan for them.
2. They were supernaturally guided, day and night, by a cloud and a pillar of fire. This corresponds to the guidance of the Holy Spirit for New Testament believers. (See Romans 8:14.)
3. They were a nation under discipline, with God-appointed leaders and God-given laws.
4. Their relationships were carefully ordered according to a divine pattern. This harmonious pattern of relationships was beautifully depicted by Balaam's own visionary description of them in Numbers 24:5-6:

> *"How lovely are your tents, O Jacob!*
> *Your dwellings, O Israel!*
> *Like valleys that stretch out,*
> *Like gardens by the riverside,*
> *Like aloes planted by the Lord,*
> *Like cedars beside the waters."*

   Obviously, this was not a literal picture of Israel, since they were encamped at that time in a desert area.
5. Much of the above was due to the fact that a whole generation of unbelieving and disobedient Israelites had been purged out from among them. (See Numbers 26:63-65.)

What are the lessons to be learned from this picture of Israel? Its main features could be summed up thus: Israel was a community divinely ordered, disciplined and guided, living in harmony with one another. To state it another way, Israel was not just an assembly of individuals each "doing his own thing."

God has not changed in what He looks for in His people; nor has Satan changed in his tactics against God's people. If the Church at this time does not fulfil the requirements for God's favour and protection, there is only one remedy: *the Church must change.*

Unfortunately, however, the record of Balaam's strategy against Israel does not end with total victory for Israel. Having failed in his attempt to bring a curse upon Israel, Balaam resorted to a second tactic. He advised Balak to use the Moabite women as a snare, to entice the men of Israel, first, into sexual immorality and, second, into idolatry. Where Balaam's first tactic had failed, his second succeeded.

After that, he had no need to pronounce a curse upon the Israelites. By breaking God's first commandment, they had brought God's own curse upon themselves, and 24,000 of them perished. (See Numbers 25.) In Numbers 31:16, Moses states specifically that this came about through the counsel of Balaam.

In 1 Corinthians 10:8 Paul holds up this incident as a warning to believers in the New Testament. The deceitful tactics of Balaam are also mentioned in three other passages of the New Testament: 2 Peter 2:15-16, Jude 11, and Revelation 2:14. Obviously the strategy of Balaam against Israel contains important warnings also for believers in the New Covenant. The central lesson is simple: Christians who are living in disciplined obedience to God and in harmony with each other can look to God for His protection against Satan. But Christians who are undisciplined, disobedient and out of harmony forfeit their claim on God's protection.

14
SOULISH TALK

It is not difficult for Christians to understand that spiritual forces directed against them from servants of Satan would be dangerous and harmful. Many Christians would be surprised, however, to learn that there are situations in which spiritual forces emanating from their fellow believers could also be harmful. Yet in James 3:14-15 the apostle is writing both to and about Christians when he warns:

> But if you have bitter envy and self-seeking in your hearts, do not boast and lie against the truth.
> This wisdom does not descend from above, but is earthly, sensual, demonic.

To describe a certain kind of "wisdom," James uses adjectives on three descending levels: first, "earthly"; below that, "sensual";

and below that, "demonic." The key to understanding the downward process lies in the second adjective, here translated "sensual." The Greek word is *psuchikos,* formed directly from *psuche,* meaning "soul." The corresponding English word would be "soulish." Translated in this way, it fits in naturally with the Bible's picture of human personality.

In 1 Thessalonians 5:23 Paul prays: "Now may the God of peace Himself sanctify you completely; and may your whole spirit, soul, and body be preserved blameless." Paul here puts together the three elements that make up a complete human personality, listing them in descending order from the highest to the lowest: first, spirit; then, soul; then, body.

The spirit is that part of human personality that was directly inbreathed by God at creation. It is therefore capable of direct union and communion with the Creator. In 1 Corinthians 6:17 Paul says: "He who is joined to the Lord is *one spirit* with Him." It would not be correct to say "one soul with Him." Only man's spirit is capable of direct union with God.

In the original pattern of creation, man's spirit related upward to God and downward to his soul. God communicated directly with man's spirit, and through man's spirit with his soul. Together, man's spirit and soul expressed themselves through his body.

At the fall, as a result of man's disobedience, his spirit was cut off from God, and at the same time his soul began to express itself independently of his spirit. This new, "disjointed" relationship was both the consequence and the expression of man's rebellion against God.

Elsewhere in the New Testament, the word *soulish* denotes the activity of man's soul when it is out of its proper relationship to his spirit. It describes, therefore, a condition that is contrary to God's highest will. This can be established by considering briefly two other passages in the New Testament where the word *psuchikos* – that is, "soulish" – occurs.

In 1 Corinthians 2:14-15 Paul says that "the natural [soulish] man does not receive the things of the Spirit of God . . . nor can he know them, because they are spiritually discerned." On the other hand, "he who is spiritual judges all things." It is obvious that "soulish" and "spiritual" are in opposition to each other. The "spiritual" person is functioning according to God's will; the "soulish" person is out of harmony with God. The "soulish" person seeks to apprehend spiritual truth in the realm of his soul, but is unable to do so. The "spiritual" person is united with God through his spirit and is thus able to receive spiritual revelation directly from God.

In Jude 16-19, the apostle describes a class of persons who are associated with the church, but are nevertheless "murmurers, complainers, walking according to their own lusts." He concludes by saying of them: "These are sensual [soulish] persons, who cause divisions, not having the Spirit [that is, the Holy Spirit]."

Taken together, these passages in 1 Corinthians and in Jude present a consistent picture of a person described as "soulish." He is apparently one who associates with the church and wears a veneer of spirituality. At the same time, his soul is not rightly related to God through his spirit. In spite of the faith he professes, he is in reality a rebel, out of harmony with God and with the people of God. He is incapable of apprehending spiritual truth. His rebellious attitude and conduct grieve the Spirit of God and cause offence in the Body of Christ.

This analysis explains the descending levels of the corrupt wisdom described in James 3:15: from earthly, to soulish, to demonic. The root problem is rebellion – some form of disobedience to God – some form of rejection of God's authority. This rebellion cuts a person's spirit off from God and from the things of heaven. He is now confined to the plane of earthly values and motives.

At the same time, his soul – out of harmony with God – is exposed by its rebellion to the influence of demons, which his blunted spiritual senses cannot identify. The outcome is a form of wisdom which appears to be "spiritual" but is, in fact, "demonic."

The whole of this third chapter of James focuses on one specific problem: the misuse of the tongue. Furthermore, the entire epistle is addressed mainly – if not exclusively – to those who profess faith in Christ. It is clear, therefore, that this corrupt, counterfeit, demonic wisdom, of which James speaks, finds its expression in words used by Christians. How does such a situation arise?

There are two main areas in which Christians are often guilty in this way on account of the words they utter. The first area is words Christians speak among themselves; the second is words which they speak to God – primarily in prayer.

The New Testament gives very clear warnings to Christians as to how they should speak about other people – and especially their fellow believers. In Titus 3:2 Paul says that we are "to speak evil of no one." The phrase *no one* applies to all other people, whether believers or unbelievers.

The Greek verb translated "to speak evil" is *blasphemo* – from which is derived the word *"blaspheme."* It is important to understand that the sin of "blasphemy" includes not only evil words spoken against God, but also evil words spoken against our fellow human beings. Whether spoken in reference to God or to other people, such language is forbidden to Christians.

In James 4:11 James deals more specifically with words that Christians speak *about one another:* "Do not speak evil of one another, brethren." The word here translated "to speak evil" is *katalalo,* which means simply "to speak against." Many Christians interpret James to mean that we are not to say anything *false* against other believers. What he actually says, however, is that we are not to speak against fellow believers at all – even if what we say about them is *true*. The sin that James is dealing with is not speaking *falsely* but speaking *against*.

One of the sins that Christians fall into most easily is *gossip*. In some Christian congregations, if gossip were excluded, scarcely any kind of conversation would be left!

Collins English Dictionary offers the two following definitions of "gossip":

1. Casual and idle chat
2. Conversation involving malicious chatter or rumours about other people

Two of the adjectives here applied to gossip are: *idle* and *malicious.* It is not enough for Christians to avoid malice in their talk. In Matthew 12:36 Jesus Himself explicitly warns us against mere idle speech: "But I say to you that for every *idle* word men may speak, they will give account of it in the day of judgement."

Although the New Testament explicitly forbids gossip, many Christians regard it as a relatively "harmless" sin. Most definitely, however, this is not how God views it. In Romans 1:29-30 Paul lists some of the consequences of man's turning away from God. Here is part of his list: "They are full of envy, murder, strife, deceit and malice. They are gossips, slanderers, God-haters, insolent, arrogant and boastful" (NIV).

The position of *gossips* in this list is significant. Some of the heart attitudes directly associated with gossip are strife, deceit and malice. Gossips themselves are classified with people who are slanderers, God-haters, insolent, arrogant and boastful. Christians who indulge in gossip may think of themselves as "exceptions," but that is not how God sees them.

The danger of this kind of talk is brought out by the descending order of adjectives in James 3:15: "earthly, soulish, demonic." Christians who permit themselves to gossip about other people – especially their fellow believers – are directly disobedient to God's Word. As a result, they find themselves on a slippery downward slope. Before they realise what is happening, they have slipped from the "earthly" to the "soulish," and then from the "soulish" to the "demonic."

The words these people speak about others would not normally be described as "curses," but their effect is the same. They are in fact channels through which demonic forces are directed against other members of Christ's Body. Furthermore, it is not only the individuals spoken about who are affected. In James 3:6 the apostle says, "The tongue is so set among our members that it defiles the whole body." The believer who is guilty of this kind of speech actually defiles both himself and that part of the Body of Christ to which he is related.

Some years ago, while in Europe on a ministry trip, I found myself in a situation which gave me vivid new insight into the dangers of soulish talk. I was preparing to speak at a very signif- icant meeting, when I was seized with a crippling pain in my lower abdomen. Fearing that I might have to cancel my commitment to speak that evening, I called out to God for help.

Immediately I had a mental picture of two Christian friends of mine, about 6,000 miles away in the United States, talking about me. There was a very warm personal relationship between the three of us, but my two friends had disagreed strongly with a recent course of action I had taken. I sensed that in their conver- sation they were criticising me for my action and that their negative words about me were producing the physical symptoms that I was struggling against. Furthermore, this was a strategy of Satan to keep me from ministering that evening.

I saw that I needed to do two things. First, by a decision of my will, I forgave my friends for the words they were speaking against me. Then I acted on the promise of Jesus in Matthew 18:18: "Whatever you bind on earth will be bound in heaven, and whatever you loose on earth will be loosed in heaven." With the authority vested in the name of Jesus, I bound the satanic forces at work against me, and then I loosed myself from the effect of my friends' words about me. Within five minutes, the pain in my abdomen had ceased entirely (and never returned!). A few hours later I was able to minister effectively in the meeting, and I had the sense that God's purpose had been fulfilled.

Later, on returning to the United States, I had a meeting with my two friends and the tension between us was resolved. Today the relationship between us is warmer than before.

In Matthew 7:1-2 Jesus says:

> *"Judge not, that you be not judged.*
> *"For with what judgement you judge, you will be judged; and with the same measure you use, it will be measured back to you."*

It is from the verb translated "to judge" that the English words *critic* and *criticise* are directly derived. When we permit ourselves to criticise other people – especially our fellow believers – in such a way that we are pronouncing judgement on them, we are disobeying Scripture and are thus guilty of a rebellious attitude toward God. This exposes us to the "syndrome" of James 3:15: "earthly, soulish, demonic."

If we find ourselves in disagreement with the conduct of a fellow Christian, it is permitted – and sometimes necessary – to follow the pattern of Paul in his disagreement with Peter concerning Judaic practices. In Galatians 2:11 Paul says, "I withstood him [Peter] *to his face."*

Paul did not criticise Peter's conduct to his own co-workers, Barnabas and Titus. Instead, he went straight to Peter himself and settled his differences with him in person. Had Paul been guilty of criticising Peter behind his back, the relationship between the two of them might have been permanently fractured. As it was, however, in 2 Peter 3:15 – written near the end of Peter's life – he spoke with warm approval of "the wisdom given to our beloved brother Paul."

In Proverbs 27:5 Solomon states this as a principle of conduct:

> *Better is open rebuke*
> *than hidden love.*
>
> NIV

A different kind of situation, in which we may have to speak about another person's wrongdoing, arises when we are legally obligated to serve as a witness. In this case, it is our duty to speak "the truth, the whole truth and nothing but the truth." No one can, however, be at the same time both a witness and a judge. In such a situation, we are not filling the role of a judge, but of a witness. We leave the responsibility of pronouncing judgement to someone else.

The specific sin that Jesus warns us against is taking the position of a judge when God has not assigned that to us. He also warns us that if we do give way to criticising other people, in due course – from one source or another – the same kinds of criticism we have spoken against others will be levelled against us in our turn.

The Bible's penetrating analysis of the harm caused by misuse of the tongue probably leaves very few among us who would dare to plead "not guilty." If we recognise that we have indeed been guilty of wounding other people with our tongues and thus defiling ourselves and the Body of Christ, we need to repent and to seek God's forgiveness and cleansing. We may also need to ask forgiveness from those we have offended.

Beyond that, we need to learn how to protect ourselves from wounding and hurtful words that others may speak against us. This issue of protection is dealt with in Section 3.

15
SOULISH PRAYERS

Many Christians are shocked when confronted with the harm they cause by speaking wrongly among themselves about other people. They are still more shocked, however, when confronted with the even greater harm they can cause when they speak wrongly about others *in their prayers to God.* They assume that prayer is always acceptable and its effects are always good. Yet this view is not supported by the Bible.

In Proverbs 28:9, for example, we are warned:

> *One who turns away his ear from hearing the law,*
> *Even his prayer shall be an abomination.*

God has laid down in the Bible the principles of prayer that are acceptable to Him. Anyone who ignores these principles and offers prayer that is contrary to them incurs God's displeasure and the rejection of his prayer. In describing God's estimate of this kind of prayer, Solomon uses one of the Bible's strongest terms of disapproval: *abomination.*

Because it is so important for us to pray the right kind of prayers, we dare not depend on our own wisdom. Mercifully, God has not left us to our own devices. He has made available to us a divine Helper: the Holy Spirit. By His enabling we can pray prayers that are acceptable to God. Apart from the Holy Spirit, however, we are incapable of praying in a way that will please God or accomplish His purposes.

In Romans 8:26-27 Paul puts these issues very clearly:

> *Likewise the Spirit also helps in our weaknesses. For we do not know what we should pray for as we ought, but the Spirit Himself makes intercession for us with groanings which cannot be uttered.*
>
> *Now He who searches the hearts knows what the mind of the Spirit is, because He makes intercession for the saints according to the will of God.*

In our fleshly nature, all of us have certain weaknesses. They are weaknesses not of the body, but of the understanding. They manifest themselves in two related ways. First, we often do not know *what* we should pray for. Second, even when we know *what* to pray for, we do not know *how* to pray for it. We are therefore shut up to total dependence on the Holy Spirit. Only He can show us both the *what* and the *how* of prayer.

In two passages in Ephesians Paul further emphasises our dependence upon the Holy Spirit to give us prayers that are acceptable to God. In Ephesians 2:18 he stresses that it is only the Holy Spirit who can give us access to God: "For through Him [Jesus] we both [Jews and Gentiles] have *access by one Spirit* [the

Holy Spirit] to the Father." Two conditions for acceptable praying are here combined: *through* Jesus and *by* the Holy Spirit. Each is essential.

There is no natural force that can carry our puny human voices from earth to the very ears of God on His throne in heaven. Only the supernatural power of the Holy Spirit can do that. Without Him, we have no access to God.

Further on, in Ephesians 6:18, Paul again stresses our need for the Holy Spirit's help, particularly in praying for our fellow believers. He says that we should be "praying always with all prayer and supplication *in the Spirit* [the Holy Spirit] . . . for all the saints." Only prayers prayed *in the Holy Spirit* can call down upon those for whom we pray the help and encouragement they need.

How, then, can we avail ourselves of the Holy Spirit's help? Two primary requirements are *humility* and *purity of motive*. First, we must humble ourselves before the Holy Spirit and acknowledge our need of Him. Then we must allow Him to purge from us all wrong motives and selfish attitudes, and to inspire us with sincere love and concern for those for whom we desire to pray.

The prayers that the Holy Spirit inspires are not necessarily lengthy or eloquent. God is not particularly impressed by fine phrases or a solemn tone of voice. Some of the most effective prayers in the Bible were amazingly simple. When Moses prayed for his sister, Miriam, who had been smitten with leprosy, he simply said, "Please heal her, O God, I pray!" (Numbers 12:13). When the tax collector prayed in the Temple, he only uttered one brief sentence: "God be merciful to me a sinner!" (Luke 18:13). Yet we know that God heard and answered both these prayers.

If you feel the need to pray, but do not know how to begin, simply ask God for help. Here are some simple words you might use:

> Lord, I need to pray, but I don't know how. Please
> help me by Your Holy Spirit to pray the kind of prayer
> You will hear and answer.

After that, accept God's response by faith, and pray whatever comes from your heart. Jesus has assured us that if we ask God for bread, He will never give us a stone (Matthew 7:9).

Suppose, however, we do not submit ourselves to the Holy Spirit and seek His direction. Instead, our prayers are motivated by envy and self-seeking (mentioned in James 3:14) or by other fleshly attitudes, such as resentment, anger, criticism or self-right-eousness. The Holy Spirit will not endorse prayers that proceed from such attitudes, nor will He present them before God the Father.

Inevitably, therefore, our praying degenerates into the James 3:15 "syndrome": earthly – soulish – demonic. The effect of such soulish prayers is like that of soulish talk: negative, not positive. It releases against those for whom we are praying invisible, indefinable pressures, which do not relieve their burdens, but rather add to them.

In particular, when we pray for our fellow believers, there are two soulish attitudes that we must guard against: we must not *accuse,* and we must not seek to *control.*

It is all too easy to see the faults of other Christians. In fact, this is often what motivates us to pray for them. It is right to pray, but we must be careful how we pray. We are not free to come before God with a catalogue of their faults.

When we begin to play the role of accusers, we are following the pattern of Satan, not of Christ. Satan's main title – *devil* – means "slanderer" or "accuser." In Revelation 12:10 he is described as the one who accuses Christians day and night before God. He has been engaged in this task from time immemorial and he is an expert at it. He needs no help from Christians!

I have observed that in almost all the prayers of Paul for his fellow Christians – whether individuals or congregations – he begins by thanking God for them. A remarkable example is provided by the opening to 1 Corinthians. According to what Paul writes later in the letter, there were many kinds of sin in that congregation: strife between the members; carnality; incest; drunkenness at the Lord's Table. Yet Paul opens his letter with eloquent thanksgiving:

> *I thank my God always concerning you for the grace of God which was given to you by Christ Jesus,*
> *that you were enriched in everything by Him in all utterance and all knowledge,*
> *even as the testimony of Christ was confirmed in you,*
> *. . . who will also confirm you to the end, that you may be blameless in the day of our Lord Jesus Christ.*
> 1 Corinthians 1:4-6, 8

Giving thanks at the beginning of a prayer has an important psychological effect. It creates a positive attitude in the one who is praying. From such a beginning, it is much easier to go on praying with positive faith, even though we are not unaware of serious faults or problems in those for whom we are praying. For my part, I make it a principle never to pray for fellow believers without first thanking God for them. If I cannot do that, then I feel it is better not to pray at all!

A missionary to India in a previous generation developed such an effective ministry of prayer that he became known as "Praying Hyde." On one occasion he was praying for an Indian evangelist whose ministry lacked both fire and fruit. He was about to say, "Lord, You know how cold that brother is." He got as far as the words, "Lord, You know how . . ." but the Holy Spirit would not allow him to complete his sentence.

Suddenly Hyde realised that it was not his business to accuse his fellow servant. Instead of focusing on the man's faults, he began to thank God for everything good he could find in him. Within months, the Indian brother was dramatically transformed. He became known throughout the whole area as a dedicated, effective winner of souls.

That is the power of prayer based on positive appreciation and thankfulness for all that is good in a person. But suppose Hyde had not been sensitive to the Holy Spirit and had continued to pray in a negative, condemnatory spirit. Could not his prayer still have been effective, but in the opposite direction? Could he not have brought upon his fellow servant such a heavy burden of condemnation that he might never have been able to rise above it?

From time to time, like most other Christians, I experience periods of spiritual "heaviness." In some undefined way, I begin to feel guilty or inadequate or unworthy. Yet I may not be aware of anything specific in my life or conduct to explain these feelings.

In such a situation, I have learned by experience that the cause may not be in me at all. My "heaviness" may be due to some other Christian – well-intentioned but misguided – who is accusing me before God. In particular, the sense of guilt is often a warning sign. After all, guilt is the logical outcome of accusation. Once I have correctly diagnosed my problem, I can turn to my High Priest, who sees all my faults and yet continually pleads my case before the Father.

There is hardly such a thing as prayer that is not effective. The question is not whether our prayers are effective. The question is whether their effect is positive or negative. That is determined by the power that works through them. Are they truly from the Holy

Spirit? Or are they a soulish counterfeit?

True intercession is based on the pattern of Jesus, as described in Romans 8:33-34:

> *Who will bring any charge against those whom God has chosen? It is God who justifies.*
> *Who is he that condemns? Christ Jesus, who died –*
> *more than that, who was raised to life – is at the right hand of God and is also interceding for us.*

NIV

Christ certainly sees our faults as believers more clearly than we see each other's. Yet His intercession on our behalf does not result in our condemnation, but in our justification. He does not establish our guilt, but our righteousness.

Our intercession for our fellow believers should follow the same pattern. Shall we dare to bring a charge against those whom God has chosen? Or to condemn those whom God has justified? Surely that would be presumption in the highest degree!

The message of Scripture is unequivocal. It leaves no room in our prayers for us to accuse our fellow believers. There is, however, a second temptation to misuse the power of prayer, which is more subtle and harder to detect. It takes the form of using prayer to *control* those for whom we pray.

There is something in our fallen, Adamic nature that makes us desire to control other people and to impose our will upon them. In chapter 6 it was pointed out that this desire to control others is the root that produces witchcraft – first as a work of the flesh, and then as an occult practice.

One of the key words that indicate the operation of this force is *manipulation*. There are countless areas in which people may resort to manipulation to get what they want from others.

Husbands manipulate their wives, and wives their husbands; children their parents; preachers their congregations; and media advertisers the general public! It is such a common practice that people do not usually recognise it – in themselves or in others.

Nevertheless, manipulation is not the will of God. God Himself never manipulates us, and He never authorises us to manipulate other people. Whenever we resort to manipulation, we have passed from the realm of the spiritual to that of the soulish. We are operating in a form of wisdom that is not from above.

Because we normally think of prayer as something good and spiritual, we assume that any results we achieve by prayer are necessarily legitimate and must represent the will of God. This is true if the power at work through our prayers is the Holy Spirit. But if our prayers are motivated by our own soulish determination, their effect will be harmful, not beneficial.

Behind this soulish kind of prayer there often lies an arrogant assumption that we have the right to "play God" in the lives of others. In reality, however, any influence that would seek to set aside God's sovereignty over an individual's life is *not* from the Holy Spirit.

There are many different situations in which Christians might be tempted to pray in a way that seems spiritual, but actually is soulish. Here are two typical examples:

1.   *Accusatory and condemnatory prayers*

A church "split" is certain to bring out the soulish element in all parties involved. In this case, Pastor Jones, of the First Full Gospel Church, discovers that his wife is having an affair with Brother Williams, the music minister. He divorces his wife and dismisses Brother Williams.

Brother Williams, however, refuses to admit the charge of

adultery. He complains of "injustice," wins over half the congregation to his side, and starts to build a new church. There follows a lengthy dispute between the two groups concerning the division of the building fund.

A year later Pastor Jones marries again. Brother Williams and his group charge that it is unscriptural for a divorced minister to remarry. They start a special prayer meeting to call down "judgement" upon him.

In the next two years Pastor Jones' new wife twice becomes pregnant, but each time her pregnancy ends in a miscarriage. The gynaecologist can find no medical reason for these miscarriages. Brother Williams and his group hail this as the answer to their prayers and God's vindication of their righteous cause.

With their first conclusion I would agree. Their prayers were responsible for the two miscarriages. But what was the power that worked through those prayers? Since the Holy Spirit in Scripture clearly warns us not to judge our fellow believers, He could never lend His authority to prayers with such a motive. The only credible diagnosis that remains is that of James 3:15. The power working through such prayers is "earthly, soulish, demonic."

2. *Dominating, manipulating prayers*

Pastor Strong is accustomed to dominating those around him. He is a widower with two sons and a daughter. He expected both sons to become ministers, but in the end they chose secular careers. Mary, the daughter, remains at home. She is devoted to her father and an active helper in the congregation.

At an evangelistic rally, Mary meets Bob, a Christian worker from another denomination, and they begin a courtship. Pastor Strong is at odds with the church Bob belongs to, however, and opposes the relationship from the beginning. Also, he is fearful of losing Mary's help, at home and in the church. Eventually Mary moves out of her father's home to share an apartment with a girlfriend. Pastor Strong calls this "rebellion." When Mary tells him she is engaged, he sets himself to pray against the planned marriage.

Bob and Mary go ahead with their plans, but the longer they know one another, the more strained their relationship becomes. Neither seems able to relax in the presence of the other. Minor misunderstandings somehow develop into painful clashes. Every activity they plan together ends in inexplicable frustration. Eventually Mary says, "Bob, this can't be God's will for us!" and hands him back his ring.

Mary concludes that the way out of her frustration is to break all contact with professing Christians. Alienated from her father and the church, she follows her brothers into a secular career. Eventually she meets and marries a man who is an agnostic.

How shall we evaluate Pastor Strong's prayers? They were certainly effective, but their effect was harmful. They were the expression of his lifelong desire to dominate those who were close to him. They were powerful enough to break up a relationship that could have brought his daughter happiness and fulfilment. Beyond that, however, they could not bring her back to her faith, or keep her from a subsequent, unscriptural marriage. The power of prayer that brings such negative results does not proceed from the Holy Spirit.

The principles illustrated by these two examples apply to many different kinds of situations in contemporary church life. The lesson they enforce is highly relevant: The power of soulish prayer is both real and dangerous. The result it produces is not a blessing, but a curse.

The sin of soulish praying must be dealt with in the same way as the sin of soulish talking, described in the previous chapter. If we have been guilty, we need to repent and seek God's forgiveness. We may also need to ask forgiveness from people who have been affected by the negative influence of our prayers.

Finally, for the future, we must firmly renounce any attempt either to accuse other people or to control them by the words we speak in prayer.

16
SUMMARY OF SECTION 2

The preceding ten chapters have dealt with many of the most important causes of curses as they are revealed in the Bible. It will be helpful to conclude the section with a summary of these causes.

Acknowledging and/or worshipping false gods
All involvement with the occult
Disrespect for parents
All forms of oppression or injustice, especially when directed against the weak and the helpless
All forms of illicit or unnatural sex
Anti-Semitism
Legalism, carnality, apostasy
Theft or perjury
Withholding from God money or other material

resources to which He has a claim

Words spoken by people with relational authority, such as father, mother, husband, wife, teacher, priest or pastor

Self-imposed curses

Pledges or oaths that bind people to ungodly associations

Curses that proceed from servants of Satan

Soulish talk directed against other people

Soulish prayers that accuse or seek to control other people.

In addition, there are curses for other causes or from other sources, mentioned in Scripture, that are not included in the above list. The most significant of these are listed below in the order in which they occur in the Bible. Various passages that merely reaffirm curses pronounced in Deuteronomy 28 and 29 are not included.

It is noteworthy that the largest category of people who incur God's curse consists of deceptive and unfaithful prophets, priests and teachers. These have been indicated by an asterisk.

A curse on the people of Meroz because they did not join Barak as leader of the Lord's army against Sisera (Judges 5:23).

A curse from Jotham on those who had murdered the sons of Gideon (Judges 9:37).

A curse on Jezebel for witchcraft and immorality (2 Kings 9:34 – compare 2 Kings 9:22).

A curse on those who reject God's commandments through pride (Psalm 119:21).

A curse on the house of the wicked (Proverbs 3:33).

A curse on the earth because its inhabitants have defiled it, changing and transgressing God's laws and covenant (Isaiah 24:6).

A curse on the people of Edom for persistent enmity and treachery toward Israel (Isaiah 34:5).

*A curse on false prophets who promised peace to people who were disobeying God (Jeremiah 29:18).

*A curse on false prophets who commit immorality (Jeremiah 29:22).

A curse on Israelites who went down to Egypt in defiance of God's warning (Jeremiah 42:18 – compare Jeremiah 44:8, 12).

A curse on any man who fails to carry out the Lord's judgement on His enemies (Jeremiah 48:10).

*A curse on the blessings of priests who reject God's discipline (Malachi 2:2).

A curse on "goat" nations who show no mercy to the brothers of Jesus (Matthew 25:41).

A curse on people who are regularly taught the truth of God, but do not produce appropriate fruit (Hebrews 6:8).

*A curse on false teachers who are guilty of covetousness, deception and immorality (2 Peter 2:14).

SECTION 3

FROM CURSE TO BLESSING

INTRODUCTION

Have you come to see by now that your life has somehow been blighted by a curse? Are you wondering if there is a way out from under that dark shadow which has been shutting off the sunlight of God's blessing?

Yes, there is a way out! *But there is only one:* through the sacrificial death of Jesus on the cross.

This section will explain in simple, practical terms how you may find and follow God's way – from shadow to sunlight, from curse to blessing.

For your further encouragement you will read – in chapter 20 – the story of a man who found the way from frustration and despair to fulfilment and fruitfulness. You can do the same!

17

THE DIVINE EXCHANGE

The entire message of the Gospel revolves around one unique historical event: the sacrificial death of Jesus on the cross. Concerning this the writer of Hebrews says: "For by one offering [sacrifice] He [Jesus] has perfected forever those who are being sanctified" (Hebrews 10:14). Two powerful expressions are combined: "perfected" and "forever." Together, they depict a sacrifice that comprehends every need of the entire human race. Furthermore, its effects extend throughout time and on into eternity.

It is on the basis of this sacrifice that Paul writes in Philippians 4:19: "And my God shall supply *all your need* according to His riches in glory *by Christ Jesus.*" "All your need" includes, specifically, the release you are seeking from the curse. But first you need to see this as part of a much larger whole – a single, sovereign act of God, which brought together all the guilt and the suffering of humanity in one climactic moment of time.

God has not provided many different solutions for the multi-tudinous problems of mankind. Instead, He offers us one all-sufficient solution which is His answer to every problem. We may come from many different backgrounds, each of us burdened with our own special need, but to receive God's solution we must all make our way to the same place: the cross of Jesus.

The most complete account of what was accomplished at the cross was given through the prophet Isaiah seven hundred years before it actually took place. In Isaiah 53:10 the prophet depicts a "servant of the Lord" whose soul was to be offered to God as a sin offering. The writers of the New Testament are unanimous in identifying this unnamed servant as Jesus. The divine purpose accomplished by His sacrifice is summed up in Isaiah 53:6:

> All we like sheep have gone astray;
> We have turned, every one, to his own way;
> And the Lord has laid on Him the iniquity of us all.

Here is the basic, universal problem of all humanity: We have turned, each of us, to our own way. There are various specific sins that many of us have never committed, such as murder, adultery, theft, and so on. But this one thing we all have in common: we have turned to our own way. In so doing, *we have turned our back on God.* The Hebrew word that sums this up is *avon* – here trans-lated "iniquity." Perhaps the closest equivalent in contemporary English would be "rebellion" – not against man, but against God. In chapter 4 we saw this as the primary cause for the curses listed in Deuteronomy 28.

No one English word, however, whether it is *iniquity* or *rebellion,* conveys the full meaning of *avon.* In its biblical use, *avon* describes not merely iniquity but also the *punishment* or the *evil consequences* that iniquity brings in its train.

In Genesis 4:13, for instance, after God had pronounced judgement on Cain for the murder of his brother, Cain said: "My punishment is greater than I can bear!" The word here translated "punishment" is *avon*. It covered not merely Cain's "iniquity," but also the "punishment" it brought upon him.

In Leviticus 16:22, concerning the scapegoat released on the Day of Atonement, the Lord said: "The goat shall bear on itself all their iniquities to an uninhabited land." In this symbolism, the goat bore not merely the iniquities of the Israelites, but also all the consequences of their iniquities.

In Lamentations 4 *avon* occurs twice with the same meaning. In verse 6 it is translated: "The *punishment of the iniquity* of the daughter of my people." Again, in verse 22: "The *punishment of your iniquity* . . . O daughter of Zion." In each case, the single word *avon* is translated by a complete phrase "the punishment of iniquity." In other words, in its fullest sense *avon* means not simply "iniquity," but also includes *all the evil consequences* God's judgement brings upon iniquity.

This applies to the sacrifice of Jesus on the cross. Jesus Himself was not guilty of any sin. In Isaiah 53:9 the prophet says, "He had done no violence, nor was any deceit in His mouth." But in verse 6 he says, "The Lord has laid on Him the iniquity of us all." Not merely was Jesus identified with our iniquity. He also endured all the evil consequences of that iniquity. Like the scapegoat that had prefigured Him, He carried them away so that they might never return again upon us.

Here is the true meaning and purpose of the cross. On it a divinely ordained exchange took place. First, Jesus endured in our place all the evil consequences that were due by divine justice to our iniquity. Now, in exchange, God offers us all the good that was due to the sinless obedience of Jesus.

Stated more briefly, the evil due to us came upon Jesus, that, in return, the good due to Jesus might be offered to us. God is able to offer this to us without compromising His own eternal justice, because Jesus has already endured on our behalf all the just punishment due to our iniquities.

All of this proceeds solely out of the unfathomable grace of God, and it is received solely by faith. There is no logical explanation in terms of cause and effect. None of us has ever done anything to deserve such an offer, and none of us can ever do anything to earn it.

Scripture reveals many different aspects of the exchange, and many different areas in which it applies. In each case, however, the same principle holds good: *the evil came upon Jesus that the corresponding good might be offered to us.*

The first two aspects of the exchange are revealed in Isaiah 53:4-5:

> *Surely He has borne our griefs* [literally, sicknesses]
>   *And carried our sorrows* [literally, pains];
> *Yet we esteemed Him stricken,*
> *Smitten by God, and afflicted.*
> *But He was wounded for our transgressions,*
> *He was bruised for our iniquities;*
> *The chastisement* [punishment] *for our peace was*
>   *upon Him,*
> *And by His stripes* [wounds] *we are healed.*

Two truths are here interwoven. The application of one is spiritual and the other physical. On the spiritual plane, Jesus received the punishment due to our transgressions and iniquities that we, in turn, might be forgiven and so have peace with God. (See Romans 5:1.) On the physical plane, Jesus bore our sicknesses and pains that we through His wounds might be healed.

The physical application of the exchange is confirmed in two passages of the New Testament. Matthew 8:16-17 refers back to Isaiah 53:4 and records that Jesus "healed all who were sick, that it might be fulfilled which was spoken by Isaiah the prophet, saying:

> *"He Himself took our infirmities*
> *And bore our sicknesses."*

Again, in 1 Peter 2:24, the apostle refers back to Isaiah 53:5-6 and says of Jesus:

> *[He] Himself bore our sins in His own body on the tree, that we, having died to sins, might live for right- eousness – by whose stripes* [wounds] *you were healed.*

The twofold exchange described in the above verses may be summed up as follows:

> Jesus was *punished* that we might be *forgiven.*
> Jesus was *wounded* that we might be *healed.*

A third aspect of the exchange is revealed in Isaiah 53:10, which states that the Lord made the soul of Jesus "an offering for sin." This must be understood in the light of the Mosaic ordinances for various forms of sin offering. The person who had sinned was required to bring his sacrificial offering – a sheep, a goat, a bull or some other animal – to the priest. He would confess his sin over the offering, and the priest would symbolically transfer the sin he had confessed from the person to the animal.

Then the animal would be killed, thus paying the penalty for the sin that had been transferred to it.

In the foreknowledge of God, all this was designed to foreshadow what was to be accomplished by the single, all-sufficient sacrifice of Jesus. On the cross, the sin of the whole world was transferred to the soul of Jesus. The outcome is described in Isaiah 53:12: "He poured out His soul unto death." By His sacrificial, substitutionary death, Jesus made atonement for the sin of the whole human race.

In 2 Corinthians 5:21 Paul refers to Isaiah 53:10 and at the same time he also presents the positive aspect of the exchange:

> *For He [God] made Him [Jesus] who knew no sin to be sin for us, that we might become the righteousness of God in Him.*

Paul does not speak here about any kind of righteousness that we can achieve by our own efforts, but about God's own righteousness – a righteousness that has never known sin. None of us can ever earn this. It is as high above our own righteousness as heaven is above earth. It can be received solely by faith.

This third aspect of the exchange may be summed up as follows:

> Jesus was made *sin* with *our sinfulness* that we might become *righteous* with *His righteousness*.

The next aspect of the exchange is a logical outworking of the previous one. The entire Bible, in both the Old Testament and the New, emphasises that the final outcome of sin is death. In Ezekiel 18:4 the Lord states, "The soul who sins shall die." In James 1:15 the apostle says, "Sin, when it is full-grown, brings forth death."

When Jesus became identified with our sin, it was inevitable that He should also experience the death that is the outcome of sin.

In confirmation of this, in Hebrews 2:9, the writer says that "Jesus . . . was made a little lower than the angels, for the suffering of death . . . that He, by the grace of God, might taste death for everyone." The death that He died was the inevitable outcome of human sin that He had taken upon Himself. He bore the sin of all men, and so died the death due to all men.

In return, to all who accept His substitutionary sacrifice, Jesus now offers the gift of eternal life. In Romans 6:23 Paul sets the two alternatives side by side: "For the wages [just reward] of sin is death, but the [unearned] gift of God is eternal life in Christ Jesus our Lord."

Thus the fourth aspect of the exchange may be summed up as follows:

Jesus died our *death* that we might share His *life*.

A further aspect of the exchange is stated by Paul in 2 Corinthians 8:9: "For you know the grace of our Lord Jesus Christ, that though He was rich, yet for your sakes He became poor, that you through His poverty might become rich." The exchange is clear: from poverty to riches. Jesus became poor that we in return might become rich.

When did Jesus become poor? Some people picture Him as poor throughout His earthly ministry, but this is not accurate. He Himself did not carry a lot of cash, but at no time did He lack anything He needed. When He sent His disciples out on their own, they likewise lacked nothing. (See Luke 22:35.) So far from being poor, He and His disciples made a regular practice of giving to the poor. (See John 12:4-8; 13:29.)

True, Jesus' methods of obtaining money were sometimes

unconventional, but money has the same value, whether withdrawn from a bank or the mouth of a fish! (See Matthew 17:27.) His methods of providing food were also at times unconventional, but a man who can provide a substantial meal for five thousand men plus women and children certainly would not be considered poor by normal standards! (See Matthew 14:15-21.)

Actually, throughout His earthly ministry, Jesus exactly exemplified "abundance," as defined in chapter 5. He always had all that He needed to do the will of God in His own life. Over and above this, He was continually giving out to others, and His supply was never exhausted.

So when did Jesus become poor for our sakes? The answer is: *on the cross.* In Deuteronomy 28:48 Moses summed up absolute poverty in four expressions: hunger, thirst, nakedness and need of all things. Jesus experienced all this in its fullness on the cross.

He was *hungry.* He had not eaten for nearly 24 hours.

He was *thirsty.* One of His last utterances was: "I thirst!" (John 19:28).

He was *naked.* The soldiers had taken all His clothes from Him (John 19:23).

He was *in need of all things.* He no longer owned anything whatever. After His death He was buried in a borrowed robe and in a borrowed tomb (Luke 23:50-53). Thus, Jesus, exactly and completely, endured *absolute poverty* for our sakes.

In 2 Corinthians 9:8 Paul presents more fully the positive side of the exchange: "And God is able to make all grace abound toward you, that you, always having all sufficiency in all things, have an abundance for every good work."[12] Paul is careful to emphasise throughout that the only basis for this exchange is God's *grace.* It can never be earned. It can only be received by faith.

---

12. Other implications of this verse were discussed in chapter 5 on page 55.

Very often our "abundance" will be like that of Jesus while He was on earth. We shall not carry large amounts of cash, or have large deposits in a bank. But from day to day we shall have enough for our own needs, and something over for the needs of others.

One important reason for this level of provision is indicated by the words of Jesus quoted in Acts 20:35: "It is more blessed to give than to receive." God's purpose is that all His children should be able to enjoy the greater blessing. He provides us, therefore, with enough to cover our own needs and also to give to others.

This fifth aspect of the exchange may be summed up:

Jesus became *poor* with our *poverty* that we might become *rich* with His *riches*.

The exchange at the cross covers also the emotional forms of suffering that follow from man's iniquity. Here again, Jesus endured the evil that we in turn might enjoy the good. Two of the cruellest wounds brought upon us by our iniquity are *shame* and *rejection*. Both of these came upon Jesus on the cross.

Shame can vary in intensity from acute embarrassment to a cringing sense of unworthiness that cuts a person off from meaningful fellowship either with God or with man. One of the commonest causes – becoming more and more prevalent in our contemporary society – is some form of sexual abuse or molestation in childhood. Often this leaves scars that can be healed only by the grace of God.

Speaking of Jesus on the cross, the writer of Hebrews says that He "endured the cross, *despising the shame* . . ." (Hebrews 12:2). Execution on a cross was the most shameful of all forms of death, reserved for the lowest class of criminal. The person to be executed was stripped of all his clothing and exposed naked to the gaze of passers-by, who jeered and mocked. This was the degree of shame Jesus endured as He hung on the cross (Matthew 27:35-44).

In place of the shame Jesus bore, God's purpose is to bring those who trust in Him to share His eternal glory. In Hebrews 2:10 the writer says: "For it was fitting for Him [God] . . . *in bringing many sons to glory,* to make the author of their salvation [that is, Jesus] perfect through sufferings." The shame which Jesus endured on the cross has opened the way for all who trust in Him to be released from their own shame. Not only that, but He then shares with us the glory which belongs to Him by eternal right!

There is another wound which is often even more agonising than shame. It is *rejection.* Usually this stems from some form of broken relationship. In its earliest form, it is caused by parents who reject their own children. The rejection may be active, expressed in harsh, negative ways, or it may be merely a failure to show love and acceptance. If a pregnant woman entertains negative feelings toward the infant in her womb, the child will probably be born with a sense of rejection – which may follow it into adulthood and even to the grave.

The break-up of a marriage is another frequent cause of rejection. This is pictured vividly in the words of the Lord in Isaiah 54:6:

> *"The Lord will call you back*
> *as if you were a wife deserted and distressed in*
> *spirit – a wife who married young,*
> *only to be rejected," says your God.*

NIV

God's provision for healing the wound of rejection is recorded in Matthew 27:46, 50, which describe the culmination of the agony of Jesus:

> *And about the ninth hour Jesus cried out with a loud
> voice, saying, "Eli, Eli, lama sabachthani?" that is,
> "My God, My God, why have You forsaken Me?"*
> *Jesus, when He had cried out again with a loud
> voice, yielded up His spirit.*

For the first time in the history of the universe, the Son of God
called out to His Father and received no response. So fully was
Jesus identified with man's iniquity that the uncompromising
holiness of God caused Him to reject even His own Son. In this
way Jesus endured rejection in its most agonising form: rejection
by a father. Almost immediately after that, He died, not of the
wounds of crucifixion, but of a broken heart. Thus He fulfilled the
prophetic picture of the Messiah given in Psalm 69:20: "Reproach
has broken my heart."

The record of Matthew continues immediately: "And behold,
the veil of the temple was torn in two from top to bottom." This
demonstrated symbolically that the way had been opened for
sinful man to enter into direct fellowship with a holy God. The
rejection of Jesus had opened the way for us to be accepted by
God as His children. This is summed up by Paul in Ephesians 1:5-
6: "Having predestined us to adoption as sons by Jesus Christ to
Himself . . . He [God] has made us *accepted in the Beloved.*" The
rejection of Jesus resulted in our acceptance.

God's remedy for shame and rejection has never been needed
more desperately than it is today. My estimate is that at least one-
quarter of the adults in America today suffer from wounds of
shame or rejection. It has given me measureless joy to point such
people to the healing that flows from the cross of Jesus.

The two emotional aspects of the exchange at the cross that

have been analysed above may be summarised as follows:

> Jesus bore our *shame* that we might share His *glory*.
> Jesus endured our *rejection* that we might have His *acceptance* as children of God.

The aspects of the exchange analysed above cover some of humanity's most basic and urgent needs, but they are by no means exhaustive. Actually, there is no need resulting from man's rebellion that is not covered by the same principle of exchange: *The evil came upon Jesus that the good might be offered to us.* Once we have learned to apply this principle in our lives, it releases God's provision for every need.

Now you must lay hold of this principle to meet that special need in your own life: *release from the curse.* Paul describes the relevant aspect of the exchange in Galatians 3:13-14:

> *Christ has redeemed us from the curse of the law, having become a curse for us (for it is written, "Cursed is everyone who hangs on a tree"),*
> *that the blessing of Abraham might come upon the Gentiles in Christ Jesus, that we might receive the promise of the Spirit through faith.*

Paul applies to Jesus on the cross an enactment of the Law of Moses, stated in Deuteronomy 21:23, according to which a person executed by hanging on a "tree" (a wooden gibbet) thereby came under the curse of God. Then he points to the resulting opposite: the blessing.

It does not require a theologian to analyse this aspect of the exchange:

Jesus became a *curse* that we might receive the *blessing*.

The curse that came upon Jesus is defined as "the curse of the Law." It includes every one of the curses, listed by Moses in Deuteronomy 28, which were examined in chapter 4. Every one of these curses, in its fullness, came upon Jesus. He has thus opened the way for us to obtain *an equally full release* and to enter into the corresponding blessings.

Try for a moment to picture Jesus as He hung there on the cross. Then you will begin to appreciate the full horror of the curse.

Jesus had been rejected by His own countrymen, betrayed by one of His disciples and abandoned by the rest (though some later returned to follow His final agony). He was suspended naked between earth and heaven. His body was wracked by the pain of innumerable wounds, His soul weighed down by the guilt of all humanity. Earth had rejected Him, and heaven would not respond to His cry. As the sun withdrew its light and darkness covered Him, His lifeblood ebbed out onto the dusty, stony soil. Yet out of the darkness, just before He expired, there came one final, triumphant cry: "It is finished!"

In the Greek text that phrase, "It is finished," consists of only one word. It is the perfect tense of a verb that means "to make something complete or perfect." In English, it could be rendered "It is completely complete" or "It is perfectly perfect."

Jesus had taken upon Himself every evil consequence that rebellion had brought upon humanity. He had exhausted every curse of God's broken Law. All this, that we in turn might receive every blessing due to His obedience. Such a sacrifice is stupendous in its scope, yet marvellous in its simplicity.

Have you been able to accept with faith this account of the

sacrifice of Jesus and of all that He has obtained for you? In particular, if you are living under the shadow of a curse, have you begun to see that Jesus, at infinite cost to Himself, has made full provision for your release?

If so, there is one immediate response that you need to make – a response which is the simplest and purest expression of true faith. It is to say, "Thank You!"

Do that right now! Say, "Thank You! Thank You, Lord Jesus, for all that You have done for me! I do not fully understand, but I do believe, and I am grateful."

Now keep on thanking Him in your own words. The more you thank Him, the more you will believe what He has done for you. And the more you believe, the more you will want to thank Him.

Giving thanks is the first step to release.

18
SEVEN STEPS TO RELEASE

There is one – and only one – all-sufficient basis for every provision of God's mercy: the exchange that took place on the cross. In the previous chapter, eight main aspects were summarised:

Jesus was *punished* that we might be *forgiven*.

Jesus was *wounded* that we might be *healed*.

Jesus was made *sin* with *our sinfulness* that we might become *righteous* with *His righteousness*.

Jesus died our *death* that we might share His *life*.

Jesus became *poor* with our *poverty* that we might become *rich* with His *riches*.

Jesus bore our *shame* that we might share His *glory*.

Jesus endured our *rejection* that we might have His *acceptance* as children of God.

Jesus became a *curse* that we might receive a *blessing*.

This list is not complete. There are other aspects of the exchange that could be added. But all of them are different facets of the provision which God has made through the sacrifice of Jesus. The Bible sums them up in one grand, all-inclusive word: *salvation.* Christians often limit salvation to the experience of having one's sins forgiven and being born again. Wonderful though this is, however, it is only the first part of the total salvation revealed in the New Testament.

The full scope of salvation is obscured – at least, in part – by problems of translation. In the original Greek text of the New Testament, the verb *sozo,* normally translated "to save," is also used in a variety of ways that go beyond the forgiveness of sins. It is used, for instance, in many cases of people being physically healed[13]. It is also used of a person being delivered from demons[14], and of a dead person being brought back to life[15]. In the case of Lazarus, it is used of recovering from a fatal illness[16]. In 2 Timothy 4:18 Paul uses the same verb to describe God's ongoing preservation and protection from evil which will extend throughout his life.

The total outworking of salvation includes every part of man's being. It is beautifully summed up in Paul's prayer in 1 Thessalonians 5:23: "Now may the God of peace Himself sanctify you completely; and may your whole spirit, soul, and body be preserved blameless at the coming of our Lord Jesus Christ."

---

13.   Matthew 9:21-22; 14:36; Mark 5:23, 28, 34; 6:56; 10:52; Luke 8:48; Acts 4:9; 14:9; James 5:15
14.   Luke 8:36
15.   Luke 8:50
16.   John 11:12

Salvation includes the total human personality – spirit, soul and body – and it is consummated only by the resurrection of the body at the return of Christ.

No one enters into all the varied provisions of salvation simultaneously, however, or by one single transaction. It is normal to progress by stages from one provision to the next. Many Christians never go beyond receiving forgiveness of their sins. They are not aware of the many other provisions that are freely available to them.

The order in which a person receives the various provisions is determined by the sovereignty of God, who deals with all of us as individuals. The starting point, generally, is forgiveness of sins, but not always. In the earthly ministry of Jesus, people often received physical healing first, and then forgiveness of their sins.

This can still happen today. In 1968 my own wife, Ruth, while still single and living as a practising Jewess, had lain sick in bed for many weeks. Then she received a miraculous visitation from Jesus in her bedroom and was instantly and totally healed. But it was two years later before she recognised her need to have her sins forgiven. Only then was she born again.

When we come to God on the basis of Christ's sacrifice for us, we need to be sensitive to the leading of the Holy Spirit. We cannot impose our priorities upon God, but we must let Him work with us in the order He chooses. A person may, for instance, be determined to seek financial prosperity, whereas God's first priority for him is righteousness. If he stubbornly insists on claiming prosperity before righteousness, he may not receive either!

Again, a person may seek physical healing, not knowing that the root of his physical sickness is an inner emotional problem – such as rejection or grief or insecurity. In response, God will move to bring the emotional healing that is needed. If the person does not open himself up to this, however, but continues to beg merely for physical healing, he may in the end receive no healing at all, either physical or emotional.

Sometimes God seeks to reveal to us a provision of salvation which is our most urgent need, and yet we are not aware of it. This applies particularly to the provision for release from a curse. Very often a curse over a person's life is the unsuspected barrier which holds him back from the other provisions of salvation. Normally, this barrier must be dealt with first, before other needs can be met.

This is the provision which we will now focus upon: *the exchange from curse to blessing.* At this point we are confronted by precisely the same issues Moses put before the Israelites as they were preparing to enter the land of Canaan: "This day I call heaven and earth as witnesses against you that I have set before you life and death, blessings and curses. Now choose life, so that you and your children may live" (Deuteronomy 30:19, NIV). The issues were so solemn, and so far-reaching in their consequences, that Moses called heaven and earth to witness Israel's response.

The alternatives were clear: life and blessings, on the one hand; death and curses, on the other. God required the Israelites to make their own choice. He urged them to make the right choice: life and blessings. But He would not make the choice for them. He also reminded them that the choice they made would affect not merely their own lives, but also the lives of their descendants. This emerges once again as a characteristic feature of both blessings and curses: They continue from generation to generation.

The choice that Israel made at that time determined their destiny. The same is true for us today. God sets before us precisely the same alternatives: life and blessings or death and curses. He leaves it to us to choose. Like Israel, we determine our destiny by the choice that we make. Our choice may also affect the destiny of our descendants.

I remember when I was first confronted by those words of Moses. As I realised that God required a response from me, I was overawed. God was waiting for me to choose! I could not evade the issue. Not to choose was, in effect, to make the wrong choice.

I thank God that He gave me the grace to make the right choice. Never, in all the years since then, have I regretted it. God soon began to show me, however, the implications of my choice. I had passed through a door leading to a lifetime walk of faith and obedience, from which there was no turning back.

All who desire to pass from curse to blessing must go through the same door. First, there must be a clear recognition of the issues which God sets before us. Then there must be a simple, positive response: "Lord, on the basis of Your Word, I make my response. I refuse death and curses, and I choose life and blessings."

Once we have made this choice, we can go on to claim release from any curses over our lives. What are the steps that we must take for this? There is no one set pattern that everyone must follow. In bringing people to the point of release, however, I have found it helpful to lead them through the seven stages outlined below.

You may be approaching this issue from the perspective of one who is concerned to help or counsel others. To receive the full benefit of this instruction, however, I recommend that you put yourself mentally in the place of the person who needs release. In so doing, you may discover that is where you actually are!

1. *Confess your faith in Christ and in His sacrifice on your behalf*

In Romans 10:9-10 Paul explains that there are two essential conditions for receiving the benefits of Christ's sacrifice: to *believe* in the heart that God raised Jesus from the dead and to *confess* with the mouth that He is Lord. Faith in the heart is not fully effective until it has been completed by confession with the mouth.

Literally, the word *confess* means "to say the same as." In the context of biblical faith, confession means saying with our mouth what God has already said in His Word. In Hebrews 3:1 Jesus is called "the High Priest of our confession." When we make the right scriptural confession concerning Him, it releases His priestly ministry on our behalf.

To receive the benefits of Christ's sacrifice, we need to make our confession specific and personal. For example:

> Lord Jesus Christ, I believe that You are the Son of God and the only way to God; and that You died on the cross for my sins and rose again from the dead.

2.   *Repent of all your rebellion and your sins*

There may have been many external factors – even going back to previous generations – that have contributed to the curse over your life. Nevertheless, the root of all your problems lies within yourself. It is summed up in that one word *avon* (iniquity): your rebellious attitude toward God and the sins that have resulted from it. For this, you must accept personal responsibility.

Before you can receive God's mercy, therefore, He requires that you *repent*. This must be a deliberate decision on your part: You lay down your rebellion and submit yourself without reservation to all that God requires of you. A person who has truly repented no longer argues with God!

The New Testament leaves no room for faith that bypasses repentance. When John the Baptist came to prepare the way before Jesus, the first word in his message was *"Repent . . . !"* (Matthew 3:2). Later, when Jesus commenced His public ministry, He took up where John had left off: *"Repent,* and believe in the gospel" (Mark 1:15). *Without repentance, no effective faith is possible.* Many professing Christians are continually struggling for faith because they have never fulfilled the prior condition of repentance. Consequently, they never receive the full benefits of Christ's sacrifice.

Here is a suggested confession that expresses the repentance that God demands:

> I give up all my rebellion and all my sin, and I submit myself to You as my Lord.

3. Claim forgiveness of all sins

The great barrier that keeps God's blessing out of our lives is *unforgiven sin.* God has already made provision for our sins to be forgiven, but He will not do this until we confess them. *"If we confess our sins,* He is faithful and just to forgive us our sins and to cleanse us from all unrighteousness" (1 John 1:9). God is *faithful* to do this because He has given us His promise, and He always keeps His promises. He is also *just* because the full penalty for our sins has already been paid by Jesus.

It may be that God has shown you certain sins which opened you up to a curse. If so, make a specific confession of those sins.

It is also possible that a curse has come upon you because of sins committed by your ancestors (especially idolatry or the occult). You do not bear the guilt of sins your ancestors committed, but you may be affected in various ways by the consequences of their sins. If you know this to be the case, ask God also for release from those consequences.

Here is a suitable prayer that covers this:

> I confess all my sins before You and ask for Your
> forgiveness – especially for any sins that exposed me to
> a curse. Release me also from the consequences of my
> ancestors' sins.

4. Forgive all other people who have ever harmed you or wronged you

Another great barrier that can keep God's blessing out of our
lives is *unforgiveness* in our hearts toward other people. In Mark
11:25 Jesus put His finger on this as something that we must deal
with, if we expect God to answer our prayers:

> *"And whenever you stand praying, if you have
> anything against anyone, forgive him, that your Father
> in heaven may also forgive you your trespasses."*

The same principle runs all through the New Testament: If we
want God to forgive us, we must be prepared to forgive others.

Forgiving another person is not primarily an emotion; it is a
decision. I sometimes illustrate this with a little "parable." You
have in your hand IOUs from another person in a total of $10,000.
In heaven, however, God has in His hand IOUs from you to Him
in the amount of $10,000,000. God makes you an offer: "You tear
up the IOUs in your hand, and I'll tear up the IOUs in Mine. On
the other hand, if you hold onto your IOUs, I'll hold onto Mine!"

Understood in this way, forgiving another person is not a
tremendous sacrifice. It is merely enlightened self-interest.
Anyone who is not willing to cancel a debt of $10,000 in order
to have his own debt of $10,000,000 cancelled is lacking in

business sense!

God may now be bringing to your mind some person or persons whom you need to forgive. If so, you can look to the Holy Spirit for help. He will prompt you to make the right decision, but He will not make it for you. While you feel His prompting, respond. Make a clear-cut decision to forgive. Then verbalise your decision. Say out loud, "Lord, I forgive . . ." and name the person or persons involved. The ones you find it hardest to name are the ones you most need to forgive! Here are some simple words you can use:

> By a decision of my will, I forgive all who have harmed me or wronged me – just as I want God to forgive me. In particular, I forgive . . . (name the person or persons).

5. Renounce all contact with anything occult or satanic

Before you come to the actual prayer for release, there is one further, important area that must be dealt with: all contact with anything occult or satanic. This includes a very wide range of activities and practices. You may need to turn back for a moment to pages 71-73 in chapter 6, where there is a list that covers some, but not all, of the forms that these may take. If you are unclear about an area that is not mentioned in the list, ask God to make it clear to you.

If you have been involved at any time in any such activities or practices, you have crossed an invisible border into the kingdom of Satan. Since that time, whether you know it or not, Satan has regarded you as one of his subjects. He considers that he has a legal claim to you. Since the kingdom of God and the kingdom of Satan are in total opposition to one another, you cannot enjoy the full rights and benefits of a citizen in God's kingdom until you have finally and forever severed all connection with Satan and totally cancelled any claim he may have against you.

In 2 Corinthians 6:14-15 Paul stresses the necessity of a complete break with Satan's kingdom: "What fellowship can light have with darkness? What harmony is there between Christ and Belial [that is, Satan]?" (NIV). In verse 17 he concludes with a direct charge from the Lord Himself:

Therefore

> *"Come out from among them*
> *And be separate, says the Lord,*
> *Do not touch what is unclean,*
> *And I will receive you."*

Making this break requires also that you deal with any "contact objects" – that is, objects that would still link you with Satan. This could include many different items. In my case, as I related in chapter 2, it was the Chinese dragons I had inherited. If you have any doubts about how this might apply in your situation, ask God to put His finger on anything that is offensive to Him. Then get rid of it in the most effective way: burn it, smash it, throw it into deep water – or whatever!

If you are ready to make this total break with Satan and his kingdom, here is an appropriate way to affirm it:

I renounce all contact with anything occult or satanic – if I have any "contact objects," I commit myself to destroy them. I cancel all Satan's claims against me.

6. *You are now ready to pray the prayer for release from any curse*

If you have been willing to commit yourself to each of the preceding five steps, you are now at the place where you can pray the actual prayer for release from any curse over your life. But remember, there is only one basis upon which God offers His mercy: the exchange that took place when Jesus died on the cross. Included in that exchange was provision for release from every curse. By being hanged on a cross, Jesus became a curse with every curse that could ever come upon you, that you in turn might be released from every curse and receive God's blessing in its place.

It is important that you base your faith *solely* upon what Jesus obtained for you through His sacrifice on the cross. You do not have to "earn" your release. You do not have to be "worthy." If you come to God with thoughts like that, you will have no solid basis for your faith. God responds to us only on the basis of what Jesus has done on our behalf, not of any merits we may fancy we have in ourselves.

If you pray with this basis for your faith, your prayer should end not merely with asking, but with actually receiving. In Mark 11:24 Jesus established this as a principle: "Therefore I tell you, whatever you ask for in prayer, *believe that you have received it, and it will be yours*" (NIV).

In this kind of prayer there are two distinct stages, related as cause and effect: *receiving* and *having*. *Receiving* is the cause, from which *having* follows as the effect. *Receiving* is in the past tense; *having* is in the future. *Receiving* takes place when we pray. Then *having* follows at a time and in a way determined by God's sovereignty. But the principle Jesus emphasises is this: If we do not *receive* at the time we pray, we have no assurance that we will ever *have*.

Here is a prayer that would be appropriate. You might first read through this prayer and then read on for further instructions.

> Lord Jesus, I believe that on the cross You took on Yourself every curse that could ever come upon me. So I ask You now to release me from every curse over my life – in Your name, Lord Jesus Christ!
> By faith I now receive my release and I thank You for it."

But now, pause for a moment! Before you pray this prayer for release, you would be wise to reaffirm each of the five preceding confessions which you have already made. To make this easier for you, they are repeated below, but without any added comments or explanation.

Read them out loud, slowly and deliberately, with undivided attention. If you feel uncertainty about any section, go back and read it again. Identify yourself with the words you utter. By the time you have read them through, *you should have the sense that you have brought yourself to God* with the words you have spoken. Then go straight on into the prayer of release which is repeated at the end.

Here, then, is the complete prayer:

> Lord Jesus Christ, I believe that You are the Son of God and the only way to God; and that You died on the cross for my sins and rose again from the dead.
> I give up all my rebellion and all my sin, and I submit myself to you as my Lord.
> I confess all my sins before You and ask for Your forgiveness – especially for any sins that exposed me to a curse. Release me also from the consequences of my

ancestors' sins.

By a decision of my will, I forgive all who have harmed me or wronged me – just as I want God to forgive me. In particular, I forgive . . .

I renounce all contact with anything occult or satanic – if I have any "contact objects," I commit myself to destroy them. I cancel all Satan's claims against me.

Lord Jesus, I believe that on the cross You took on Yourself every curse that could ever come upon me. So I ask You now to release me from every curse over my life – in Your name, Lord Jesus Christ!

By faith I now receive my release and I thank You for it.

Now don't stop at saying "Thank You" just once or twice. Your *mind* cannot grasp a fraction of what you have asked God to do for you, but respond to God with your *heart!* This could be the time to release hurts or pressures or inhibitions that have built up inside you over the years. If a dam breaks inside you, don't try to hold back the tears which are the outflow of your heart.

Don't be held back by self-consciousness or embarrassment! God has known all along the things that you kept shut up inside you – and He is not the least embarrassed by them. So why should you be? Tell God how much you really love Him. The more you express your love, the more real it will become to you.

On the other hand, there is no set pattern for responding to God which everyone has to follow. The key to release is not some particular type of response. Faith can be expressed in many different ways. Just be your real self with God. Open your whole being to God's love as a flower opens its petals to the sun.

7.   *Now believe that you have received, and go on in God's blessing!*

Do not try at this stage to analyse what form the blessing will take or how God will impart it to you. Leave that in God's hands. Let Him do it just how and when He will. You do not have to concern yourself with that. Your part is simply to open yourself, without reservation, to all that God wants to do in you and for you through His blessing.

Remember that God "is able to do exceedingly abundantly above all that we ask or think" (Ephesians 3:20). So do not limit God to doing only what you think.

Here is a simple form of words that you can use:

> Lord, I now open myself to receive Your blessing in every way You want to impart it to me.

It will be exciting for you to see just how God will respond!

19

FROM SHADOWS TO SUNLIGHT

If you followed the instructions in the previous chapter, you have crossed an invisible boundary. Behind you now is a territory overshadowed by curses of many different kinds and from many different sources. Before you lies a territory made bright by the sunshine of God's blessings. Before you go any further, cast your mind back to the summary of the list Moses gave in Deuteronomy 28:2-13:

Exaltation	Prosperity
Health	Victory
Reproductiveness	God's favour

These are all parts of your inheritance in Christ, waiting for you to explore and to claim.

It could help you to repeat these key words over to yourself several times – preferably out loud. Living under a curse often makes it difficult for a person to envisage what it would be like to enjoy the corresponding blessing. Ask God to make your new inheritance real and vivid to you. You may need to go on repeating these words frequently – even many times a day – until you really know they are yours!

As you repeat them, pause and thank God that each one is now part of your inheritance. Remember that giving thanks is the purest and simplest expression of faith. If you have had a long struggle with a curse over your life, there may be areas of your mind from which the darkness is not immediately dispelled. Repeating these positive words that describe the blessings will be like seeing the first rays of the sun shining into a dark valley, then spreading until the whole valley is illuminated.

The transition from the dark to the sunlit territory may take many different forms. There is no single pattern that is standard for everyone. Some people experience an almost instantaneous release and seem to enter immediately into the blessings that Scripture promises. For others, who are equally sincere, there may be a long, hard struggle. The more deeply people have been involved in the occult, the harder may be their struggle to escape. Satan regards them as his legitimate prey, and he is determined to hold onto them. On their part, they must be even more determined to assert their claim to the freedom which has been purchased for them by the sacrifice of Jesus.

Also, Satan has at least some foreknowledge of what God has prepared for those who escape from his oppression. The greater the blessings in store for a person, the more determined will be Satan's attempt to hold him back. Viewed in this light, as foreshadowings of blessings ahead, our struggles can actually become a source of encouragement.

Over and above these factors, we are confronted with the sovereignty of God. God's perspective is different from ours. He takes into account factors in a situation about which we know nothing. He always keeps His promises, but in most cases there are two things He does not reveal in advance: the precise way that He will work in each life, and the precise time that He will take. No one can dictate to God exactly how to fulfil His promises. What we must do is maintain an attitude of firm, unwavering trust that God will move when and how He sees fit.

We need to look once more at the positive side of the exchange described by Paul in Galatians 3:13-14:

> *Christ has redeemed us from the curse of the law, having become a curse for us (for it is written, "Cursed is everyone who hangs on a tree"),*
> *that the blessing of Abraham might come upon the Gentiles in Christ Jesus, that we might receive the promise of the Spirit through faith.*

Paul points out three important facts concerning the promised blessing:

First, it is not something vague or undefined. It is quite specific: *the blessing of Abraham.* In Genesis 24:1 its extent is defined: "The Lord had blessed Abraham in *all things.*" God's blessing covered every area of Abraham's life. He has a corresponding blessing prepared for each person who fulfils His conditions.

Second, the blessing comes only *in Christ Jesus.* It cannot be earned by our own merits. It is offered solely upon the basis of our relationship to God through Jesus Christ. There is no other channel through which the blessing can flow into our lives. If the relationship with Christ is ruptured by unbelief or disobedience, the blessing will cease to flow. But thank God, it can be restored immediately by sincere repentance!

Third, the blessing is further defined as *"the promise of the [Holy] Spirit."* Concerning this, Jesus tells us in John 16:13-15:

> *"But when he, the Spirit of truth, comes, he will guide you into all truth . . . He will bring glory to me by taking from what is mine and making it known to you. All that belongs to the Father is mine. That is why I said the Spirit will take from what is mine and make it known to you."*
>
> NIV

What wonderful words of encouragement! All three Persons of the Godhead – Father, Son and Holy Spirit – are united in their purpose to share with us all that has been purchased for us by the sacrifice of Jesus. Because this is far greater than the natural mind can comprehend, we must depend upon the Holy Spirit to guide us into our full inheritance and to show us how to appropriate what God has provided for us.

In Romans 8:14 Paul again emphasises the unique role of the Holy Spirit: "For as many as are led by the Spirit of God, these are sons of God." Paul is careful to use here the continuing present tense: "as many as *are continually led* by the Spirit of God." To be "led by the Holy Spirit" is not a single, once-for-all experience. It is something on which we must depend moment by moment. It is the only pathway to spiritual maturity. Through it we grow up from being little children to become *mature sons* of God.

Unfortunately, many Christians never fully enjoy the guidance and companionship of the Holy Spirit for one basic reason: they do not realise that He is a *Person*. "The Lord is that Spirit" (2 Corinthians 3:17). Just as God the Father is Lord, and God the Son is Lord, so also God the Spirit is Lord. He is not just a theological abstraction, nor a set of rules, nor half a sentence at the end of the Apostles' Creed. He is a Person, and He wants us to cultivate an intimate, *personal* relationship with Him.

The Holy Spirit has His own distinctive characteristics. He is not aggressive or "pushy," nor does He shout at us. He usually speaks in soft tones and directs us by gentle impulses. To receive His direction, we must be attentive to His voice and sensitive to His impulses.

Furthermore, the Holy Spirit deals with each of us as individuals. To enter into God's blessings, there is no single set of rules that everybody must follow. Each of us has a special, distinctive personality with unique needs and aspirations, unique strengths and weaknesses. The Holy Spirit respects our uniqueness. Someone has said that God never makes one believer a carbon copy of another. Nor does He produce Christians on a factory assembly line.

Only the Holy Spirit knows the special dangers that threaten us in any situation or the particular blessings that will meet our individual needs. He guides us faithfully through the dangers and opens up to us the blessings. If we begin to follow some religious system or to model ourselves on some other Christian, we shall miss some of the choicest blessings that God has marked out for us.

You would be wise, therefore, to pause for a moment and offer up a brief prayer:

> Holy Spirit, I open my heart and mind to You. Reveal to me the blessings that Jesus has obtained for me and how I may receive them.

In Hebrews 10:14 – already quoted in chapter 17 – the writer uses two contrasted tenses to depict two opposite sides of the exchange that took place on the cross. To describe what Jesus accomplished, he uses the *perfect* tense: "By one offering He *has perfected* forever." What Jesus has done is absolutely and eternally complete. Nothing need ever be added, and nothing can ever be taken away.

On the other hand, to describe the outworking of the sacrifice in those who accept it for themselves, the writer uses the *continuing present:* "those who *are being sanctified.*" Our appropriation of the sacrifice is not immediately complete; it is *progressive.* The process by which we appropriate it is described as "being sanctified" – that is, being set apart to God in holiness. As we bring our lives progressively into line with God's requirements of holiness, we are able to enter into His blessings more fully.

When confronted with this challenge, Christians sometimes respond, "But I thought I got everything when I was born again!" The answer to that is yes – and no. There are two sides to this issue: the legal and the experiential. The answer will differ according to which side we view it from.

Legally, you did indeed "get everything" when you were born again. According to Romans 8:17, when you became a child of God, you were made "an heir of God and a joint heir with Christ." Legally, from that point on, you were entitled to share Christ's whole inheritance with Him.

Experientially, however, you were only at the beginning of a process that takes a lifetime to complete. The Christian life could be described as a progression from the legal to the experiential. Step by step, in faith, we must appropriate in experience all that is already ours by legal right through our faith in Christ. This is what the writer of Hebrews calls "being sanctified."

In John 1:12-13 the apostle says, concerning those who have been born again through receiving Jesus, that God has given them *"the right to become children of God."* The Greek word translated "right" is exousia, usually translated "authority." That is what a person actually receives at the new birth: *authority to become a child of God.*

Authority is effective, however, only insofar as it is exercised. The potential of the new birth is unlimited, but the actual results depend on the exercise of the authority that goes with it. What a person will become through the new birth is determined by the extent to which he exercises his God-given authority.

There is a close parallel between the experience of believers entering into the blessings of God in the New Covenant and that of the Israelites entering into Canaan under the Old Covenant. In the first covenant, under a leader named Joshua, God brought His people into *a promised land.* In the second covenant, under a leader named Jesus (which is another form of Joshua), God brings His people into *a land of promises.* Just as the land of Canaan was the physical inheritance appointed for Israel, so the promises of God, offered through Jesus, are the spiritual inheritance appointed for Christians in this dispensation. The same principles that applied to Israelites then apply to Christians now.

In Joshua 1:2-3 God gave Joshua instructions on how the Israelites were to take possession of their inheritance:

> *"Moses My servant is dead. Now therefore, arise, go over this Jordan, you and all this people, to the land which I am giving to them – the children of Israel.*
> *"Every place that the sole of your foot will tread upon I have given you, as I said to Moses."*

There is precisely the same contrast of tenses here as in Hebrews 10:14. In verse 2, the Lord uses the continuing present: "I *am giving* [the land]." But in verse 3 He uses the perfect tense: "I *have given* [the land]." From verse 3 onward, the legal ownership of Canaan was settled: It belonged to Israel. Experientially, however, nothing had changed. The Canaanites were still in occupation of the land.

The challenge to Joshua and his people was to move from the legal to the experiential. This they were to do one step at a time. As they placed their feet on each place, it became theirs not just legally, but in actual experience.

Had the Israelites responded to God's promise in the same way that some Christians would like to, history would have been very different. They would have lined up on the east bank of the Jordan, folded their arms, looked westward and said, "It's all ours!" But the Canaanites would have laughed at them. They knew who still had possession of the land.

As it was, Joshua and his people acted very differently. First, they crossed the Jordan by a miracle that God performed in response to their obedience. Then they besieged and captured Jericho – again by a miracle. But after that their further progress was mainly by battles, not by miracles. They moved out in every direction across Canaan and fought a long series of battles against the various inhabitants of the land. Even after much arduous warfare, their task had not been completed. A long time later, God said to Joshua, "There remains very much land yet to be possessed" (Joshua 13:1).

Precisely the same challenge confronts us as believers in the New Testament: to move from the legal to the experiential. Like Israel, we must progress one step at a time. Like Israel, too, we will face opposition. Our progress will continually be contested by satanic forces, and we must learn to overcome them with the spiritual weapons God has provided for us. Ultimately, Christ's promises in the New Covenant are given to only one kind of person: "to him who overcomes." (See Revelation 2 and 3.) The right to the inheritance is summed up in Revelation 21:7: "He who *overcomes* shall inherit all things."

To further strengthen and encourage us, God has also set before us the example of Abraham, who is called "the father of us all." Through Abraham, God did not merely establish the measure of the blessing He has prepared for each of us, which is "in all things." He also marked out ahead the path that leads to that blessing. The life of Abraham is both an example and a challenge in three main areas: his prompt obedience, his complete confidence in God's word and his steadfast endurance.

In Hebrews 11:8 the writer emphasises Abraham's prompt, unquestioning obedience: "By faith Abraham obeyed when he was called to go out to the place which he would afterward receive as an inheritance. And he went out, not knowing where he was going."

Abraham did not ask for any explanation of why he should go, or any description of the place he was going to. He simply did what God told him to do, promptly, without questioning. The same kind of obedience characterised his entire life: for instance, when God required him and all his household to be circumcised (Genesis 17:9-14, 23-27); and even when God asked him to offer up his son, Isaac, as a sacrifice (Genesis 22:1-14). At no time did Abraham ever hesitate in his obedience or question God concerning what he was asked to do.

In Romans 4:16-21 Paul points out that when God called Abraham "a father of many nations," he had only one son by Hagar, a slave woman, while Sarah, his wife, had been barren for many years. Yet he reckoned God's description of him as true from the moment it was spoken. Because he thus accepted God's word without questioning, even against the evidence of his own senses, ultimately there came a physical fulfilment which was confirmed by his senses.

Actually, about 25 years passed from the time God first

promised Abraham that his descendants would be as numerous as the stars, until the birth of the son who was the promised heir. Through all those years he had nothing to hold onto but God's promise. He must have faced endless temptations to discouragement. Yet he never gave up or abandoned his faith. Finally, the reward of his steadfastness is summed up in Hebrews 6:15: "And so, after he had patiently endured, he obtained the promise."

In Romans 4:11-12 Paul tells us that we are children of Abraham "if we walk in the steps of Abraham's faith." This is the scriptural requirement for entering into "the blessing of Abraham" promised in Galatians 3:14. Like Abraham, we must accept God's Word as the one sure, unchanging element in our experience. All the variable opinions of men, and all the fluctuating impressions of our senses, are just "grass that withers. But the Word of our God stands forever" (Isaiah 40:8).

Our acceptance of God's Word, however, must not be purely intellectual or theoretical. We must demonstrate it in our actions just as Abraham did: by prompt, unquestioning obedience and by steadfast endurance in the face of all discouragement. In this way, we shall find that God's Word will ultimately be proved true in our experience. We shall come to know God's blessing – just as Abraham did – "in all things."

Satan will continually oppose us with mental and emotional pressures: doubts, fear, guilt, confusion, and so on. He may also assail our bodies with various forms of physical infirmity. Against all this God has provided us with one supremely effective weapon: His Word. In Ephesians 6:17 Paul directs us: "Take . . . the sword of the Spirit, which is the word of God."

This requires the interplay of the human and the divine. The sword is the sword of the Holy Spirit, but it is our responsibility to "take" it. If we take it, the Holy Spirit will wield it. But if we do not take it, the Holy Spirit has nothing to wield.

The Greek word Paul uses here to describe God's Word is rheum. This is primarily *a word that is spoken*. It becomes effective only when it is spoken through believing lips. It is not the Bible in our bookshelves, or even on our nightstands, that Paul is speaking about. It is the Bible when we take it on our lips *and speak it out with bold faith*.

Our great pattern in the use of this sword is the Lord Jesus Himself, as He demonstrated in His temptation by Satan in the wilderness. (See Matthew 4:1-11.) Each of Satan's three temptations contained the word *if*. In other words, it was aimed to produce *doubt*.

The first two temptations each began with the phrase *"If* You are the Son of God . . ."* Shortly before, when Jesus was baptised by John in the Jordan, God the Father had publicly declared, "This is My beloved Son, in whom I am well pleased" (Matthew 3:17). Now Satan was tempting Jesus to doubt what the Father had said about Him.

The third temptation also began with *if,* but it was no longer a temptation merely to doubt, but also to direct disobedience: *"If* You will fall down and worship me . . ." Satan now challenged Jesus to commit the greatest of all sins: the breaking of the first commandment.

The temptations which Satan brings against us, as disciples of Jesus, will follow a similar pattern. First, he will tempt us to doubt what God has said about us; to doubt that our sins have been forgiven, that God really loves us, that we have been accepted into God's family as His children, that we have been released from the curse and have entered into the blessing. But always the final thrust of his temptation will be to direct disobedience.

Jesus used only one weapon to defeat Satan: the *rhema* – the spoken Word of God. He countered each temptation with the same phrase: "It is written." Each was a direct quotation from the

Scriptures of the Old Testament. Satan has no defence against the Word of God thus quoted directly at him. He has to withdraw, defeated.

In all of this, Jesus is our perfect example. He did not rely on any wisdom or arguments of His own. He used precisely the same weapon which God has given to us: the Word of God. Our security depends on following the example of Jesus. We would certainly be foolish to rely on our own wisdom or strength or righteousness. Satan is a thousand times wiser and stronger than we are. He can point to a thousand flaws in our own righteousness. But there is one weapon against which he has no defence: the Word of God spoken in faith.

Such, then, is the path that leads us out of the territory overshadowed by curses into the territory that enjoys the sunlight of God's blessings. Its first requirement is determined, unswerving faith, based on the exchange that took place on the cross. Faith of this kind reckons God's promises as effective from the moment they are apprehended. We do not wait for confirmation from the senses. By prompt, unquestioning obedience and patient endurance, we move from our legal rights in Christ into the full, experiential enjoyment of them. We meet all satanic opposition with "the sword of the Spirit": the spoken Word of God.

20
FORCEFUL MEN
LAY HOLD OF IT

When Joshua was commissioned as the leader who would bring Israel into their inheritance in Canaan, he received the same admonition three times: "Be strong and of good courage" (Joshua 1:6, 9, 18). The first two admonitions came from the Lord Himself; the third came from his fellow Israelites. After the third admonition Joshua must surely have understood one thing: entering into the Promised Land would not be easy!

The same applies to Christians today who set out to appropriate the promised blessings of the New Covenant. God assures us that He will be with us and fulfil all His promises to us. At the same time, He warns us that we will face various forms of opposition, which will test our faith and our commitment.

In Matthew 11:12 Jesus spoke of the Gospel dispensation He had come to initiate: "From the days of John the Baptist until now, the kingdom of heaven has been forcefully advancing, and forceful men lay hold of it" (NIV). In Luke 16:16 He emphasised the same point: "The Law and the Prophets were proclaimed until John. Since that time, the good news of the kingdom of God is being preached, and everyone is forcing his way into it" (NIV).

Clearly the promise of the Kingdom is not for those who merely indulge in wishful thinking or religious talk. It demands "forcefulness" – an attitude of fixed determination that presses ahead regardless of every kind of difficulty or discouragement.

In Acts 14:22 Paul and Barnabas gave a similar warning to a group of new converts: "We must through many tribulations enter the kingdom of God." Any road that bypasses the tribulations will not take us into the Kingdom. Once we have settled this issue in our own minds, then the tribulations will not deter us.

Otto Aguiar is one man who set out to lay hold of God's promises with forceful determination. Otto is a Brazilian who was born with curses over his life that went back many generations. He had also brought further curses upon himself by his own foolishness. Nevertheless, he has finally crossed over from the dark territory of curses to the sunlit land of God's blessings, which is where he now lives.

Otto Aguiar tells his story:

> I was born fifty years ago in Rio de Janeiro, Brazil. My father was a well-known general from mixed European and Indian stock; my mother came from a family of governors and statesmen. Both sides of my family had been in spiritism for generations.
>
> I was the seventh of ten children – a fourteen-pound breech birth. For several years I was accused of almost killing my mother. I was guilt-ridden and withdrawn. I

would sit, hiding my head in my arms, reliving the gruesome experience of being dragged out with forceps, and not ready to cope. I repeated first grade *four* times. By the time I was promoted to second grade, I was almost the size of my teacher.

Ancestral curses began to affect the older members of my family while I was still a child. My eldest sister, while in a strict Catholic school, was taken to a spiritist centre, and began to "receive spirits of saints," as they say in Brazil. She has spent most of her life in mental institutions.

The second child, my eldest brother, a brilliant student, took a fall on his head at age ten, and became an epileptic. In Brazil at that time it was commonly believed that epilepsy was contagious, so he was moved, with all his belongings, from the main house to the servants' quarters. When he would have an attack, my mother would become totally distraught and scream, "There is no God!" He has been institution-alised for the past fifteen years.

When I was sixteen I began to have all the symptoms of epilepsy – foaming at the mouth, fainting, vomiting, in complete confusion. Yet brain scans showed nothing.

My father, an excellent leader of men, was extremely passive with his seven sons, and exercised no real authority. I cannot remember his even speaking to me until I became a man – yet I adored him. He frequented a spiritist centre. I never felt good about spiritism, but would on occasion go myself.

I don't really understand how it happened, but I was accepted for study at a fine arts school – where I obtained a master's degree, with honours in graphic arts! But I never pursued that career. I chose to become a fashion model, and travelled from Brazil to Paris, modelling.

I was heavily involved in drugs and a fast-paced lifestyle. Sometimes I would spend time alone at my family's beach house. I would look at the sky and think of the One who put the stars in the sky and caused the sun to rise. I hungered to know who He was, but I didn't know where to look.

Then I met Ellen, a Jewess from the U.S.A., also a fashion model. When I met her, I decided to change my lifestyle, but I couldn't do it. She went away for five days on an assignment, and I went to the beach with my friends. We were high on drugs and when I entered the rough water, I was immediately dragged in by a powerful wave. Wave after wave slammed on me. I couldn't get my breath. I thought, "*O, God*, now that I've met Ellen and I want to change, am I going to *die?*" This was the first time in my 37 years that I had called on God, but He heard me – and suddenly I was on the sand, trembling and bruised all over, in total panic, yet amazed to be alive.

Within eleven months I not only had a wife, but also a baby – and I could not cope. Instead of hiding my head in my arms as I did as a small boy, I would "phase out" and stare at the ceiling in a trance . . . I was still a model, and everything else I tried failed . . . so I decided to take my wife and son to Fort Lauderdale, Florida.

My first job was working part-time in a men's clothing shop on fashionable Las Olas Boulevard. I was terrified – I couldn't speak proper English – so I also dug ditches, cracked holes in cement, cleaned bathrooms, and washed cars. I had a serious problem with pornography and was in total depression. I could not adjust to American culture, and most of the people I worked for cheated me or didn't pay me at all.

Then we were invited to Good News Church; Ellen was brought to her knees and received the Lord with no intellectual understanding – just fear and trembling! I went forward for salvation the next week, but nothing seemed to happen. The trances got worse; I couldn't keep a job for even one week; my depression was worse; Ellen and I fought constantly because we had no money.

Since Ellen had been involved in the occult, she knew she needed deliverance – and she got it when she renounced everything occult. I could not believe that I needed deliverance from evil spirits – and I also could not believe that God wanted to bless me the way I saw Him blessing others.

By this time, I had done almost every menial task a general's son would never do! People would say, "Why don't you use your creative abilities?" But I was afraid – anything good seemed unattainable.

I went to Derek Prince's seminar on "Curses: Cause and Cure," but nothing happened. I got the tapes and played them over and over. I could see my need, and I desperately wanted to be set free – but it seemed that it didn't work for me.

I got delivered gradually. After two and a half years as a Christian, with no progress, I decided to fast and ask God to help me and deliver me. I was able to fast ten days, and when some Christian friends prayed for me, I received partial deliverance.

For the first time in my life I had some JOY . . . but it didn't last. We had numerous car accidents; I was never able to support my family; I worried about my father in Brazil, who was dying, but we could not possibly afford to go to visit him.

People who tried to help me thought my situation was impossible – I was so passive. I was very uncomfortable with Christian men . . .

Ellen and two friends began to meet and pray for their husbands at 6:00 A.M. at the prayer house. She would say, "I'm going to pray that you will be a success in all that you put your hand to, and that the Lord will give you a job that you'll love and use the gifts He's set within you." I could not believe that God would answer such a prayer; how could she? (Since then all three women have seen their prayers answered: One husband is now in full-time ministry, one was delivered from alcoholism and I got exactly what my wife prayed for.)

Finally, after six years as a Christian, I went to the pastor for deliverance from evil spirits (after years of being too proud to admit I needed it). Then I went to "Evangelism Explosion" training. When I discovered what Jesus Christ had done for me, I was totally amazed. I had so much JOY – I was in love with God – my co-workers and clients in the store began to come to church to find out what had happened to me!

Again, after a while, my joy dwindled – my job, my finances, my concern for my dying father . . . I was still passive, still frustrated. I began to get an urge to paint – but I was so scared, so afraid of failing. Finally I tried – and I did such primary work that people thought my son, age eight, had done it! But God was stirring up ideas – I began to create in my mind . . .

I decided to go on a forty-day fast. I felt God wanted me to leave my job in the clothing store, but I wanted to be *sure*. I said I wouldn't eat until He spoke to me. After forty days I still had heard nothing. So I ate for two weeks and fasted for two weeks all summer. That was the hardest summer of my life. It was so hard that I learned to cry out to God for His mercy. I *begged* Him to speak to me. *I needed to know His will.* My wife and my children would lay hands on me and pray that God would do a miracle in my life . . .

Then an artist friend gave me some canvas stretched on boards . . . One Sunday I sent my family to church, and did my first painting.

Two days later, seated in the clothing shop, the Lord spoke to me: *Otto, do you believe that I really want to bless you?*

I said, "Yes, Lord . . ."

Then why are you sitting here? You are here because you do not want to be blessed. It is your choice. You have never really trusted Me to completely control your life.

I said, "Take it! My life is Yours."

He said, *Take your bag and go home.* (For me, it was as if He had said, "Take up your pallet and walk.")

I got up, walked out, and never looked back.

That first painting sold within one week for $80. Within two weeks I was paid $900 for six paintings. After two months my paintings brought $600 each; within one year $1800; before two years up to $6500.

I have sold everything I have ever painted and I cannot keep up with the demand – and *I love my work!*

After nine months of painting, not only was I able to support my family, but we had enough money to go to Brazil. My father had *never* heard the Gospel, but when he heard, he believed! I had the joy of seeing my 89-year-old father gather up every ounce of strength to pray the sinner's prayer, and I also led several of my brothers and sisters, plus nurses and strangers, to the Lord. Two weeks after we returned to the U.S., my father died with joy on his face! What a privilege God gave me.

The main changes in my life seem obviously financial – but, far more important, God completed the revelation of what Jesus did for me on the cross. Now I fully believe He set us free from the curse and that His desire is to bless us, and that He wants us to give Him *complete* control over all that concerns us. That without His power, His grace, I cannot do anything – much less create. I am totally dependent upon His anointing. I *know that He loves me!*

God now speaks to me in dreams and very clearly . . . I am confident if He wants me to stop painting, it will be to do something better. I'll continue praising Him and trusting.

I now have three precious healthy children, a happy marriage, wonderful friends, and consider myself blessed among men. *I have seen the enemy completely defeated in my own life*, and God has given me a testimony that has encouraged multitudes of Christians and baffled the unsaved.

Otto's story contains a number of features that are typical of people whose lives are overshadowed by curses. It can also encourage those who are seeking to help loved ones in a similar condition. Here are some of the main lessons to be learned.

The root cause of the curses over Otto's life was his ancestors' deep involvement in spiritism over many generations. It has been my observation that curses follow this type of involvement as surely as night follows day.

The ensuing curses did not just affect Otto as an individual. They affected almost all his brothers and sisters, but in various ways. He states that two of them have spent long periods in psychiatric institutions.

One of the first steps in Otto's release was a *correct diagnosis* of his condition. Once he understood clearly that his life was under a curse, he was motivated to seek the release that Jesus had purchased for him through the exchange on the cross.

But, like many others, Otto had lived so long under a curse that he could not envisage God's blessing as a reality in his own life. Left to himself, he probably would never have been able to enter into the blessing. He was too timid and withdrawn. He lacked the "forcefulness" needed to press into God's Kingdom. But persistent intercession by Otto's wife and children, and by others, gradually released him from his timidity and built up in him the determined faith that enabled him to pass from the curse to the blessing.

This should encourage other Christians who are concerned about family members or other loved ones under a curse. Patient, persistent intercession – motivated by love – can release those who are not able to exercise faith for themselves.

Perhaps parents are reading this who realise with deep anguish that their trespassing into the occult has brought curses upon their children, causing them to become captives of Satan. For such parents who repent and seek God with their whole hearts, He has a special promise in Isaiah 49:24-25:

> *Can plunder be taken from warriors,*
> *or captives rescued from the fierce?*
> *But this is what the Lord says:*
> *"Yes, captives will be taken from warriors,*
> *and plunder retrieved from the fierce;*
> *I will contend with those who contend with you,*
> *and your children I will save."*

NIV

Finally, it is encouraging to look at the extent of the blessings Otto now enjoys. God has blessed him – just as He blessed Abraham – "in all things."

21
BEYOND CONFESSION: PROCLAMATION, THANKSGIVING, PRAISE

In the prayer of release in chapter 18, the initial focus was on the truth revealed in Hebrews 3:1: Jesus is "the High Priest of our confession." This principle should also govern our ongoing relationship with the Lord. In every situation we encounter, we must respond with an appropriate scriptural confession in order to invoke on our behalf the continuing ministry of Jesus as our High Priest.

In most situations we have three possibilities: to make a positive, scriptural confession; to make no confession; to make a negative, unscriptural confession. If we make a positive confession, we release the ministry of Jesus to help us and to meet our need. If we make no confession, we are left at the mercy of our circumstances. If we make a negative confession, we expose ourselves to evil, demonic forces. In chapter 12, on the theme of "self-imposed curses," various examples were given, showing how negative words release evil and negative forces into people's lives.

It is important to distinguish between the scriptural confession of genuine faith and such things as wishful thinking or irreverent presumption or some kind of "mind-over-matter" philosophy. There are three main differences. First of all, "confession" in the biblical sense is limited to the statements and promises of the Bible. It consists in saying with our mouth what God has already said in His Word. Beyond this confession cannot go.

Second, confession is also limited by the conditions attached to any particular promise. The great majority of the promises in the Bible are *conditional*. God says, in effect, "If you will do this, then I will do that." If we have not done the appropriate "this," then we have no right to expect that God will do the corresponding "that." Confession is valid only if the appropriate conditions have been fulfilled. It is never a substitute for obedience.

Third, confession cannot be reduced to a convenient "system," operated by human will. According to Romans 10:10, confession is effective only if it proceeds from faith in the *heart*. There is a radical difference between faith in the heart and faith in the mind. Faith in the mind is produced by our own mental processes; all it can produce is words, devoid of power. On the other hand, faith in the heart is produced only by the Holy Spirit, and it produces *words charged with power* to accomplish what is confessed. What God has promised to faith in the heart is out of the reach of mere mental faith.

In imparting faith to the heart, the Holy Spirit jealously guards His own sovereignty. He is not amenable to "witchcraft." No one can manipulate Him or intimidate Him or make Him do anything contrary to His own will. Concerning this kind of faith, Paul tells us in Ephesians 2:8-9 that it is "not of yourselves; it is the gift of God, not of works, *lest anyone should boast.*" Mental faith often tends to be boastful and self-assertive. Genuine faith in the heart, on the other hand, humbly acknowledges its total dependence upon God.

With these qualifications, however, confession – rightly understood and practised – can be a decisive factor in the Christian life. In James 3:4-5 the apostle compares the tongue to the rudder of a ship. Although tiny in comparison to the whole structure of the ship, the rudder determines the course that the ship will follow. Used rightly, it will guide the ship safely to its appointed harbour. Used wrongly, it will cause shipwreck.

This applies to the way we express our faith. Right confession can bring us into all the blessings God has promised to faith. Wrong confession can take us further and further away – into perilous, uncharted seas where some kind of shipwreck awaits us.

People are often unwilling to accept responsibility for the words they speak. According to Jesus, however, there is no way to escape the issue: "For by your words you will be justified, and by your words you will be condemned" (Matthew 12:37). Our words will either confirm our righteousness in God's sight, or they will bring us under condemnation. There is no middle ground.

According to Romans 10:10, faith in the heart becomes fully effective only when it is confessed with the mouth. This is also true of unbelief. When we express our unbelief in words, we release its negative power to work against us, and to withhold from us the blessings which God has promised to faith.

The writer of Hebrews offers two further warnings concerning the importance of right confession. In Hebrews 4:14:

Seeing then that we have a great High Priest who has passed through the heavens, Jesus the Son of God, let us hold fast our confession.

Again, in Hebrews 10:21, 23:

> . . . *And having a High Priest over the house of God . . .*
> *Let us hold fast the confession of our hope without wavering, for He who promised is faithful.*

In each of these passages, there is a direct link between our confession and the ministry of Jesus as our High Priest. The same principle holds true throughout the New Testament: It is our confession that unites us to Jesus as our High Priest and releases His priestly ministry on our behalf.

The other main emphasis in these passages is on the words *hold fast*. It is important to make the right initial confession, but that is not sufficient by itself. In every subsequent situation where the same issues apply, we must consistently reaffirm our original confession.

In Hebrews 10:23 the writer challenges us not merely to hold fast our confession, but to hold it fast *without wavering*. Clearly he envisages various possible situations that might cause us to waver. "Wavering" might express itself in failing to maintain the initial right confession, or even in changing a positive confession to a negative one. In any case, the warning against wavering indicates that the pressures directed against us all have one objective: to make us retract, or even deny, our original right confession.

The concept of right confession seems so simple, perhaps even simplistic: just to say concerning each problem or each test exactly, and only, what the Bible says about it, and to keep on saying it. Yes, it is simple, but it is not easy! In fact, I have concluded – both from experience in my own life and from observation in the lives of others – that it is perhaps the most searching test of Christian character and commitment.

It is the test that has confronted every martyr. Faced by accusation, threats, torture, he has one supreme commitment: to maintain his confession of the truth *to the end.*

When the accusations come from visible, human enemies, the issues at least are clear. But there is another kind of test, less easy to discern, in which the accusations are inward, directed against the mind by invisible demonic powers. Yet the issue is the same: to maintain the confession of the truth with unwavering determination until those invisible forces are silenced and routed.

Any Christian who successfully passes this test can be assured that he will be an overcomer, and that, as such, he will inherit the blessings that God has promised to those who overcome.

To give full, victorious expression to faith, however, there is one further biblical concept that takes us beyond confession. It is "proclamation." Derived from a Latin verb meaning to "shout forth" or to "shout aloud," *proclamation* suggests strong, confident assertion of faith, which cannot be silenced by any form of opposition or discouragement. It implies a transition from a defensive posture to one of *attack.*

In Psalm 118:11-17 the psalmist describes such an experience. His enemies had surrounded him on every side and were about to destroy him, but the Lord intervened and gave him victory. His transition from defence to attack is described in verses 15 and 17:

> *Shouts of joy and victory*
> > *resound in the tents of the righteous:*
> > *"The Lord's right hand has done mighty things! . . ."*
> *I will not die but live,*
> > *and will **proclaim** what the Lord has done.*

NIV

It was the psalmist's joyful, confident proclamation of what the Lord had done for him that set the seal on his victory. Rightly practised, it will do the same for us.

As we practice the confident proclamation of all that God has provided for us through the sacrifice of Jesus, it will naturally lead us on to two further forms of expression: thanksgiving and praise. If we truly believe what we proclaim, this is the only appropriate response! Wherever there is genuine faith, proclamation will always be followed by thanksgiving and praise.

Although thanksgiving and praise are closely related, there is a distinction between them. Simply stated, we thank God for what He *does;* we praise Him for who He *is.* Joined together, thanksgiving and praise give us direct access to God's presence.

This is depicted vividly in the imagery of Psalm 100:4:

> *Enter into His gates with thanksgiving,*
> *And into His courts with praise.*
> *Be thankful to Him,*
> *and bless His name.*

The psalmist pictures two stages in approaching God. First, we enter His *gates* with *thanksgiving;* then, we pass through His *courts* with *praise.* This brings us into the immediate presence of God. If we do not fulfil these requirements for access, we can still cry out to God – but only from a distance. In His mercy He will respond to our cry, but we have no direct access into His presence.

Thanksgiving and praise are the two most immediate ways in which our faith can respond to God. Whenever God gives us a promise of blessing or reveals a provision that He has made for us, we need to respond like Abraham and accept God's Word to us as true from the moment it is spoken. Logically, therefore, we begin to thank and praise Him immediately. We do not wait until we have actually experienced the fulfilment of the promise or the provision.

In 2 Chronicles 20, this principle is illustrated by an event in the reign of Jehoshaphat, king of Judah. Word had come to the king that a vast invading army was advancing against him from the south. Jehoshaphat knew that he did not have the military resources to oppose this army. Consequently, he summoned all his people together to seek God's help by united prayer and fasting.

God responded to their prayer by a prophetic utterance, given through a Levite, which directed Jehoshaphat to lead his people against the enemy by a certain route. It also contained words of assurance and encouragement: "Do not be afraid or dismayed because of this great multitude, for the battle is not yours, but God's . . . You will not need to fight in this battle. Position yourselves, stand still and see the salvation of the Lord, who is with you."

Nothing had changed at this point in the military situation, but Jehoshaphat received God's promise *by faith*, without demanding further evidence. The next day "he appointed those who should sing to the Lord, and who should praise the beauty of holiness, as they went out before the army and were saying,

> *'Praise the Lord,*
> *For His mercy endures forever.' "*

This was certainly not the conventional way for an army to go into battle – but it worked! As soon as the Lord heard the praises of His people, He intervened sovereignly and supernaturally by sending a spirit of division among the various national groups within the invading army. Suddenly, and for no apparent reason, they began to fight each other, until all were totally destroyed. The people of Judah did not need to fight, but only to gather the booty from their slain enemies! God intervened in this way because His people responded to His promise by faith, without waiting for further confirmation.

Two important principles are illustrated by this account. First, God expects us to praise Him for the promises He gives us, without waiting to see them fulfilled. Second, praise offered in faith releases the supernatural intervention of God on our behalf. Briefly stated: Faith begins to praise God *before* the promised victory, not merely after it.

In the New Testament, in Acts 16, the experience of Paul and Silas in Philippi dramatically illustrates the same principles. As a result of casting a demon out of a slave girl, they had been unjustly arrested, savagely abused and beaten, and then thrown into the maximum security section of the jail, with their feet in stocks. There was no ray of light in their darkness, no source of comfort or encouragement in their physical situation, no assurance as to what the future held.

Yet in their spirits they knew that nothing could change the eternal faithfulness of God, and nothing could rob them of the victory Christ had won for them. The logic of their faith triumphed over the logic of their circumstances. At midnight – the darkest hour – they were singing hymns of praise to God!

Their praises did the same for them as for Jehoshaphat's army: They released the supernatural intervention of God on their behalf. "Suddenly there was a great earthquake, so that the foundations of the prison were shaken; and immediately all the doors were opened and everyone's chains were loosed" (Acts 16:26).

The lesson of Jehoshaphat's army, and of Paul and Silas in the jail is summed up by the Lord Himself in Psalm 50:23:

"He who sacrifices thank offerings honours me,

and he prepares the way
so that I may show him the salvation of God."

NIV

God's salvation is already complete through the sacrifice of Jesus on the cross. Nothing we say or do can ever change that. But when we respond with sacrifices of thanksgiving and praise, we open the way for salvation's benefits to be manifested in our lives. Like Jehoshaphat, and like Paul and Silas, we must learn to offer these sacrifices in faith, before we have actually experienced the benefits.

In Psalm 20:5 David said, "In the name of our God we will set up our banners." Again, in Song of Solomon 6:10, the Bride of Christ is portrayed "awesome as an army with banners." Three of the most effective "banners" God has given us are *proclamation, thanksgiving* and *praise.*

First, we raise the banner of *proclamation.* We boldly speak out, in faith, the promise or the provision of God's Word that applies to our particular situation or meets our particular need. Then we go on to thank God — still in faith – for the truth we have proclaimed. Finally, we move from *thanksgiving* to jubilant *praise.* All this we do *in pure faith,* without waiting for any visible change in our situation.

In His own way and time, God responds to our faith, just as He did to that of Abraham. The truth, which we have proclaimed and for which we have thanked and praised Him, becomes a reality in our experience.

By raising these three banners of proclamation, thanksgiving and praise, we achieve two purposes at one and the same time. First, we secure for ourselves the promised blessings of God which we have proclaimed. Second, we shut out the satanic forces which would resist us and seek to withhold the blessings from us.

In this way, marching together into our inheritance, we fulfil Solomon's prophetic picture of "an army awesome with banners."

22
PROCLAMATIONS FOR CONTINUING VICTORY

The truths I have been sharing in this book are much more than the outcome of an intellectual pursuit of knowledge in the abstract. On the contrary, I have "mined" them out of intense, persistent prayer and spiritual conflict, in which Ruth and I have shared together for at least three years. Every main truth unfolded in this book has been subjected first to the test of our own experience. I have not felt free to pass on to others theories which have not worked for us.

In the previous chapter I explained how proclamation, thanksgiving and praise, working together, can release into our lives the promised blessings of God. In this chapter I am going to share briefly how Ruth and I have been learning to apply this principle in our own lives. The regular practice of proclaiming God's Word, and then thanking and praising Him for it, has become an integral part of our personal spiritual discipline. We regard this as one of

the most valuable truths that God has opened to us from the
Scriptures.

God has led us to establish a central "bank" of Scriptures,
which we have memorised and which we draw upon in our times
of prayer, or whenever we become involved in spiritual conflict.
Proclaiming these in faith invariably releases corresponding
expressions of thanksgiving and praise.

Normally, we speak these out loud, alone or together. We are
not talking to one another, however, nor to the walls or the ceiling
of our room. We are speaking to a vast, invisible world of spirit
beings: first of all, to God the Father, the Son and the Spirit; then
to all the heavenly beings who worship and serve God, and who
have been appointed "ministering spirits, sent out to render
service for the sake of those who will inherit salvation" (Hebrews
1:14, NASB). We are also conscious that we are surrounded by a
"great cloud of witnesses," made up of the saints of all ages who
have victoriously completed their earthly pilgrimage (Hebrews
12:1).

We believe that this is a legitimate application of Hebrews
12:22-24:

> But you have come to Mount Zion, to the heavenly
> Jerusalem, the city of the living God. You have come to
> thousands upon thousands of angels in joyful assembly,
> to the church of the firstborn, whose names are written
> in heaven. You have come to God, the judge of all men,
> to the spirits of righteous men made perfect, to Jesus the
> mediator of a new covenant, and to the sprinkled blood
> that speaks a better word than the blood of Abel.
>
> NIV

Also included in our audience, however, are Satan and all the evil angels and other demonic beings under his control. These operate in a way exactly opposite to God's ministering angels. Their purpose is to inflict every form of harm and evil on the entire human race, but first and foremost on those who are serving the true God.

In this context, our proclamation has two effects. On the one hand, it invokes on our behalf the help of God and His angels. On the other hand, it protects us from the schemes and assaults of Satan and his demonic forces.

This form of proclamation is continually building up our faith. According to Romans 10:17, "Faith comes by hearing . . . the word [the *rhema,* the spoken word] of God." Hearing others speak God's word is helpful, but hearing ourselves speak it is even more effective. As we both speak and hear, both edges of the sword of God's Word are at work in us simultaneously. (See Hebrews 4:12.)

Finally, when we make the same proclamation together, in harmony, supernatural power is released. Jesus says, "If two of you agree [harmonise] . . . concerning anything . . . it will be done for them by My Father in heaven" (Matthew 18:19). The power of one believer making a proclamation on his own is tremendous, but the power of two or more making the same proclamation together in harmony increases by geometric progression.

There are many times and situations, of course, when it would be out of place to make a proclamation out loud. The alternative is to make the same proclamation inaudibly in one's mind. Inaudible words can also make a powerful impact in the spiritual realm.

This is probably the most effective way to deal with lies and accusations with which the enemy bombards our minds. The mind is the main field of battle in all conflicts of this kind. When our minds are actively responding to the Word which we are proclaiming inwardly, no room is left for the enemy's negative thoughts and insinuations.

In all of this, however, we must be careful to recognise our continuing dependence on the Holy Spirit. Otherwise, the carnal mind can reduce these principles to a "system" in which God plays the role of a "heavenly vending machine." We simply insert the right proclamation, and out comes any brand of carnal gratification that we select! Obviously, this is a caricature of a believer's relationship with God.

There may be a wide gap between the way we view ourselves and the way the Holy Spirit views us. We may be conscious of what we *want,* whereas the Holy Spirit sees what we *need.* He alone can be trusted to direct each of us to the type of proclamation that applies to our individual situation and level of faith. In this way, God can accomplish His purpose in our lives.

With this caution, I feel it would be helpful for me to list below, simply as patterns, some of the proclamations which Ruth and I make regularly, together with the situations in which they would be appropriate. So far as possible, we "personalise" the Scriptures we quote. For instance, if a statement is addressed to believers and introduced with the pronoun "you," we normally change it to "I" or "we," and also make any other grammatical changes that are indicated.

My list opens with Scriptures that are directly connected with the theme of this book, but continues with others that have a more general application. Some comments and words of explanation are interspersed. In each case, the relevant Scripture reference is given.

1.   As a result of praying the prayer for release from curses (see chapter 18)

> *Through the sacrifice of Jesus on the cross, I have passed out from under the curse and entered into the blessing of Abraham, whom God blessed in all things.*
>
> See Galatians 3:13-14

Ruth has received release from many curses over her life, but she has had a continuing battle walking it out in experience. This proclamation has therefore become particularly significant for us. We often make it several times in a day. Over the past two or three years we have repeated these words many hundreds of times. Each time we do so, we move further away from effects of curses and into the blessing which is our inheritance.

2.   When becoming aware of negative forces directed against us, either from servants of Satan or from soulish utterances of Christians (see chapters 13, 14 and 15)

> *No weapon formed against me shall prosper, and every tongue which rises against me in judgement I do now condemn. This is my heritage [my inheritance right] as a servant of the Lord, and my righteousness is from You, O Lord.*
>
> See Isaiah 54:17

There are two important points to note in connection with this proclamation. First, we are not directed to ask God to condemn any tongue that speaks against us. God has given us the authority to do this for ourselves, and He expects us to exercise it.

Second, our right to exercise this authority depends on the fact that we are not acting out of our own righteousness, but because

God's righteousness is imputed to us on the basis of our faith. Clearly this proceeds out of the exchange by which Jesus, on the cross, was made sin with our sinfulness that we might become righteous with His righteousness. The various benefits of that exchange are all interrelated, and should not be separated from each other.

But God requires more of us than just turning back the evil words spoken against us. After that, He instructs us to forgive those who seek to harm us. Finally, He expects us to move from the negative to the positive: to respond to a curse with a blessing[17].

Blessing those who curse us, just like forgiving those who harm us, does not depend on our emotions. It proceeds from a firm decision of our will, made in obedience to God's Word. Here is a suitable form of words that covers both forgiving and blessing:

> Lord, I forgive all who have spoken evil against me,
> and having forgiven them, I bless them in Your name.

Altogether, we need to follow three successive steps in responding to those who curse us. First, we condemn the tongue that has uttered the curse. Second, we forgive the person from whom the curse proceeded. Third, we ask God to bless the person. By carrying out these three steps, we can dissipate any spiritual darkness or heaviness that a curse has brought on us.

3.   *When pressures of sin or guilt or unworthiness pursue us from our past*

> *I am in Christ, and therefore I am a new creation. All those old things have passed away. Everything in my*

---

17.   This is dealt with more fully in chapter 24.

life has become new, and everything is from God.
                                    See 2 Corinthians 5:17-18

God accepts total responsibility for the new creation. It is all His doing. Nothing is carried over from the old creation which has been marred and corrupted by sin.

When the past reasserts its claims over us, we need to meditate on the picture John gives us in Revelation 21:5:

> *Then He who sat on the throne said, "Behold, I make all things new." And He said to me, "Write, for these words are true and faithful."*

These words come from the One who sits on the throne, the One who has under His control the entire universe and everything in it. That includes every detail of our lives. He reaffirms that He makes *everything* new.

It seems that John might have wondered inwardly whether this was too stupendous a claim, even for God. But the Lord assures him: "Write, for these words are true and faithful." It is as if He says: "Yes, John, you really can assure My people: I do exactly what I say."

4.   *When oppressed by hopelessness and gloomy forebodings of death*

> *I will not die but live, and will proclaim what the Lord has done.*
>
> See Psalm 118:17, NIV

Of course, this does not mean "I will never die" – but only "I will not die before God's appointed time – I will not allow myself

to be murdered by Satan." Proclaimed with faith and understanding, this verse can deliver and protect those who are assailed
by the spirit of death. It can be used to revoke the negative utterances by which people expose themselves to that spirit. (For
examples, see chapter 12.)

For some people it may be necessary to repeat this proclamation many times over, until it becomes more real than all their
previous negative thought patterns. Remember that Jesus required
Peter to reaffirm his love for Him just as many times as he had
previously denied Him.

5. *When assailed by physical sickness or infirmity*

> *Jesus Himself bore my sins in His own body on the
> tree, that I, having died to sins, might live for right-
> eousness – by whose wounds I was healed.*
>
> See 1 Peter 2:24

I have also prepared the following special proclamation, which
combines truths from many different Scriptures and which has
helped Christians in many areas of the world:

> *My body is a temple for the Holy Spirit, redeemed,
> cleansed and sanctified by the blood of Jesus. My
> members – the parts of my body – are instruments of
> righteousness, presented to God for His service and for
> His glory. The devil has no place in me, no power over
> me, no unsettled claims against me. All has been settled
> by the blood of Jesus.*
>
> *I overcome Satan by the blood of the Lamb and by
> the word of my testimony, and I do not love my life to
> the death. My body is for the Lord, and the Lord is for*

my body.

Based on: 1 Corinthians 6:19; Ephesians 1:7;
1 John 1:7; Hebrews 13:12; Romans 6:13; 8:33-34;
Revelation 12:11; 1 Corinthians 6:13

Someone might ask: Is it honest for me to make proclamations such as these, when I see in my body the physical evidences of sickness, or when I feel in my soul the oppositions of sin? The answer depends on your point of view. If you are looking at yourself in your own natural condition, then it is not honest. But if you are looking at yourself as God sees you in Christ, then you have the right to make such a proclamation.

Once we have repented of our sins and committed ourselves to Christ, God no longer looks at us as we are in our natural state. Instead, He looks at us from the perspective of the exchange that took place on the cross. Spiritually, He sees us as made righteous; physically, He sees us as made whole.

It is significant that, in the Scriptures, the healing provided through the sacrifice of Jesus is never spoken of in the future tense. In Isaiah 53:5, written more than seven hundred years before the death of Jesus, healing is already presented as an accomplished fact: "By his wounds *we are healed*" (NIV). In the New Testament, in 1 Peter 2:24 (quoted above), the apostle refers to Isaiah 53:5, but uses the past tense: "By whose stripes *you were healed.*"

When the words we speak about ourselves agree with what God says about us in Christ, then we open the way for Him to make us in actual experience all that He says we are. But if we fail to make the appropriate confession – or proclamation – about ourselves, we are confined to the prison of our own natural state. We have shut ourselves off from the supernatural, transforming grace of God, which works only through faith.

Again, someone might ask: What about someone who says and does all the right things, and yet the promised results do not follow? An answer is to be found in the words of Moses in Deuteronomy 29:29: "The secret things belong to the Lord our God, but those things which are revealed belong to us and to our children forever, that we may do all the words of this law."

The reason some people do not receive some part of the promised blessings often belongs in the category of "secret things." It is vain for us to seek to pry God's secrets from Him. It is also irreverent. If God withholds an answer, it is more important to trust than to understand.

On the other hand, the words of Moses remind us of our responsibility, as God's people, to believe, to proclaim and to act upon those things He has clearly revealed in His Word. Central to these is the provision God has made for us through the sacrifice of Jesus on the cross. We must not let our concern about the secret things keep us from believing and obeying the things which are revealed.

6.   When Satan attacks an area for which God holds us responsible – our home, our family, our business, our ministry, etc.

> *The bolts of our gates will be iron and bronze, and our strength will equal our days.*
>
> *There is no one like the God of Jeshurun, who rides on the heavens to help us and on the clouds in his majesty.*
>
> *The eternal God is our refuge, and underneath are the everlasting arms. He will drive out our enemy before us, saying "Destroy him!"*
>
> See Deuteronomy 33:25-27, NIV

By this proclamation we are enabled to move from defence to attack. First of all, "our gates" represent our defence system. God promises that this will be strong enough to keep out our enemy's attack. Then there is a wonderful picture of God intervening supernaturally on our behalf: "He rides on the heavens to help us." Our proclamation is one way that we invoke His intervention.

Finally, there is assurance of our enemy's defeat: "He [God] will drive out our enemy before us." God requires us to play our part in this final stage; therefore, He says, "Destroy him!" He has equipped us with the spiritual weapons we need to do this.

7. *When we awaken to the realisation that the mind is a battlefield in which the lies of Satan are at war with the truths of God's Word*

> *The weapons of my warfare are mighty in God. With them I pull down the strongholds which Satan has built in my mind. I bring all my thoughts into obedience to Christ. Three of my mightiest weapons are proclamation, thanksgiving and praise.*
>
> See 2 Corinthians 10:3-5

It is important to remember, however, that our "enemies" in the Christian life are not our fellow human beings. Our enemies are the evil spiritual forces directed against us from the kingdom of Satan. Paul makes this clear in Ephesians 6:12: "For we are not fighting against people made of flesh and blood, but against persons without bodies – the evil rulers of the unseen world . . . and against huge numbers of wicked spirits in the spirit world" (TLB).

In this strange kind of warfare to which God has called us, the standards of measurement are different from those we use in the world of the senses. Measured by the spiritual scale, *forgiving* is stronger than *resenting; blessing* is stronger than *cursing; giving thanks* is stronger than *complaining; praise* is stronger than *accusation;* and *loving* is stronger than *hating.*

Based on this paradox, here are two proclamations that unlock God's strength and God's enabling when our own resources fail.

8.   When confronted by a task too big for me

I can do all things through the One who empowers me within.

See Philippians 4:13

9.   When my own strength fails or is insufficient

God's strength is made perfect in my weakness, and so when I am weak, then I am strong.

See 2 Corinthians 12:9-10

Finally, here are two proclamations that cover needs that arise at some time or other in the lives of almost all of us.

10.   When exercising faith for financial needs

God is able to make all grace abound toward us, that we, always having all sufficiency in all things, may have an abundance for every good work.

See 2 Corinthians 9:8

The level of God's provision for His people is revealed as abundance, not mere sufficiency. Ruth and I make this proclamation regularly, as the financial base for Derek Prince Ministries.

11. *When assailed by fear*

> *God has not given me a spirit of fear, but of power and of love and of a sound mind.*
>
> See 2 Timothy 1:7

> *In the name of Jesus I submit to God and I resist the spirit of fear. Therefore it has to flee from me.*
>
> See James 4:7

The above Scriptures are only a few examples. There is no limit to the number of scriptural proclamations we can make. Each of us must rely on the Holy Spirit to guide us to those that suit our particular situations.

Choosing and making appropriate proclamations based on Scripture has one very important result. We receive and apply God's Word in the *active,* not the passive mode. We no longer just read a Scripture and then pass on. Instead, we go through three successive stages. First, we ask the Holy Spirit to direct us to Scriptures that are especially appropriate for us. Second, we fix them firmly in our minds. Third, by proclaiming them, we release their power into the areas of our lives where we need them.

Perhaps you are one of the many Christians today who feel the need to "take the sword of the Spirit" – referred to in chapter 19 – but do not know of a simple and practical way to do this. If so, Ruth and I would like to recommend to you this method of selective proclamation of Scriptures. We have practised it in our own lives, and we can say, *It works!*

But let me add one final word of warning! Do not put your faith in your proclamation, or in any other method or procedure. *Our faith must be in God alone* – not in anyone or anything else. Our proclamation is merely an effective way to express the faith we have in God.

So now, as you set your face toward the land of God's blessings, receive the admonition given three times to Joshua:

"Be strong and of good courage!"

IMPORTANT AFTERWORDS

INTRODUCTION

The theme of *blessings* and *curses* is central to the whole of God's dealings with the human race. It can be compared to the trunk of a tree whose branches reach out in many different directions. A systematic study raises important, practical questions about various other main areas of biblical truth.

This section deals with two of these questions:

1. Is it possible at this present time, through faith, to experience release from all the curses that sin has brought upon the human race? If not, when – and how – will this finally be accomplished?

2. The Old Testament contains many examples of God's servants who pronounced curses on His enemies. What should the Christian response be when we are opposed and mistreated?

23
CURSES NOT YET REVOKED

On the cross Jesus took upon Himself all the evil consequences that disobedience to God had brought upon the human race. These fall into two main categories: those brought upon man by his original disobedience in the Garden; and those pronounced later in connection with the Law given through Moses.

In Galatians 3:13 Paul refers to this latter category. He states specifically that "Christ has redeemed us from *the curse of the law.*" He relates this to the fact that the Law had declared that anyone executed by hanging on a tree had – by that very fact – become a curse. The same Law that pronounced the curse thus opened the way for deliverance from the curse through the substitutionary sacrifice of Christ.

In chapter 4 we summarised "the curse of the Law" as follows: humiliation; barrenness, unfruitfulness; mental and physical sickness; family breakdown; poverty; defeat; oppression; failure; God's disfavour.

According to the clear statement of Paul in Galatians 3:13, the death of Christ on the cross offers deliverance from all these consequences of the broken Law. Paul does not here include, however, the various forms of the original curse that God pronounced upon Adam and Eve after their disobedience in the Garden. This curse – recorded in Genesis 3:16-19 – falls into two main sections, the first spoken to Eve, and the second spoken to Adam.

The curse spoken to Eve relates to her unique function as a woman and it again falls into two sections:

1. Childbearing would be arduous and painful.
2. She would be subject to her husband's authority and dependent upon him for the fulfilment of her basic feminine desire for children.

The curse spoken to Adam relates primarily to the original task assigned to him by God in Genesis 2:15 to "tend and keep the garden" – that is, to cultivate the soil. This curse can be divided into three main sections:

1. The nature of the soil would undergo a change. Henceforth, it would yield its produce only by hard, sweat-producing labour.
2. The evidence of the change in the soil would be seen in a change in the vegetation it would produce – specifically in the growth of two unproductive forms of vegetation: thorns and thistles.
3. Man himself would be subject to decay and death, doomed ultimately to return to the dust from which he

was taken. Though directed to Adam, this third section actually affected Eve as well, together with their descendants.

It is clear that the curses pronounced at this time also affected the earth itself. This followed from the close connection between Adam and his environment, which is indicated by the Hebrew word for earth: *adamah*. Adam himself was made from the earth. He was also held responsible by God for the care of the earth.

In addition, a special curse was placed upon the serpent, which thereafter distinguished it from all other members of the animal kingdom.

In Ecclesiastes 1:2 and in Romans 8:20, the condition of the earth and its inhabitants produced by these curses is described by two words that have the same meaning: *vanity* and *futility*.

The redemption from "the curse of the law," to which Paul refers in Galatians 3:13, does not include the curses described above. These resulted from the original disobedience of Adam and Eve in the Garden. At this time there was no God-given system of law, and consequently no curse pronounced for breaking it.

In Romans 5:13-14 Paul says: "For until the law sin was in the world, but sin is not imputed when there is no law. Nevertheless death reigned from Adam to Moses, even over those who had not sinned according to the likeness of the transgression of Adam."

During this period "from Adam to Moses" humanity was without any God-given system of law. All men suffered, however, from the effects of the curse pronounced originally upon Adam and Eve, and each person paid the penalty for his own individual sin, which was death.

The beginning of the period of the Law is indicated in John 1:17: "The law was given through Moses." In connection with the giving of the Law, a long series of curses was pronounced on those who came under the Law, but then failed to keep it. These are the curses that are listed primarily in Deuteronomy 28:15-68. Collectively, they are called "the curse of the law." When Paul says in Galatians 3:13 that "Christ has redeemed us from the curse of the law," it is to these curses that he refers.

What about the curses pronounced originally on Adam and Eve? Has God provided redemption also from these? And if so, upon what basis?

To answer these questions, we need to recognise two different ways in which Jesus, when He came to earth, was identified with those whom He came to redeem. The New Testament depicts two different aspects of His identification with humanity, which are indicated by the two different genealogies given for Him.

In Matthew His genealogy is traced back to Abraham. As the promised "seed of Abraham," He identified with Abraham's descendants, the nation of Israel, who were under the Law. In Galatians 4:4-5 Paul says that Jesus was "born under the law, to redeem those who were under the law."

In Luke, however, the genealogy of Jesus is traced back to Adam, and He is thus identified with the whole race descended from Adam. During His earthly life the title which He applied to Himself more than any other was "Son of man." In Hebrew the name *Adam* is also the word for *man*. Thus, "Son of man" is also "Son of Adam." By using this title, therefore, Jesus continually emphasised His identification with all of Adam's descendants – the whole human race.

Because of this identification, the substitutionary sacrifice of Jesus on the cross did not merely provide redemption from the curse of the broken Law. It also provided deliverance from all the evil consequences that the original sin of Adam had brought upon all his descendants – whether under the Law or not.

This is brought out by two different titles that Paul gives to Jesus in 1 Corinthians 15. In verse 45 he calls Him "the last Adam," and in verse 47 "the second Man." These two titles refer respectively to the death and the resurrection of Jesus.

On the cross Jesus died as "the last Adam." He took upon Himself all the evil consequences that Adam's disobedience had brought upon the entire human race. When He died, they were terminated. When He was buried, they were forever put away.

Then on the third day Jesus rose again from the dead as "the second Man." He thus became the Head of an entirely new race – the Immanuel race – the God-man race – a race in which the nature of God and man are blended together in a new creation.

All those who by faith and commitment are identified with Jesus in His death, His burial and His resurrection become members of this new race. In 1 Peter 1:3-4 the apostle says of these: "God . . . has begotten us again to a living hope through the resurrection of Jesus Christ from the dead, to an inheritance incorruptible and undefiled and that does not fade away.

There were, therefore, two complementary aspects to the redemption from the curse provided through the death of Jesus. As "the seed of Abraham," born under the Law, He took upon Himself all the curses of the broken Law summed up in Deuteronomy 28:15-68. As "the last Adam," He also took upon Himself the curses pronounced upon Adam and Eve for their original act of disobedience. As we have seen, these extended also to earth's soil and its vegetation, being specifically manifested in two unproductive forms of vegetation: thorns and thistles.

The New Testament uses very beautiful imagery to reveal how Jesus took upon Himself not merely the curses upon Adam and Eve, but also the curse upon the earth. In John 19:5 the apostle records the scene when Pilate brought Jesus out before His accusers:

*Then Jesus came out, wearing the crown of thorns
and the purple robe. And Pilate said to them, "Behold
the Man!"*

The phrase *the Man* pointed out Jesus as a descendant of Adam
– unique in His perfection, yet representative of the whole race.
At the same time, Jesus' attire represented the double curse that
Adam had brought upon the earth. The crown on His head represented the curse of *thorns;* the purple colour of His robe
represented the curse of *thistles.*

This brief but vivid scene revealed Jesus as "the last Adam," who
took upon Himself both the curse that had come upon Adam and
Eve, and also the curse that their sin had brought upon the earth.

From every point of view, therefore, the redemption from the
curse provided by the death of Jesus was complete. It covered
every curse that had ever come upon humanity. It covered the
curse pronounced upon Adam and Eve for their disobedience; it
covered the curse their disobedience had brought upon the earth;
and it covered all the curses subsequently pronounced in
connection with the Law of Moses.

Further study of Scripture indicates, however, that full
redemption from the curse will be worked out in successive
phases. Redemption from "the curse of the law" is already offered
in this present age to those who can appropriate it by faith. It will
be manifested in its completeness only upon the return of Christ.
At that time, too, those who are caught up to meet Him will finally
and forever be released from the Adamic curse.

In Philippians 3:20-21 Paul describes the change that will take
place at this time in the body of each redeemed believer:

*For our citizenship is in heaven, from which we also
eagerly wait for the Saviour, the Lord Jesus Christ,*

*who will transform our lowly body that it may be
conformed to His glorious body, according to the
working by which He is able even to subdue all things
to Himself.*

Paul here contrasts two kinds of bodies: "our lowly body" and
"His [Christ's] glorious body." More literally, these phrases could
be rendered "the body of our humiliation" and "the body of His
glory." The curse pronounced upon Adam confined him – and his
descendants – in "a body of humiliation." As such, it reminds each
of us continually of our fallen condition.

From the moment of birth, this body is continually subject to
decay, depending on many external factors for life and well-
being. By luxury and self-indulgence we may briefly seek to
forget our inherent weaknesses, yet within a matter of moments
we are inevitably confronted once more with our body's humiliating limitations.

We may put on the most elegant and expensive clothes, but as
soon as we became physically active, the smell of our sweat
reminds us that we are confined in "a body of humiliation." Or we
may fill our stomachs with the finest of food and drink. Within a
few hours, however, we will be compelled to empty our bladders
and our bowels – actions that leave no room for pomp or
arrogance.

For those who have accepted the redemption provided by
Christ, all these humiliating features of our present body will be
changed not gradually or progressively, but in one single, glorious
moment. In 1 Corinthians 15:51-53 Paul describes this supernatural transformation:

*We shall not all sleep [in death], but we shall all be
changed –*

> *in a moment, in the twinkling of an eye, at the last*
> *trumpet. For the trumpet will sound, and the dead will*
> *be raised incorruptible, and we shall be changed.*
> *For this corruptible must put on incorruption, and*
> *this mortal must put on immortality.*

Altogether, in 1 Corinthians 15, Paul sums up the following five changes that will take place in the body of each believer at the return of Christ:

1. From corruptible to incorruptible
2. From mortal to immortal
3. From dishonour to glory
4. From weakness to power
5. From natural – literally, "soulish" – to spiritual.

All the five negative features in the above list are the effects of the original curse on Adam. Full deliverance from all of them will come first to the believers who are caught up to meet Christ at His return. In James 1:18 these are described as "a kind of firstfruits of [God's] creatures." The transformation they undergo will serve as a guarantee of the redemption that will ultimately come to the whole creation.

In the period that will follow for earth's remaining inhabitants, the righteousness and justice of Christ's Millennial reign will minimise, but not abolish, the curse of the Law. Human life will be greatly extended, but the Adamic curse also will still prevail. Earth, too, as well as the animal creation will experience a period of fruitfulness and abundance without parallel since the Fall – but "futility" will not yet be done away with. The full and final abolition of every curse must wait until the period of "a new heavens and a new earth" (2 Peter 3:13).

All this will be the outworking of the exchange by which Jesus on the cross was made a curse in order to cancel every curse that man's disobedience had brought on himself and on creation. In Revelation 22:3 its consummation is summed up in one brief, but comprehensive, statement: "And there shall be no more curse."

24
TO BLESS OR TO CURSE?

Suppose that people revile us, curse us, oppose us and persecute us for our faith in Christ. Suppose that they spread malicious lies about us and use all sorts of dishonest and illegal means to do us harm. Are we free to retaliate by pronouncing some kind of curse against them? To this the answer of the New Testament is a clear, emphatic NO!

In Romans 12:9-21 Paul lists various principles that should govern Christian behaviour. In verse 9 he begins with the one supremely important motivation: "Let *love* be without hypocrisy." All the other directions that follow are simply different ways in which Christian love expresses itself.

In verse 14 he instructs Christians how to respond to those who seek to do them harm: "Bless those who persecute you; bless and do not curse."

In verse 21 he closes with a more general application of the same principle: "Do not be overcome by evil, but overcome evil with good." There is only one power strong enough to overcome evil, and that is *good*. Whatever form of evil confronts us, we must always respond with the corresponding form of good. Otherwise we shall find evil too strong for us.

In 1 Peter 3:8-9, Peter gives a similar warning against the wrong kind of reaction to evil:

> *Finally, all of you be of one mind, having compassion for one another; love as brothers, be tender-hearted, be courteous;*
> *not returning evil for evil or reviling for reviling, but on the contrary blessing, knowing that you were called to this, that you may inherit a blessing.*

By thus overcoming evil with good, we share in Christ's own triumph over evil, as depicted in 2 Corinthians 2:14-15:

> *Now thanks be to God who always leads us in triumph in Christ, and through us diffuses the fragrance of His knowledge in every place.*
> *For we are to God the fragrance of Christ among those who are being saved and among those who are perishing.*

Like Mary of Bethany, who poured costly ointment on the head of Jesus, we fill the whole area around us with a sweet fragrance. Even those who oppose us and criticise us are nevertheless blessed by the fragrance. (See Mark 14:3-9.)

This brings out a basic difference between the Old and the New Covenants. In the Old Testament God frequently used His people as instruments of judgement against other people. In bringing

Israel into the land of Canaan, for instance, God used Joshua and his army as the instruments of His judgement on the Canaanites who had previously occupied the land. There are also many other instances in the Old Testament in which God's servants pronounced curses on people who opposed or disobeyed Him, and the effect was the same as if God Himself had uttered them.

In Joshua 6:26, for instance, after the Israelites had captured and destroyed Jericho, Joshua pronounced the following curse on anyone who would ever afterward rebuild a city on the same site:

> *"Cursed be the man before the Lord who rises up and builds this city Jericho; he shall lay its foundation with his firstborn, and with his youngest he shall set up its gates."*

About five hundred years later, during the reign of Ahab king of Israel, this curse was fulfilled, as recorded in 1 Kings 16:34:

> *In his [Ahab's] days Hiel of Bethel built Jericho. He laid its foundation with Abiram his firstborn, and with his youngest son Segub he set up its gates, according to the word of the Lord, which He had spoken through Joshua the son of Nun.*

In the margin of the New King James the phrase "with his son" is rendered "at the cost of the life of . . ." The NASB renders it "with the loss of . . ." The NIV renders it "at the cost of . . ."

This is a vivid example of the invisible forces that are continually at work in human history, and yet are so often ignored. How many secular historians today, when describing this incident, would trace the death of these two young men to words spoken by a servant of God five hundred years earlier?

It is important to notice, in 1 Kings 16:34, that the writer emphasises that the curse was fulfilled *"according to the word of the Lord,* which He had spoken through Joshua the son of Nun." Joshua was the channel through which the curse came, but the Lord was its source. This – and this alone – accounts for its effect.

David was another servant of God who pronounced curses that took effect many generations later. In Psalm 69:22-25, and again in Psalm 109:6-13, he pronounced a lengthy series of curses on some unnamed person, or persons, on account of treachery and disloyalty to a righteous man who had been unjustly accused and condemned. About one thousand years later, after the death and resurrection of Jesus, the apostles recognised that these curses of David had found their fulfilment in Judas Iscariot, who had been the betrayer of Jesus. (See Acts 1:15-20.)

Some of the prophets who followed David also pronounced curses that released God's judgements in various ways. In 2 Kings 1:9-12, for instance, Elijah called down fire from heaven that destroyed two successive bands of soldiers sent to arrest him. In 2 Kings 2:23-24, his successor, Elisha, cursed a group of youths who had mocked him, with the result that 42 of them were mauled by bears.

Subsequently, God used Elisha to bring miraculous healing of leprosy to the Syrian general, Naaman, who in turn offered Elisha a variety of lavish presents. Elisha, however, refused to accept any of them, thus showing Naaman that there was no way he could "pay" for his healing from God. Later, Elisha's servant, Gehazi, motivated by covetousness, ran after Naaman and, on false pretences, persuaded Naaman to give him a substantial gift of silver and clothing (2 Kings 5:1-27).

When Gehazi returned, Elisha – by supernatural revelation – confronted him with his covetousness and dishonesty. Then he pronounced God's judgement on him:

"Therefore the leprosy of Naaman shall cling to you and your descendants forever." And he went out from his presence leprous, as white as snow.

The effect of Elisha's curse was visible and instantaneous. Gehazi found himself afflicted by leprosy in the same advanced stage from which Naaman had just been healed. Furthermore, the same disease would continue to afflict Gehazi's descendants, so long as there was one of them remaining on earth.

There is one important feature common to all the curses referred to above – whether uttered by Joshua, David, Elijah or Elisha. Each of them expressed a sovereign judgement of Almighty God. *They did not proceed from the mind or will of the men who uttered them.* They were not the expression of mere human anger or vindictiveness. God sovereignly chose human channels through whom to administer His justice. There is no suggestion in Scripture that God has ever renounced His right to do this.

In the New Testament, however, God has chosen to use His servants primarily as instruments of mercy and not of judgement. The contrast between the two covenants is brought out in an incident in Luke 9:51-56. Jesus had sent messengers ahead of Him to prepare for His reception in a Samaritan village through which He intended to pass, but the Samaritans refused to receive Him. In response, James and John had asked, "Lord, do You want us to command fire to come down from heaven and consume them, just as Elijah did?"

In reply, Jesus rebuked them for their attitude, saying: "You do not know what manner of spirit you are of. For the Son of Man did not come to destroy men's lives but to save them."

Jesus did not deny that Elijah had called down fire to destroy his enemies. Nor did He question that James and John might have been able to do the same. Instead, He reminded them that they were in a period when God was using His servants in a different way. They were called to be instruments of God's mercy, rather than His judgement.

Nevertheless, there are a few instances in the New Testament of curses pronounced by God's servants. Jesus Himself provided one of the most dramatic examples. On His way into Jerusalem, becoming hungry, He went up to a fig tree to get some of the early fruit which would have been appropriate at that season. Discovering that the tree was full of leaves, but had produced no fruit, He said to it, "Let no fruit grow on you ever again" (Matthew 21:19).

Next day, when He and His disciples passed by, the fig tree had withered from the roots. Peter commented: "Rabbi, look! The fig tree which You cursed has withered away" (Mark 11:21). In reply, Jesus delegated to His disciples the same authority that He Himself had demonstrated in cursing the fig tree: "Assuredly, I say to you, if you have faith and do not doubt, you will not only do what was done to the fig tree . . ." (Matthew 21:21). In other words, He gave them authority to pronounce curses similar to that which He had pronounced on the fig tree.

Many commentators see in this fig tree a type of the form of religion into which the practice of the Law of Moses had degenerated. It was full of "leaves" – that is, the outward forms of religion – but it did not yield the true fruit of the Law, which Jesus summed up as "justice and mercy and faith" (Matthew 23:23). As a result, sincere seekers who looked to that form of religion to satisfy their spiritual hunger were turned away, empty and disappointed. Within a generation, under the judgement of God, the whole system was destined to "wither from the roots."

The disciples apparently saw no significance in the fruitless fig tree, and would have passed it by. It was Jesus who took action against it, and then commissioned His disciples to take similar action. In succeeding generations, this lesson seems to have been lost on most Christians. Certainly there are times when we encounter such "fruitless fig trees" – that is, deceptive religious systems that disappoint hungry seekers after the reality of the Gospel. Do we merely pass "fig trees" by, unconcerned? Or do we take the same kind of aggressive action that Jesus demonstrated?

In Matthew 10:14-15, when Jesus sent out the first apostles to preach the Gospel, He gave them authority of a similar kind to deal with those who rejected them and their message:

> *"And whoever will not receive you nor hear your words, when you depart from that house or city, shake off the dust from your feet.*
> *"Assuredly, I say to you, it will be more tolerable for the land of Sodom and Gomorrah in the day of judgement than for that city!"*

By this act of shaking off the dust from their feet, the apostles would, in effect, hand over those who rejected them to the judgement of God, which would ultimately be more severe than that on the inhabitants of Sodom and Gomorrah.

The apostles of the New Testament took this command of Jesus literally. In Pisidian Antioch, after Paul and Barnabas had ministered for some time with great effect, their adversaries finally drove them out of the city. Acts 13:51 records the apostles' response:

> *But they shook off the dust from their feet against them, and came to Iconium.*

Incidents such as these confirm a principle already established in the Old Testament: Blessings and curses are never far separated from one another. When blessings are offered, but rejected, curses almost inevitably follow in their place. When Israel entered Canaan under the law of Moses, God required them to invoke upon themselves either the blessings promised for obedience, or the curses that followed disobedience. There was no third option. The same applies to those who have the Gospel with its blessings proclaimed to them, but deliberately and consciously reject it. Almost inevitably they expose themselves to corresponding curses.

Earlier, on the island of Cyprus, God had opened the way for Paul and Barnabas to bring the Gospel to the Roman proconsul[18], Sergius Paulus. However, a sorcerer – that is, a practitioner of the occult – named Elymas sought to keep them from speaking to the proconsul. Paul's response to this challenge from Satan is described in Acts 13:9-12:

> *Then Saul, who also is called Paul, filled with the Holy Spirit, looked intently at him*
> *and said, "O full of all deceit and all fraud, you son of the devil, you enemy of all righteousness, will you not cease perverting the straight ways of the Lord?*
> *"And now, indeed, the hand of the Lord is upon you, and you shall be blind, not seeing the sun for a time."*
> *And immediately a dark mist fell on him, and he went around seeking someone to lead him by the hand.*
> *Then the proconsul believed, when he saw what had been done, being astonished at the teaching of the Lord.*

The effect of Paul's words on Elymas was as immediate and dramatic as the curse of leprosy which Elisha had pronounced

18. A senior Roman official.

upon Gehazi. The writer of Acts emphasises that at this moment Paul was "filled with the Holy Spirit." Therefore, his words were not the product of his own fleshly reaction to opposition, but represented God's sovereign judgement on the sorcerer, uttered by the Holy Spirit. The proconsul was so impressed by this demonstration of the supremacy of Jesus over Satan that he became a believer.

This incident brings out the decisive issue in determining whether or not there are situations in which it is right for Christians to pronounce a curse. If the motive is some reaction of our fleshly nature, such as resentment or anger, or the desire for revenge or self-justification or self-glorification, then to utter a curse in such a situation would be a sin. Furthermore, it would do much greater harm to the one who utters the curse than to the one who is cursed.

In Romans 6:16 Paul emphasises the danger of yielding to this kind of satanic motivation:

> *Don't you know that when you offer yourselves to someone to obey him as slaves, you are slaves to the one whom you obey – whether you are slaves to sin, which leads to death, or to obedience, which leads to right-eousness?*

NIV

It can be tempting to seek momentary gratification of some evil impulse by allowing a curse to pass through our lips, but in so doing we offer ourselves as slaves to the author of the temptation: Satan. He is not content with merely temporary influence over us. He uses the temptation as an opening through which he can move in and take permanent control of our lives. Our temporary yielding to him thus becomes permanent enslavement. In this way, *the one who uses a curse to bring evil upon others brings a far greater and more enduring evil upon himself.*

On the other hand, the New Testament gives clear examples of situations in which the Holy Spirit sovereignly chose to pronounce a curse through a servant of God. If we refuse to acknowledge this possibility, we shut ourselves off from one of the ways in which God might wish to use us. Our only safeguard is to cultivate a relationship with the Holy Spirit in which we are sensitive both to His prompting and to His restraining. If we have any doubts as to the purity of our motives or the leading of the Holy Spirit, we should most certainly keep silent.

The possibility that the Holy Spirit may in certain circumstances prompt us to utter a curse was made very real to me by an incident that occurred in my ministry in the mid-1960s. At that time I was part of the ministerial staff of a church located in the inner city of Chicago. The building immediately adjoining the church was a pub. This had become a centre for various forms of vice, which included drug-peddling, knife fights and prostitution – both male and female.

One evening I was on the platform of the church, leading a meeting of people gathered to pray for the city of Chicago. In the midst of the prayer, without any premeditation on my part, I heard myself make a loud declaration: "I put the curse of the Lord on that pub!" After that, the meeting continued along its normal course. Personally, I gave little further thought to what I had said.

About two months later, I was awakened at 3 A.M. by an urgent phone call to say that the church was on fire. I dressed and hurried to the scene, to discover that it was not the church, but the pub next door, that was on fire. The wind off Lake Michigan, however, was blowing the flames onto the church. Just when it seemed inevitable that the church would be destroyed along with the pub, the direction of the wind suddenly changed 180 degrees and blew the flames away from the church.

In the end, the pub was completely destroyed and the church suffered only smoke damage, which was fully covered by insurance. No lives were lost, and no one was injured. After surveying the scene and what had taken place, the fire chief commented to the senior elder of the church: "You people must have a special relationship with the Man upstairs!"

My personal reaction was one of awe, mingled with fear. I had no doubt that what I had witnessed was the outworking of the curse on the pub that I had pronounced two months earlier. I did not regret what I had done. I felt that God had intervened in righteous judgement, tempered with mercy. At the same time, I realised in a new way the awesome power that could be released through words spoken by a servant of God. I resolved that, for my part, I would seek God for His grace never to misuse that power.

On a small scale, the destruction of that pub by fire reinforces a truth of Scripture that is central to this whole theme of blessings and curses: *the power of the tongue is measureless – whether for good or for evil.* With our tongue we can bless and we can curse; we can build up and we can break down; we can wound and we can heal; we can do great good, and just as great harm.

The power of the tongue is also frightening, because we ourselves cannot control it. Again and again, our experience compels us to acknowledge the truth of James 3:8: "But no man can tame the tongue." There is therefore only one safe course: to yield the tongue to God through the Holy Spirit and ask Him to control it for us. To help us do this, here are two prayers of David that are patterns for us to follow:

> *Set a guard, O Lord, over my mouth;*
> *Keep watch over the door of my lips.*
>
> Psalm 141:3

Let the words of my mouth
    and the meditation of my heart
Be acceptable in Your sight,
O Lord, my strength and my redeemer.

Psalm 19:14

FOR FURTHER STUDY

Curses: Cause and Cure

Many people experience continual frustration in areas such as marriage, health or finance, yet never discern the underlying cause: a curse. This series reveals both cause and cure.

To order further materials by Derek Prince, contact your local bookshop or write to the address below for a Resource Guide.

Derek Prince Ministries – UK
PO Box 77
Harpenden
Herts AL5 1PJ
United Kingdom

FREE!

Teaching cassette by Derek Prince

Release From The Curse – Part 1

4285

Are you frustrated? Bewildered? Defeated? Never fully satisfied? You can pass from the dark shadow of a curse into the sunlight of God's blessing!

❏ I would like to join the Derek Prince Ministries–UK mailing list and receive a copy of the audio cassette *Release From The Curse – Part 1*.

Name _____

Address _____

_____

_____

Postcode _____ Tel No _____

Please complete your details above and return this postcard to the address overleaf.

B56RC

affix
stamp
here

DPM–UK
PO Box 77
Harpenden
Herts
AL5 1PJ
United Kingdom

KU-443-652

THE WORLD'S CLASS

CASTLE RACKRENT

MARIA EDGEWORTH was born in Oxfordshire in 1767 or 1768. On her father's second marriage in 1773, she went with him to Ireland. Her father employed her in keeping accounts and in dealing with his tenants. She also acquired a familiarity with fashionable people, and with Irish peasantry, all of which was to be of use in her novels. Her father made her a confidential friend, and he also became her literary advisor. Much of her early writing was for children, and it was not until 1800 that she appeared as a novelist for adult readers with the publication of *Castle Rackrent*. Its vigorous descriptions of Irish characters made the book an instant success. In 1798 the marriage of her father to his fourth wife brought her an intimate friend for fifty-one years in her new stepmother. Maria Edgeworth showed great business talent, and took a keen personal interest in the poor upon the estate. She was of diminutive stature, with a vivacious and amiable character. After some years of illness she died in the arms of her stepmother on 22 May 1849.

GEORGE WATSON is Fellow in English of St. John's College, Cambridge. He is editor of the *New Cambridge Bibliography of English Literature* (1969–73) and author of *The Literary Critics* (1962), *Politics and Literature in Modern Britain* (1977) and *The Story of the Novel* (1979).

THE WORLD'S CLASSICS

MARIA EDGEWORTH
Castle Rackrent

Edited with an Introduction by
GEORGE WATSON

Oxford New York

OXFORD UNIVERSITY PRESS

Oxford University Press, Walton Street, Oxford OX2 6DP

Oxford New York Toronto
Delhi Bombay Calcutta Madras Karachi
Kuala Lumpur Singapore Hong Kong Tokyo
Nairobi Dar es Salaam Cape Town
Melbourne Auckland Madrid

and associated companies in
Berlin Ibadan

Oxford is a trade mark of Oxford University Press

Editorial matter © Oxford University Press 1964, 1969

First published by Oxford University Press 1964
First issued as a World's Classics paperback 1980

All rights reserved. No part of this publication may be reproduced,
stored in a retrieval system, or transmitted, in any form or by any means,
without the prior permission in writing of Oxford University Press.
Within the UK, exceptions are allowed in respect of any fair dealing for the
purpose of research or private study, or criticism or review, as permitted
under the Copyright, Designs and Patents Act, 1988, or in the case of
reprographic reproduction in accordance with the terms of the licences
issued by the Copyright Licensing Agency. Enquiries concerning
reproduction outside these terms and in other countries should be
sent to the Rights Department, Oxford University Press,
at the address above

This book is sold subject to the condition that it shall not, by way
of trade or otherwise, be lent, re-sold, hired out or otherwise circulated
without the publisher's prior consent in any form of binding or cover
other than that in which it is published and without a similar condition
including this condition being imposed on the subsequent purchaser

British Library Cataloguing in Publication Data
Data available
ISBN 0-19-281539-3

11 13 15 17 19 20 18 16 14 12

Printed in Great Britain by
BPCC Paperbacks Ltd
Aylesbury, Bucks

CONTENTS

———

CONTENTS

INTRODUCTION

Castle Rackrent (1800) is the first regional novel in English, and perhaps in all Europe; and, as Scott saw at once, the regional novel is the gateway to the ampler world of the historical novel, since it represents whole societies and conceives of individual characters as composing societies. After 1800 it was no longer a matter of occasional regional types, like the stage Scotsmen and Irishmen of some eighteenth-century plays, or the provincial grotesques of Smollett's novels—all those whom Scott laughingly called 'the "Teagues" and "dear joys" who so long, with the most perfect family resemblance to each other, occupied the drama and the novel' before Maria Edgeworth. *Rackrent* pictures a world identified in time and place; and *Waverley* (1814), the first historical novel, was begun by Scott in 1805 under its direct inspiration, 'so as in some distant degree to emulate the admirable Irish portraits drawn by Miss Edgeworth'.[1] The informed study of societies which for

---

[1] *Waverley* (1814), ch. lxxii ('A Postscript, which should have been a Preface'). The passage was read to Maria Edgeworth by her stepmother in 1814, interrupting her as she wrote an admiring letter (23 Oct. 1814) to Scott, whom she guessed to be the author of the anonymous novel. Their friendship began here. Cf. R. F. Butler, 'Maria Edgeworth and Sir Walter

a century we have called sociology, from the rash, pioneer mid-century attempts by Marx and Comte to the more pragmatic inquiries of our own age, all spring from here. It is an aspect of human knowledge which novelists and poets, not historians, inaugurated, and the novels of Maria Edgeworth and of her first pupil are decades in advance of the historians in their social concern, though they have antecedents in the regional travel-books and economic surveys of the Georgian age such as Arthur Young's *Tour in Ireland* (1780) and in such regional poems as those of Burns and Crabbe. This vast literary revolution, which inspired Scott and perhaps Turgenev,[1] and which informed the historical sensibility of a whole century and more, was set on foot (in the novel at least) by a diminutive thirty-year-old Anglo-Irish spinster in a remote house in the middle of Ireland in the last years of the eighteenth century, and it is a triumph that is still largely unknown. The best studies of the historical novel do not mention it.[2] It is difficult to believe, even now, but Scott himself, who called her 'the great Maria', seems to have been in no doubt where the credit lay.

Maria Edgeworth (1767-1849), who was born in

Scott: Unpublished Letters, 1823', *Review of English Studies*, N.S. ix (1958).

    [1] Cf. Appendix p. 115.

    [2] e.g. Herbert Butterfield, *The Historical Novel*, Cambridge (1924), and George Lukács, *The Historical Novel*, London (1962), which first appeared in Russian in 1937. Both of these valuable studies—the first an historical essay, the second a comprehensive study by a Hungarian Marxist critic—fail to mention Maria Edgeworth at all.

Oxfordshire, saw Ireland for the first time, apart from infancy, at the age of fifteen, when she settled at her father's estate at Edgeworthstown in County Longford. There she spent almost all the remainder of a long life, unmarried but never solitary, in the company of numerous brothers and sisters and, successively, of her second and third stepmothers. To arrive in Ireland in 1782 was in itself to experience an historical moment: the Independency was established in that year by a constitution whereby the Irish Parliament at last achieved the power to legislate—'a natural, cheerful alliance' with England, as Burke called it—and the mood of confidence lasted well into the 1790's, until it was shattered by the war with France and the rising of 1798. 'Ireland is now a Nation', Grattan told the new parliament in Dublin in 1782, and the year remained a watershed in the memory of Maria Edgeworth, as the title-page to *Rackrent* shows—rather like the year 1745 in the historical imagination of Scott. Her father, in the *Memoirs* (1820) which she finished after his death, confidently claimed that, since before the Independency, 'the people of Ireland have improved more than any other people in Europe' (i. 234). His future father-in-law, Dr. Beaufort, in his *Memoirs of a Map of Ireland* (1792), claimed that the population of Ireland had more than trebled in the course of the century to nearly four million, which is almost equivalent to its present population. It is difficult for us now, with our knowledge of the Famine and the growth of nationalism, to conceive of the confidence with which the Anglo-Irish governed Ireland in the last years of the eighteenth century. *Rackrent* is a novel of optimism: it is about a bad old day that is dead and gone, however much may remain to be done. Maria's literary career belongs to this world of confident Protestant leadership. It began, and long continued, in apprenticeship to her father, Richard Lovell Edgeworth, an infinitely energetic and talkative squire of reforming instincts who knew something of the worlds of politics and of letters, a Fellow of the Royal Society and a crony of Thomas Day, Sir Joseph Banks, Sir Humphry Davy, and Erasmus Darwin. It is Maria's tutelage to her father, which persisted devotedly until his death in 1817, that makes her the least feminine of female novelists. She steals a long march over Jane Austen in the credibility of her male characters, as well as in her knowledgeable interest in whole societies and in the relations between classes as well as within them; though she never equals Jane Austen in economy of literary design. To the end, her novels breathe an air of faintly mannish concern, of the more practical talk of the dinner-table and the utterly practical talk of the estate. For all that Richard Lovell Edgeworth survives for us now as a kind of parody of the European Enlightenment, with his Rousseau-esque theories of education and government, he served his eldest daughter well for more than twenty years as a literary consultant, and she kept only one thing from him. That was *Castle Rackrent*, her first independent novel, which she scribbled down fast and in secret—almost the only novel she ever wrote without her father's help, and her best.

Even here she was not alone: the notion of turning her father's steward, John Langan, into the mouthpiece of a novel seems to have sprung from her father's sister Mrs. Ruxton. 'How many things we have talked over together!' Maria wrote many years after. ' "Rackrent" especially, which you first suggested to me, and encouraged me to go on with.'[1] The novel may have taken rise from Maria's amused account to her aunt of the ways of an Irish 'character' on her father's estate who provided the narrator-figure of Thady Quirk, a memory of adolescence that came to her with the first shock of Ireland:

The only character drawn from the life in 'Castle Rackrent' is Thady himself, the teller of the story. He was an old steward (not very old, though, at that time; I added to his age, to allow him time for the generations of the family). I heard him when I first came to Ireland, and his dialect struck me, and his character; and I became so acquainted with it, that I could think and speak in it without effort; so that when, for mere amusement, without any idea of publishing, I began to write a family history as Thady would tell it, he seemed to stand beside me and dictate; and I wrote as fast as my pen could go, the characters all imaginary.[2]

This, if Maria's memory is to be trusted, must refer to

[1] Letter to Mrs. Ruxton (7 Aug. 1822); *Memoir* (1867), ii. 206. For John Langan, who survived well into the nineteenth century, cf. *Memoir*, i. 22, 47 and n., 59, 188, 219.
[2] Letter to Mrs. Stark on Maria Edgeworth's 'habits of composition' (6 Sept. 1834); *Memoir* (1867), iii. 152.

the first third of the novel, and it pushes this sudden
creative burst back in time into the middle of the 1790's,
well before the Wolfe Tone rising of 1798; for in the
same letter she tells us how the longer 'Continuation',
or the history of Sir Condy Rackrent, 'was added two
years afterwards: it was not drawn from life, but the
good-natured and indolent extravagance were suggested
by a relation of mine long since dead'. There is no
certain way of knowing who this might be,[1] but this
late letter of 1834, in separating the work into two
distinct periods of composition, usefully destroys the
myth that *Rackrent* is a novel occasioned by the rebellion
of 1798, when French revolutionary troops, landing in
County Mayo in support of the Irish rebels, frightened
the Edgeworths and other county families into taking
refuge in Longford. We know that the novel appeared
as early as January 1800—perhaps even in December
1799—and if the manuscript was delivered to the publisher Johnson late in 1799, then the 'Continuation'
cannot have been written later than 1799, or the first
part of the novel later than 1797. *Rackrent*, in fact, in its
first conception, is a novel of the last, confident days of
the Irish Independency, though the Preface and Glossary, written late in 1799 when the Union of 1800 already

---

[1] Sir Condy might be a broad portrait of Maria's maternal grandfather,
Paul Elers of Black Bourton, Oxfordshire, a poor English lawyer who
married an Oxfordshire heiress and stood for Parliament though (unlike Sir
Condy) he did not get in. Richard Lovell Edgeworth, in his unfinished
Memoirs (1820), mentions that his first father-in-law, who was indifferent to
all money matters, had 'a very old steward' who 'managed all the business
of the estate' (i. 84).

seemed a bitter and inevitable necessity, darken the
novelist's own view of her novel and perhaps the tone
of the later narrative as well. Beyond this, in dating, we
cannot go. The novel may have been written at any time
between 1797 and 1799, or even earlier,[1] and there are
periods here when Maria's contact with her father may
have been less than usually intimate: early in 1798, for
example, when he was courting his fourth wife, Frances
Beaufort, who was to become Maria's closest friend.
These were the years when the *Lyrical Ballads* were
being written in Somerset; and though Maria Edgeworth never showed the faintest respect for Wordsworth,
either as a poet or as an acquaintance, the kinship of
interest, condescending yet informed, in the naïve and
the poor that unites two books is bound to seem significant to us now.

Though written, almost uniquely, without her father's
help and even without his prior knowledge, *Rackrent*
may easily have been written as an apt gift for him, perhaps a birthday present or as a surprise to greet him on

[1] A dinner-table conversation nearly twenty years after publication would
put the date of composition as early as 1792. Joseph Farington, R.A., in
his diary under March 1819, records a remark by the brother of Maria's
stepmother. The manuscript at Windsor Castle reads: '[Lestock] Wilson's
I dined at . . . Capt. [Francis] Beaufort spoke of Miss Edgeworth. He told
me that Her Novel *Castle Rackrent* was written 8 years before it was published, and witht. any intention to publish it, which she was induced to do
by an Aunt, a Sister of Her Father, who, being an invalid, Miss Edgeworth
sent Her the manuscript to read, & she was delighted with it. . . .' Cf. *The
Farington Diary*, ed. James Greig, vol. viii, London (1928), p. 217. But
even if Farington's memory is to be trusted, the tradition may be far from
reliable—especially since Beaufort (1774-1857) is unlikely to have known
the Edgeworths as early as 1792.

his return from a journey. And yet it remained stub-bornly Maria's book, and to the end she successfully resisted his encouragements to add to it. 'My father wishes to have some *additions* made to it,' she wrote to her brother Sneyd years later, '& I fear in this instance *additions* will not according to the Irish usage be synonymous with improvements. I am inclined to think that I could say better all my father wishes to have said about the modern manners of the Irish McQuirks in the story I am now writing of *Patronage*.'[1] This suggests that her father was asking for a second 'Continuation' to bring the book up to date by describing the modern Irish of the first years of the Union; and there is, in principle, no limit to the number of sequels that the book might bear. But, in the end, *Rackrent* was left alone, and the Irish scenes written for *Patronage* (1813) were transferred to *The Absentee* (1812) and told without the device of an Irish narrator. Perhaps the demands of dialect were irksome to Maria, or a doubtful advantage in the English market. At all events, the novel itself was never added to and never radically altered. Even the Glossary, hastily prepared as it evidently was, suffered little change. Richard Lovell Edgeworth's surviving copy of the first edition shows an abundance of notes scribbled in the endpapers, all materials for additions to the Glossary. They are in Maria's hand, and since they are in her father's copy of her book they may have been

---

[1] Letter to C. Sneyd Edgeworth of Mar. 1810 (unpublished).

taken down at his dictation. And yet only one of them was ever used,[1] being enlarged into a new note on Irish land-disputes for a later edition; while an unpublished letter to her brother Sneyd in October 1802, addressed by Maria from Sittingbourne on the way to Dover and Paris, suggests that she had also dictated a new note for the book to her aunt:

> Will you beg dear Aunt Mary to look in my bureau for a note about *fairies* for Castle Rackrent. It is written in her own hand—if she finds it she will be so kind to send it to Johnson—he is going to publish a *4th Ed of Rackrent*.

This too was never printed; indeed it has not survived at all. *Rackrent*, though it suffered some minor revisions for the collected edition of 1832, remained to the end essentially what it was at the start: two linked narratives describing the decline and fall of a dynasty of Irish landlords of the mid eighteenth century, furnished with a commentary designed to explain Irish allusions to English readers.

In terms of technique, *Rackrent* is original too. After a fashion, it is a memoir-novel, supposedly based on the autobiography of an imaginary hero 'edited' by the novelist—the oldest of novel-techniques in the eighteenth century, and familiar to all English readers since *Robinson Crusoe* (1719). In the late eighteenth century it had tended to be superseded in vogue by the epistolary novel, which Richardson had popularized in England with *Pamela* (1740); but by 1800 this too was passing

[1] Cf. p. 124, below.

out of fashion, and Maria was to use it only twice—
once in her first book, *Letters for Literary Ladies* (1795),
which includes a letter-novel; and years later in *Leonora*
(1806), which celebrates the only love-attachment she
ever experienced, and that tragically renounced, during
the visit to Paris in 1802–3. The rest of her novels, such
as the brilliant, melodramatic society-novel *Belinda*
(1801), or *The Absentee* (1812), the finest of her later
Irish novels, are all (like Jane Austen's six) pure fiction
and in the third person. *Rackrent* remains unique: a kind
of memoir-novel in which the narrator is not, like
Crusoe, the central actor in the drama, but an observer
merely—a technique impossible to parallel in English
before 1800, and rare even in French. Even the fashionable *Paul et Virginie* (1787) of Bernardin de Saint-Pierre,
which employs it, hardly provides a convincing source—
the narrator there is merely a colourless bystander.
Thady, on the contrary, though an observer, is the life
of *Rackrent*, and all the blood of the book flows through
the figure of this absurdly loyal family retainer—a full,
affectionately ironic vision of a dying system, and an
enriching device which, for some odd reason, Maria
never again essayed. It adds both flavour and authenticity: the novel is not only the livelier in detail because it
is recounted in the Irish dialect, it is the more informa-
tive as well. This was the prescription for its great and
immediate success in 1800. It instructed by pleasing.
'We hear from good authority', wrote Maria's father
proudly to his father-in-law, Dr. Beaufort, shortly after

the book appeared, 'that the King was much pleased with *Castle Rackrent*—he rubbed his hands and said what what—I know something now of my Irish subjects—I am more flattered by its being so well received by the Irish themselves—We were lately told by a very sensible man that it was considered by all the people he had met as representation of past manners which should flatter the present generation—In reality the family from whom the picture was chiefly taken has ceased to exist these forty years.' The novel is historical as well as regional, in fact—and if we hesitate to call it an 'historical novel' it is only because, unlike *Waverley*, it celebrates no great public event like the Forty-Five. It is about a way of life, not an event. As often happens, the world beyond (including George III) mistook it for a contemporary portrait. It was hailed, too, as a novelty, and that it was. For though the large shadow of Rousseau hangs over much that Maria and her father thought and did, and though *La Nouvelle Héloïse* (1761), with its sentimental picture of country life in the Vaud, has good claim to be considered a pioneer, there had clearly been nothing like it in English. It is true that the late eighteenth-century English novel, and still more the late eighteenth-century stage comedy such as Charles Macklin's *True-Born Irishman* (1793), had increasingly exploited regional types. In the 1780's, according to Dr. Tompkins, 'gradually the novel—even the library novel—ceases to move within the traditional world and opens to the world without', though she adds that, in the English novel, 'there is no sudden demand for realism in the 'eighties, and no demand at all for realism unadulterated. What there is, is a gradually increasing proportion of common-sense'.[1] The wider movement is from the sensational fantasy of Horace Walpole's *Castle of Otranto* (1765) and its Gothic successors towards realism and eventually, in Maria Edgeworth and Scott, towards something more pedantic than realism, something that almost deserves the pompous name of documentation. In the late eighteenth century the European memory suddenly grows more precise. Scott, in the 1829 preface to *Waverley*, is clear, looking back on his momentous career as a novelist, that the effort has in many ways been a scholarly one—or rather one in which the creative instinct, almost for the first time in Europe, mastered the scholarly and used it to a creative end. At the age of fifteen, driven by illness into 'becoming a glutton of books', Scott tells us how he 'read almost all the romances, old plays, and epic poetry, in that formidable collection [the Edinburgh circulating library], and no doubt was unconsciously amassing materials for the task in which it has been my lot to be so much employed'. Maria Edgeworth's documentation, though equally significant, is not like this sort of bookishness. She undoubtedly read widely, and the novels are laced with quotations from Shakespeare, Pope, Sheridan, and minor eighteenth-century poets, as well as refer-

---

[1] J. M. S. Tompkins, *The Popular Novel in England, 1770–1800*, London (1932), pp. 174-5; on regional characters, cf. p. 187 n.

ences to seventeenth- and eighteenth-century studies of Ireland. But it is not this that makes for realism, since the period described in *Rackrent* is the immediate past. It is not a remote age like Scott's Middle Ages, or even his Covenanting and Jacobite wars; it is a world of which her father, and John Langan, and many others, could inform her. Her real sources in *Rackrent* are not literary at all, but hearsay. Hence her engagingly naïve footnotes such as 'Fact', or 'Verbatim'. The story of *Rackrent* is an invention; but many of the details are openly offered as real.

The telling reality of *Rackrent*, of course, lies in the narrator-figure of Old Thady himself, and the device is so expertly used as to make us wonder why Maria Edgeworth never used it again. Unlike Lord Colambre in *The Absentee*, or Scott's Captain Waverley, who are both essentially outsiders in the Ireland or the Scotland which they visit, Thady is not only an observer, but an observer fully within a society he exemplifies as well as describes. He does not possess the liberty, or suffer the hard necessity, of choosing between two civilizations, as they do: 'Under which King, Bezonian? Speak, or die!', as the Shakespearian tag has it on Scott's title-page. Within the frame created by the Preface and the Glossary, which make it clear that the world which Thady and his four mad masters represent is dying or dead, and well deserves to die, is a rich prospect of laziness, generosity, and trickery; and above all of obsession, for each master of the estate is destroyed by a demon within himself: Sir Patrick by drink, Sir Murtagh by the law, Sir Kit by gambling, and Sir Condy, in the amplest portrait of all, by the spendthrift life of politics. The obsessions are mainly generous, and all ridiculous. We are shown good reason why Thady should love his masters, none at all why he should respect them as he does.

This large device of irony gives *Rackrent* a coherence which no other of Maria Edgeworth's novels achieves, and one which fully compensates for an episodic design. It is a more powerful unifying force than her attempt to put on paper a plausible example of the Irish dialect. No doubt we now see this aspect of the novel through the wrong end of the telescope. *Rackrent* is the first consistent attempt to compose a novel in any dialect of English; and alarmed at her experiment, Maria fitted it out first with explanatory footnotes and then, as an afterthought, with a 'Glossary' (in fact a commentary) as well. Conditioned as we now are by Scott, Dickens, and Kipling, we are inclined to find her over-solicitous; and conditioned by political doctrines of equality, we are inclined to find her patronizing as well. It is only by a large effort of the historical imagination that the modern reader can now see how little, in 1800, these can have seemed reasonable charges to bring against her. Her excuses to the 'English reader' in the preliminary pages, like Wordsworth's apologetic 'Advertisement' before the *Lyrical Ballads* of 1798, remind us how improbable both experiments must have seemed in Regency Lon-

don. The nature of the Anglo-Irish dialect had never
been so much as mentioned by any grammarian until
Thomas Sheridan's *Rhetorical Grammar of the English
Language* (1781), and no one in 1800 could have dreamed
that the remote world of an Irish country estate could
furnish matter for a whole novel—still less that it could
furnish the manner as well. But Maria Edgeworth, like
Wordsworth and Burns before him, is only a little ahead
of contemporary taste, and unlike them she did not have
to pause while it caught up with her. The world of belief
she represents, though instantly recognizable to anyone
acquainted with Regency taste, is not easy to pin down.
She was not a romantic but, in her literary tastes, a late
Augustan, and the resemblance between her first novel
and the *Lyrical Ballads* is only a profound coincidence.[1]
And yet, deeply influenced by the Enlightenment
through her father, she is not (like him) simply a product
of that world. Nor is she, at the other extreme, an anti-
romantic, a partisan of pious conservative Anglican sense
like Jane Austen. It is true that, like Jane Austen and
almost everyone in that age who was not subject to some
dangerous jacobinical influence such as Godwin or Tom
Paine, she believed that distinctions of class are a fact,
and on the whole a neutral fact, about human society.
She never doubted the principle of landlordism, con-
demning only absenteeism and putting her faith in

---

[1] Cf. *Readings on Poetry* (1816) by Maria Edgeworth and her father, a
handbook of explications of poems by Milton, Joseph Warton, and Gray.
Her letters suggest a lively contempt for Wordsworth and Byron.

benevolence—convinced of 'not only what could be done, but what had been done, by the influence of great proprietors residing on their own estates, and encouraging the people by judicious kindness'.[1] She knows her world by virtue of accepting it, and her perceptions are those of the intelligent insider. 'The question, whether society could exist without the distinction of ranks, is a question involving a variety of complicated discussions, which we will leave to the politician and the legislator', as she wrote early in life, in the preface to her collection of children's stories, *The Parent's Assistant* (1796). 'At present it is necessary that the education of different ranks should, in some respects, be different. They have few ideas, few habits in common.' Slight as this seems, it is a good deal nearer to a political comment than anything Jane Austen ever dares; and the intelligently detailed interest that Maria reveals, in the course of her Irish novels, in the duties of a landlord suggest something outside Jane Austen's range altogether. More than that, there is a compassion for human sentiment, especially after the visit to Paris in 1802, which is simply alien to Jane Austen's world of sensible choices. The devastating portrait of the snobbish Lady Clonbrony in *The Absentee*, which appeared a year after *Sense and Sensibility* (1811), seems determined to guy the notion of 'sense' as an absolute arbiter of conduct:

Lady Clonbrony knew nothing of love—she had read of it, indeed, in novels, which sometimes, for fashion's sake, she

[1] *The Absentee* (1812), ch. ix.

had looked at, and over which she had been obliged to doze; but this was only love in books—love in real life she had never met with—in the life she led, how should she? She had heard of its making young people, and old people even, do foolish things; but those were foolish people; and, if they were worse than foolish, why it was shocking, and nobody visited them. But lady Clonbrony had not, for her own part, the slightest notion how people could be brought to this pass, nor how any body out of Bedlam could prefer, to a good house, a decent equipage, and a proper establishment, what is called love in a cottage.   (ch. iv).

Not everything in Maria Edgeworth's novels is as morally permissive as this appears to be. But the common charge that she is stuffily edifying cannot really be sustained over wide areas of her major novels. (The stories for children and for young girls are, of course, another matter.)[1] Love in a cottage, like Sir Condy's last, heroic residence as a pauper in the Lodge of his own castle, is decidedly part of her scheme of virtue. It is this strain of intelligent compassion that makes the portrait of the servant Thady both a possibility and a triumph. His simplicity makes him a butt, but it also makes him a reporter, an accurate lens through which the life of the

---

[1] The distinction is best illustrated by her attitude to the picaresque novel, which she defends for the purposes of adult reading. 'In many engaging characters in society', she or her father wrote in *Practical Education* (1798), a treatise on the upbringing of children, 'and in many entertaining books, deceit and dishonesty are associated with superior abilities, with ease and gaiety of manners, and with a certain air of frank carelessness which can scarcely fail to please. Gil Blas, Tom Jones, Lovelace, Count Fathom, are all of this class of characters; they should not be introduced to our pupils till their habits and integrity are thoroughly formed' (p. 216). Cf. *Ormond* (1817), chaps. vii–viii.

Castle in which he serves is seen. 'The lower Irish', wrote Maria some twenty years after, in her continuation to her father's unfinished *Memoirs* (1820), 'are such acute observers, that there is no deceiving them as to the state of the real feelings of their superiors. They know the signs of what passes within, more perfectly than any physiognomist, who ever studied the human face, or human head' (ii. 241). This describes minutely what Thady does: it is an unrepeated triumph of observation and of instinct.

Enlightened, romantic, anti-romantic—no one word will describe what Maria Edgeworth is like, even in bare outline. The paradox is repeated in her disciple Scott, who is at once Tory-Unionist and sentimentally Jacobite. Both novelists stand about half-way in the spectrum which Jane Austen called Sense and Sensibility, and both predict more accurately than she the nature of the Victorian compromise. Lockhart tells an exemplary story of how Scott, walking in the park of Edgeworthstown on his visit to Maria in August 1825, claimed that 'higher sentiments' were to be heard from the poor and the uneducated than are to be found in the Bible or among the great. 'We shall never learn to feel and respect our real calling and destiny, unless we have taught ourselves to consider everything as moonshine, compared with the education of the heart.' Maria, says Lockhart, who was walking with them, 'did not listen to this without some water in her eyes—her tears are always ready when any generous string is touched—. . . but she brushed them gaily aside, and said, "You see how it is—Dean Swift said he had written his books, in order that people might learn to treat him like a great lord. Sir Walter writes his, in order that he may be able to treat his people as a great lord ought to do".' The two paradoxes revealed in this exchange between like minds are the foundations upon which Maria Edgeworth's fiction is largely built: what both called 'the education of the heart',[1] or the conviction that the human emotions and instincts, as well as the intelligent faculty of man, can be educated; and the social paradox that the poor, though distinct, are not in all respects inferior. *Rackrent*, in its abundant gaiety, celebrates them both, and roots them firmly in a time and a place. Without it, and without the more imposing novels of dead, dying, and living societies which it directly inspired, the novel of the nineteenth century could not have been made.

G. W.

---

[1] Cf. preface to *Practical Education* (1798): 'With respect to what is commonly called the education of the heart, we have endeavoured to suggest the easiest means of inducing [in children] useful and agreeable habits, well regulated sympathy and benevolent affections' (p. vii).

NOTE ON THE TEXT

NOTE ON THE TEXT

within all his argues, written the authorly is made.

THE text is printed from the British Museum copy of the first edition of the novel, published by Joseph Johnson (London, 1800), except that the position of Maria Edgeworth's Glossary, added as an afterthought following the Preface when the novel was already in the press, has been moved to its natural position at the end of the novel—the position it was accorded in the second London edition of 1800, and in all subsequent editions— with its page-references adjusted to the present text. Corrections in the author's hand in the Butler copy of the first edition have been incorporated in the text for the first time and recorded in the commentary; and obvious misprints have been corrected.

The publishing history of *Rackrent* after 1800 is not marked by any large changes in the text, in spite of family persuasions, though there is some loss of individuality in punctuation—an individuality which we may fairly attribute to Maria herself, since she wrote the novel, exceptionally, without the advice of her father, and boasted to an aunt of the clearness of her manuscript: 'There was literally not a correction,' she wrote to Mrs. Ruxton on 29 January 1800, 'not an alteration, made in the first writing, no copy, and, as I recollect, no interlineation; it went to the press just as it was written.' This argues well for the authority of *1800*. The first Dublin edition of 1800 is merely a reprint, with many minor differences in spelling. The third London edition, with some corrections, appeared in 1801, with Maria Edgeworth's name for the first time on the title-page; the fourth in 1804, all octavos; and the duodecimo fifth (with an addition to the Glossary and footnotes deleted) in 1810, all published by Johnson. The fifth was reprinted by Johnson's successor, Hunter, as a sixth edition in 1815. The first collected edition (1825) was carelessly made. The second (1832–3) undoubtedly includes a number of minor corrections made by the novelist or with her approval: spelling is altered and punctuation further simplified, following the trend of the second and later editions, especially by reducing the rather feminine dashes of *1800* and by reducing one of the features of the first edition, the use of brackets within dialogue around phrases like 'says he'. Three footnotes are dropped, and some new misprints introduced. Altogether, *1832* is largely a reprint of the early editions in a more modern, or less idiosyncratic, dress, and for this reason it is clearly of less interest than the epoch-making octavo of January 1800. In an original-spelling edition such as this, it has seemed better to reproduce the conventions of the day in which the novel was written and first read rather than those of a generation and more later. *Rackrent* is a late-eighteenth-century novel; and, for the first time, it is reproduced here in its original form.

SELECT BIBLIOGRAPHY

THE place of publication, unless otherwise stated, is London.

There are texts of *Castle Rackrent* with introductions by Anne Thackeray Ritchie (1895) and by Brander Matthews (1910) (Everyman's Library), both with *The Absentee*; and by A. Norman Jeffares (Edinburgh, 1953). There has been no collected edition of the novels in this century.

The chief published source of information concerning Maria Edgeworth remains *A Memoir of Maria Edgeworth, with a Selection from her Letters by the late Mrs.* [*Frances*] *Edgeworth*, 3 vols. (1867) (privately printed). This was supplemented by Augustus J. C. Hare, *The Life and Letters of Maria Edgeworth*, 2 vols. (1894); by *Chosen Letters*, edited by F. V. Barry (1931), a selection from the *Memoir* of 1867 with eight unpublished letters; and by H. W. Häusermann, *The Genevese Background* (1952), which prints for the first time a number of letters now preserved in or near Geneva. There are many letters still unpublished in the possession of Mrs. Margaret Butler of Richmond, Surrey, and of the National Library of Ireland in Dublin. The posthumous *Memoirs of Richard Lovell Edgeworth*, 2 vols. (1820), which his daughter finished, and *The Black Book of Edgeworthstown and other Edgeworth Memories, 1585-1817*, edited by H. J. and H. E. Butler (1927), both contain information about the family background.

There have been four studies of Maria Edgeworth in this century: an English Men of Letters biography by the Hon. Emily Lawless (1904); *Maria Edgeworth*, by P. H. Newby (1950); *Maria Edgeworth : her Family and Friends*, by Isabel C. Clarke [1950]; and *The Great Maria*, by Elisabeth Inglis-Jones (1959). For a critical essay, see Donald Davie, *The Heyday of Sir Walter Scott* (1961), ch. vi. There is a bibliography by Bertha Coolidge Slade, *Maria Edgeworth : a Bibliographical Tribute* (1937) (limited edition).

Note (1980). Three highly important contributions have been published since this book was first published in the Oxford English Novels series, 1964: *Maria Edgeworth: a Literary Biography* by Marilyn Butler (Oxford, 1972), the best life of the novelist; and two collections drawn from her manuscript letters, both edited by Christina Colvin: *Letters from England* (Oxford, 1972) and *Maria Edgeworth in France and Switzerland* (Oxford, 1979).

ACKNOWLEDGEMENTS

ACCESS to the manuscript of the Farington diary at Windsor Castle was granted by the gracious permission of H.M. the Queen.

In making this edition I have found myself pleasantly indebted to several members of the Butler family: to Mrs. Margaret Butler, widow of Harold Edgeworth Butler of London University, who gave me permission to use the marked copy of the first edition of *Rackrent* and the Edgeworth papers in her possession, and offered advice as well; to her daughter, Mrs. Christina Colvin of Oxford, who helped me to find my way through the haystack of unpublished Edgeworth letters, of which she has an unrivalled knowledge; to Mrs. Marilyn Butler, who generously discussed with me her plans for a critical study of the novelist; to Dr. Richard Freeborn of Brasenose College, Oxford, for guidance on Turgenev; and to Dr. V. G. Mylne of University College, Swansea, for advice about the background of eighteenth-century fiction. My thanks, too, are due to the National Library of Ireland for the use of some of the Edgeworth papers, and to the Bodleian Library, which made them available to me. The General Editor of the Oxford English Novels series, Professor Herbert Davis, has shown me how to be a better editor, and not for the first time.

CHRONOLOGY OF
MARIA EDGEWORTH

Recent evidence suggests ME may have been born on 1 January 1768. See M. Butler and C. Colvin, *Notes and Queries* (September 1971).

CASTLE RACKRENT[1]

AN
HIBERNIAN TALE

TAKEN FROM FACTS,
AND FROM
THE MANNERS OF THE IRISH SQUIRES,
BEFORE THE YEAR 1782[2]

PREFACE[3]

THE prevailing taste of the public for anecdote has been censured and ridiculed by critics, who aspire to the character of superior wisdom: but if we consider it in a proper point of view, this taste is an incontestible proof of the good sense and profoundly philosophic temper of the present times. Of the numbers who study, or at least who read history, how few derive any advantage from their labors! The heroes of history are so decked out by the fine fancy of the professed historian; they talk in such measured prose, and act from such sublime or such diabolical motives, that few have sufficient taste, wickedness or heroism, to sympathize in their fate. Besides, there is much uncertainty even in the best authenticated antient or modern histories; and that love of truth, which in some minds is innate and immutable, necessarily leads to a love of secret memoirs and private anecdotes. We cannot judge either of the feelings or of the characters of men with perfect accuracy from their actions or their appearance in public; it is from their careless conversations, their half finished sentences, that we may hope with the greatest probability of success to discover their real characters. The life of a great or of à little man written by himself, the familiar letters, the diary of any individual published by his friends, or by his enemies after his decease, are esteemed important literary curiosities. We are surely justified in this eager desire to collect the most minute facts relative to the domestic lives, not only of the great and good, but even of the worthless and insignificant, since it is only by a comparison of their actual happiness or misery in the privacy of domestic life, that we can form a just estimate of the real reward of virtue, or the real punishment of vice. That the great are not as happy as they seem, that the external circumstances of fortune and rank do not constitute felicity, is asserted by every moralist; the historian can seldom, consistently with his dignity, pause to illustrate this truth, it is therefore to the biographer we must have recourse. After we have beheld splendid characters playing their parts on the great theatre of the world, with all the advantages of stage effect and decoration, we anxiously beg to be admitted behind the scenes, that we may take a nearer view of the actors and actresses.

Some may perhaps imagine, that the value of biography depends upon the judgment and taste of the biographer; but on the contrary it may be maintained, that the merits of a biographer are inversely as the extent of his intellectual powers and of his literary talents. A plain unvarnished tale[4] is preferable to the most highly ornamented narrative. Where we see that a man has the power, we may naturally suspect that he has the will to deceive us, and those who are used to literary manufacture know how much is often sacrificed to the rounding of a period or the pointing an antithesis.[5]

That the ignorant may have their prejudices as well as the learned cannot be disputed, but we see and despise vulgar errors; we never bow to the authority of him who has no great name to sanction his absurdities. The partiality which blinds a biographer to the defects of his hero, in proportion as it is gross ceases to be dangerous; but if it be concealed by the appearance of candor, which men of great abilities best know how to assume, it endangers our judgment sometimes, and sometimes our morals. If her Grace the Duchess of Newcastle, instead of penning her lord's elaborate eulogium, had undertaken to write the life of Savage,[6] we should not have been in any danger of mistaking an idle, ungrateful libertine, for a man of genius and virtue. The talents of a biographer are often fatal to his reader. For these reasons the public often judiciously countenances those, who without sagacity to discriminate character, without elegance of style to relieve the tediousness of narrative, without enlargement of mind to draw any conclusions from the facts they relate, simply pour forth anecdotes and retail conversations, with all the minute prolixity of a gossip in a country town.

The author of the following memoirs[7] has upon these grounds fair claims to the public favor and attention: he was an illiterate old steward, whose partiality to *the family* in which he was bred and born must be obvious

to the reader. He tells the history of the Rackrent family
in his vernacular idiom, and in the full confidence that
Sir Patrick, Sir Murtagh, Sir Kit,[8] and Sir Condy Rackrent's affairs, will be as interesting to all the world as
they were to himself. Those who were acquainted with
the manners of a certain class of the gentry of Ireland
some years ago, will want no evidence of the truth of
honest Thady's narrative: to those who are totally un-
acquainted with Ireland, the following Memoirs will
perhaps be scarcely intelligible, or probably they may
appear perfectly incredible. For the information of the
ignorant English reader a few notes have been subjoined
by the editor, and he had it once in contemplation to
translate the language of Thady into plain English; but
Thady's idiom is incapable of translation, and besides,
the authenticity of his story would have been more
exposed to doubt if it were not told in his own characteristic manner. Several years ago he related to the editor
the history of the Rackrent family, and it was with some
difficulty that he was persuaded to have it committed to
writing; however, his feelings for '*the honor of the family*,'
as he expressed himself, prevailed over his habitual
laziness, and he at length completed the narrative which
is now laid before the public.

The Editor hopes his readers will observe, that these
are 'tales of other times;' that the manners depicted in
the following pages are not those of the present age: the
race of the Rackrents has long since been extinct in
Ireland, and the drunken Sir Patrick, the litigious Sir

Murtagh, the fighting Sir Kit, and the slovenly Sir Condy, are characters which could no more be met with at present in Ireland, than Squire Western or Parson Trulliber[9] in England. There is a time when individuals can bear to be rallied for their past follies and absurdities, after they have acquired new habits and a new consciousness. Nations as well as individuals gradually lose attachment to their identity, and the present generation is amused rather than offended by the ridicule that is thrown upon their ancestors.

Probably we shall soon have it in our power, in a hundred instances, to verify the truth of these observations.

When Ireland loses her identity by an union with Great Britain, she will look back with a smile of good-humoured complacency on the Sir Kits and Sir Condys of her former existence.[10]

AN HIBERNIAN TALE

CASTLE RACKRENT

Monday Morning[g]

HAVING out of friendship for the family, upon whose estate, praised be Heaven! I and mine have lived rent free time out of mind, voluntarily undertaken to publish the Memoirs of the Rackrent Family, I think it my duty to say a few words, in the first place, concerning myself. —My real name is Thady Quirk, though in the family I have always been known by no other than '*honest Thady*'—afterwards, in the time of Sir Murtagh, deceased, I remember to hear them calling me '*old Thady ;*' and now I'm come to 'poor Thady'—for I wear a long great coat* winter and summer, which is very handy, as

* The cloak, or mantle, as described by Thady, is of high antiquity.— Spencer,[11] in his 'View of the State of Ireland,' proves that it is not, as some have imagined, peculiarly derived from the Scythians, but that 'most nations of the world antiently used the mantle; for the Jews used it, as you may read of Elias's mantle, &c.; the Chaldees also used it, as you may read in Diodorus; the Egyptians likewise used it, as you may read in Herodotus, and may be gathered by the description of Berenice, in the Greek Commentary upon Callimachus; the Greeks also used it anciently, as appeareth by Venus's mantle lined with stars, though afterwards they changed the form thereof into their cloaks, called Pallia, as some of the Irish also use: and the ancient Latins and Romans used it, as you may read in Virgil, who was a very great

I never put my arms into the sleeves, (they are as good as new,) though, come Holantide next, I've had it these seven years; it holds on by a single button round my neck, cloak fashion—to look at me, you would hardly think 'poor Thady' was the father of attorney Quirk; he is a high gentleman, and never minds what poor Thady says, and having better than 1500 a-year, landed estate, looks down upon honest Thady, but I wash my hands of his doings, and as I have lived so will I die, true and loyal to the family.[14]—The family of the Rackrents is, I am proud to say, one of the most ancient in the kingdom.—Every body knows this is not the old family name, which was O'Shaughlin, related to the Kings of

antiquary, that Evander, when Eneas came to him at his feast, did entertain and feast him, sitting on the ground, and lying on mantles; insomuch as he useth the very word mantile for a mantle,

———— Humi mantilia sternunt.

so that it seemeth that the mantle was a general habit to most nations, and not proper to the Scythians only.'

Spencer knew the convenience of the said mantle, as housing, bedding, and cloathing.

'Iren. Because the commodity doth not countervail the discommodity; for the inconveniences which thereby do arise, are much more many; for it is a fit house for an outlaw, a meet bed for a rebel, and an apt cloak for a thief.— First, the outlaw being, for his many crimes and villainies, banished from the towns and houses of honest men, and wandering in waste places, far from danger of law, maketh his mantle his house, and under it covereth himself from the wrath of Heaven, from the offence of the earth, and from the sight of men. When it raineth, it is his pent-house; when it bloweth, it is his tent; when it freezeth, it is his tabernacle. In summer he can wear it loose; in winter he can wrap it close; at all times he can use it; never heavy, never cumbersome. Likewise for a rebel it is as serviceable; for in this war[12] that he maketh (if at least it deserve the name of war), when he still flieth from his foe, and lurketh in the *thick woods*, (*this should be black bogs*,)[13] and straight passages waiting for advantages; it is his bed, yea, and almost his household-stuff.'

Ireland—but that was before my time.—My grandfather was driver to the great Sir Patrick O'Shaughlin, and I heard him, when I was a boy, telling how the Castle Rackrent estate came to Sir Patrick—Sir Tallyhoo Rackrent was cousin-german to him, and had a fine estate of his own, only never a gate upon it, it being his maxim, that a car was the best gate.—Poor gentleman! he lost a fine hunter and his life, at last, by it, all in one day's hunt.—But I ought to bless that day, for the estate came straight into *the* family, upon one condition, which Sir Patrick O'Shaughlin at the time took sadly to heart, they say, but thought better of it afterwards, seeing how large a stake depended upon it, that he should, by Act of Parliament, take and bear the sirname and arms of Rackrent.

Now it was that the world was to see what was *in* Sir Patrick.—On coming into the estate, he gave the finest entertainment ever was heard of in the country—not a man could stand after supper but Sir Patrick himself, who could sit out the best man in Ireland, let alone the three kingdoms itself.ᵍ—He had his house, from one year's end to another, as full of company as ever it could hold, and fuller; for rather than be left out of the parties at Castle Rackrent, many gentlemen, and those men of the first consequence and landed estates in the country, such as the O'Neills of Ballynagrotty, and the Moneygawls¹⁵ of Mount Juliet's Town, and O'Shannons of New Town Tullyhog, made it their choice, often and often, when there was no moon to be had for love or money, in

long winter nights, to sleep in the chicken house, which
Sir Patrick had fitted up for the purpose of accommo-
dating his friends and the public in general, who
honoured him with their company unexpectedly at
Castle Rackrent; and this went on, I can't tell you how
long—the whole country rang with his praises—Long
life to him!—I'm sure I love to look upon his picture,
now opposite to me; though I never saw him, he must
have been a portly gentleman—his neck something
short, and remarkable for the largest pimple on his nose,
which, by his particular desire, is still extant in his
picture—said to be a striking likeness, though taken
when young.—He is said also to be the inventor of
raspberry whiskey, which is very likely, as nobody has
ever appeared to dispute it with him, and as there still
exists a broken punch-bowl at Castle-Stopgap, in the
garret, with an inscription to that effect—a great
curiosity.—A few days before his death he was very
merry; it being his honour's birth-day, he called my
great grandfather in, God bless him! to drink the company's health, and filled a bumper himself, but could
not carry it to his head, on account of the great shake in
his hand—on this he cast his joke, saying, 'What would
my poor father say to me if he was to pop out of the grave,
and see me now?—I remember, when I was a little boy,
the first bumper of claret he gave me after dinner, how
he praised me for carrying it so steady to my mouth—
Here's my thanks to him—a bumper toast'—Then he
fell to singing the favourite song he learned from his

father—for the last time, poor gentleman—he sung it
that night as loud and hearty as ever, with a chorus—

He that goes to bed, and goes to bed sober,
Falls as the leaves do, falls as the leaves do, and dies in October—
But he that goes to bed, and goes to bed mellow,
Lives as he ought to do, lives as he ought to do, and dies an honest
    fellow.[16]

Sir Patrick died that night—just as the company rose
to drink his health with three cheers, he fell down in a
sort of a fit, and was carried off—they sat it out, and
were surprised, on enquiry, in the morning, to find it
was all over with poor Sir Patrick—Never did any
gentleman live and die more beloved in the country by
rich and poor—his funeral was such a one as was never
known before nor since in the county!—All the gentlemen in the three counties were at it—far and near, how
they flocked![17]—my great grandfather said, that to see
all the women even in their red cloaks, you would have
taken them for the army drawn out.—Then such a fine
whillaluh![g] you might have heard it to the farthest end
of the county, and happy the man who could get but
a sight of the hearse!—But who'd have thought it?[18]
Just as all was going on right, through his own town
they were passing, when the body was seized for debt—
a rescue was apprehended from the mob—but the heir
who attended the funeral was against that, for fear of
consequences, seeing that those villains acted[19] under
the disguise of the law—So, to be sure, the law must
take its course—and little gain had the creditors for their
pains. First and foremost, they had the curses of the

country; and Sir Murtagh Rackrent the new heir, in the next place, on account of this affront to the body, refused to pay a shilling of the debts, in which he was countenanced by all the best gentlemen of property, and others of his acquaintance, Sir Murtagh alledging in all companies, that he all along meant to pay his father's debts of honor; but the moment the law was taken of him, there was an end of honor to be sure. It was whispered, (but none but the enemies of the family believe it) that this was all a sham seizure to get quit of the debts, which he had bound himself to pay in honor.

It's a long time ago, there's no saying how it was, but this for certain, the new man did not take at all after the old gentleman—The cellars were never filled after his death—and no open house, or any thing as it used to be—the tenants even were sent away without their whiskey*g*—I was ashamed myself, and knew not what to say for the honor of the family—But I made the best of a bad case, and laid it all at my lady's door, for I did not like *her* any how, nor any body else—she was of the family of the Skinflints, and a widow—It was a strange match for Sir Murtagh; the people in the country thought he demeaned himself greatly*g*—but *I* said nothing—I knew how it was—Sir Murtagh was a great lawyer, and looked to the great Skinflint estate; there, however, he overshot himself; for though one of the co-heiresses, he was never the better for her, for she outlived him many's the long day—he could not foresee that, to be sure, when he married her. I must say for her,

she made him the best of wives, being a very notable
stirring woman, and looking close to every thing. But
I always suspected she had Scotch blood in her veins,
any thing else I could have looked over in her from a
regard to the family. She was a strict observer for self
and servants of Lent, and all Fast days, but not holidays.
One of the maids having fainted three times the last day
of Lent, to keep soul and body together we put a morsel
of roast beef into her mouth, which came from Sir
Murtagh's dinner, who never fasted, not he; but somehow or other it unfortunately reached my lady's ears,
and the priest of the parish had a complaint made of it
the next day, and the poor girl was forced as soon as she
could walk to do penance for it, before she could get any
peace or absolution in the house or out of it. However,
my lady was very charitable in her own way. She had
a charity school for poor children, where they were
taught to read and write gratis, and where they were
kept well to spinning gratis for my lady in return; for
she had always heaps of duty yarn from the tenants, and
got all her houshold linen out of the estate from first to
last; for after the spinning, the weavers on the estate took
it in hand for nothing, because of the looms my lady's
interest could get from the Linen Board to distribute
gratis. Then there was a bleach yard near us, and the
tenant dare refuse my lady nothing, for fear of a law-suit
Sir Murtagh kept hanging over him about the water
course. With these ways of managing, 'tis surprising
how cheap my lady got things done, and how proud she

was of it. Her table the same way—kept for next to
nothing—duty fowls, and duty turkies, and duty geese, [g]
came as fast as we could eat 'em, for my lady kept
a sharp look out, and knew to a tub of butter every
thing the tenants had, all round. They knew her way,
and what with fear of driving for rent and Sir Murtagh's law-suits, they were kept in such good order,
they never thought of coming near Castle Stopgap
without a present of something or other—nothing
too much or too little for my lady—eggs—honey—
butter—meal—fish—game, growse, and herrings, fresh
or salt—all went for something. As for their young
pigs, we had them, and the best bacon and hams they
could make up, with all young chickens in spring;
but they were a set of poor wretches, and we had nothing but misfortunes with them, always breaking and
running away—This, Sir Murtagh and my lady said,
was all their former landlord Sir Patrick's fault, who
let 'em all get the half year's rent into arrear—there
was something in that, to be sure—But Sir Murtagh
was as much the contrary way—For let alone making
English tenants[g] of them, every soul—he was always
driving and driving, and pounding and pounding,
and canting[g] and canting, and replevying and replevying, and he made a good living of trespassing cattle—
there was always some tenant's pig, or horse, or cow,
or calf, or goose, trespassing, which was so great a
gain to Sir Murtagh, that he did not like to hear me
talk of repairing fences. Then his herriots[20] and duty

work^g brought him in something—his turf was cut—his potatoes set and dug—his hay brought home, and in short all the work about his house done for nothing; for in all our leases there were strict clauses with heavy penalties, which Sir Murtagh knew well how to enforce—so many days duty work of man and horse, from every tenant, he was to have, and had, every year; and when a man vexed him, why the finest day he could pitch on, when the cratur was getting in his own harvest, or thatching his cabin, Sir Murtagh made it a principle to call upon him and his horse—so he taught 'em all, as he said, to know the law of landlord and tenant. As for law, I believe no man, dead or alive, ever loved it so well as Sir Murtagh. He had once sixteen suits pending at a time, and I never saw him so much himself — roads — lanes — bogs — wells — ponds — eel-wires — orchards — trees — tythes — vagrants — gravel-pits — sandpits — dung-hills and nuisances—every thing upon the face of the earth furnished him good matter for a suit. He used to boast that he had a law-suit for every letter in the alphabet. How I used to wonder to see Sir Murtagh in the midst of the papers in his office—why he could hardly turn about for them. I made bold to shrug my shoulders once in his presence, and thanked my stars I was not born a gentleman to so much toil and trouble—but Sir Murtagh took me up short with his old proverb, 'learning is better than house or land.'[21] Out of forty-nine suits which he had, he never lost one but seventeen^g;

the rest he gained with costs, double costs, treble costs sometimes—but even that did not pay. He was a very learned man in the law, and had the character of it; but how it was I can't tell, these suits that he carried cost him a power of money—in the end he sold some hundreds a year of the family estate—but he was a very learned man in the law, and I know nothing of the matter except having a great regard for the family. I could not help grieving when he sent me to post up notices of the sale of the fee simple of the lands and appurtenances of Timoleague.—'I know, honest Thady,' says he to comfort me, 'what I'm about better than you do; I'm only selling to get the ready money wanting, to carry on my suit with spirit with the Nugents of Carrickashaughlin.'

He was very sanguine about that suit with the Nugents of Carrickashaughlin. He would have gained it, they say, for certain, had it pleased Heaven to have spared him to us, and it would have been at the least a plump two thousand a year in his way; but things were ordered otherwise, for the best to be sure. He dug up a fairy-mount* against my advice, and had no luck afterwards. Though a learned man in the law, he was a little too incredulous in other matters. I warned him that I heard

* 22 These fairy-mounts 8 are called ant-hills in England. They are held in high reverence by the common people in Ireland. A gentleman, who in laying out his lawn had occasion to level one of these hillocks, could not prevail upon any of his labourers to begin the ominous work. He was obliged to take a *loy*23 from one of their reluctant hands, and began the attack himself. The labourers agreed, that the vengeance of the fairies would fall upon the head of the presumptuous mortal, who first disturbed them in their retreat.

the very Banshee* that my grandfather heard, before I was born long, under²⁴ Sir Patrick's window a few days before his death. But Sir Murtagh thought nothing of the Banshee, nor of his cough with a spitting of blood, brought on, I understand, by catching cold in attending the courts, and overstraining his chest with making himself heard in one of his favorite causes. He was a great speaker, with a powerful voice; but his last speech was not in the courts at all. He and my lady, though both of the same way of thinking in some things, and though she was as good a wife and great economist as you could see, and he the best of husbands, as to looking into his affairs, and making money for his family; yet I don't know how it was, they had a great deal of sparring and jarring between them.—My lady had her privy purse— and she had her weed ashes, ᵍ and her sealing money ᵍ upon the signing of all the leases, with something to buy gloves besides; and besides again often took money from the tenants, if offered properly, to speak for them to Sir Murtagh about abatements and renewals. Now the weed ashes and the glove money he allowed her clear perquisites; though once when he saw her in a new gown saved out of the weed ashes, he told her to my face, (for he could say a sharp thing) that she should not

---

* The Banshee is a species of aristocratic fairy, who in the shape of a little hideous old woman has been known to appear, and heard to sing in a mournful supernatural voice under the windows of great houses, to warn the family that some of them are soon to die. In the last century every great family in Ireland had a Banshee, who attended regularly, but latterly their visits and songs have been discontinued.

put on her weeds before her husband's death. But it
grew more serious when they came to the renewal busi-
nesses. At last, in a dispute about an abatement, my lady
would have the last word, and Sir Murtagh grew mad;[g]
I was within hearing of the door, and now wish I had
made bold to step in. He spoke so loud, the whole
kitchen was out on the stairs[g]—All on a sudden he
stopped, and my lady too. Something has surely happened, thought I—and so it was, for Sir Murtagh in his
passion broke a blood-vessel, and all the law in the land
could do nothing in that case. My lady sent for five
physicians, but Sir Murtagh died, and was buried. She
had a fine jointure settled upon her, and took herself
away to the great joy of the tenantry. I never said any
thing, one way or the other, whilst she was part of the
family, but got up to see her go at three o'clock in the
morning—'It's a fine morning, honest Thady, says she;
good bye to ye'—and into the carriage she stept, without
a word more, good or bad, or even half-a-crown; but
I made my bow, and stood to see her safe out of sight
for the sake of the family.

Then we were all bustle in the house, which made me
keep out of the way, for I walk slow and hate a bustle, but
the house was all hurry-skurry, preparing for my new
master.—Sir Murtagh, I forgot to notice, had no childer,* so the Rackrent estate went to his younger
brother—a young dashing officer—who came amongst

* *Childer*—this is the manner in which many of Thady's rank, and others
in Ireland, *formerly* pronounced the word *children*.

us before I knew for the life of me whereabouts I was, in a gig or some of them things, with another spark along with him, and led horses, and servants, and dogs, and scarce a place to put any Christian of them into; for my late lady had sent all the feather-beds off before her, and blankets, and household linen, down to the very knife cloths, on the cars to Dublin, which were all her own, lawfully paid for out of her own money—So the house was quite bare, and my young master, the moment ever he set foot in it out of his gig, thought all those things must come of themselves, I believe, for he never looked after any thing at all, but harum-scarum called for every thing as if we were conjurers, or he in a public-house. For my part, I could not bestir myself any how; I had been so used to my late master and mistress, all was upside down with me, and the new servants in the servants' hall were quite out of my way; I had nobody to talk to, and if it had not been for my pipe and tobacco should, I verily believe, have broke my heart for poor Sir Murtagh.

But one morning my new master caught a glimpse of me as I was looking at his horse's heels, in hopes of a word from him—and is that old Thady! says he, as he got into his gig—I loved him from that day to this, his voice was so like the family—and he threw me a guinea out of his waistcoat pocket, as he drew up the reins with the other hand, his horse rearing too; I thought I never set my eyes on a finer figure of a man— quite another sort from Sir Murtagh, though withal *to* *me*, a family likeness—A fine life we should have led, had he stayed amongst us, God bless him!—he valued a guinea as little as any man—money to him was no more than dirt, and his gentleman and groom, and all belonging to him, the same—but the sporting season over, he grew tired of the place, and having got down a great architect for the house, and an improver for the grounds, and seen their plans and elevations, he fixed a day for settling with the tenants, but went off in a whirlwind to town, just as some of them came into the yard in the morning. A circular letter came next post from the new agent, with news that the master was sailed for England, and he must remit 500l. to Bath for his use, before a fortnight was at an end—Bad news still for the poor tenants, no change still for the better with them— Sir Kit Stopgap, my young master, left all to the agent, and though he had the spirit of a Prince, and lived away to the honour of his country abroad, which I was proud to hear of, what were we the better for that at home? The agent was one of your middle men,* who grind the

* *Middle men.*—There was a class of men termed middle men in Ireland, who took large farms on long leases from gentlemen of landed property, and set the land again in small portions to the poor, as under tenants, at exorbitant rents. The *head-landlord*, as he *was* called, seldom saw his *under tenants*, but if he could not get the *middle man* to pay him his rent punctually, he *went to the land, and drove the land for his rent*, that is to say, he sent his steward or bailiff, or driver, to the land, to seize the cattle, hay, corn, flax, oats, or potatoes, belonging to the under-tenants, and proceeded to sell these for his rent; it sometimes happened that these unfortunate tenants paid their rent twice over, once to the *middle man*, and once to the *head landlord*.

The characteristics of a middle man *were*, servility to his superiors, and tyranny[25] towards his inferiors—The poor detested this race of beings. In

6 # AN HIBERNIAN TALE

face of the poor, and can never bear a man with a hat upon his head—he ferretted the tenants out of their lives—not a week without a call for money—drafts upon drafts from Sir Kit—but I laid it all to the fault of the agent; for, says I, what can Sir Kit do with so much cash, and he a single man? but still it went.—Rents must be all paid up to the day, and afore—no allowance for improving tenants—no consideration for those who had built upon their farms—No sooner was a lease out, but the land was advertised to the highest bidder—all the old tenants turned out, when they had spent their substance in the hope and trust of a renewal from the landlord.—All was now set at the highest penny to a parcel of poor wretches who meant to run away, and did so, after taking two crops out of the ground. Then fining down the year's rent *g* came into fashion—any thing for the ready penny, and with all this, and presents to the agent and the driver, *g* there was no such thing as standing it—I said nothing, for I had a regard for the family, but I walked about, thinking if his honour Sir Kit, (long may he live to reign over us!) knew all this, it would go hard with him, but he'd see us righted—not that I had any thing for my own share to complain of, for the agent was always very civil to me, when he came down into the

speaking to them, however, they always used the most abject language, and the most humble tone and posture—'*Please your honour,—and please your honour's honour,*' they knew must be repeated as a charm at the beginning and end of every equivocating, exculpatory, or supplicatory sentence—and they were much more alert in doffing their caps to these new men, than to those of what they call *good old families.*—A witty carpenter once termed these middle men *journeymen-gentlemen.*

country, and took a great deal of notice of my son Jason. —Jason Quirk, though he be my son, I must say, was a good scholar from his birth, and a very 'cute lad—I thought to make him a priest, g but he did better for himself—Seeing how he was as good a clerk as any in the county, the agent gave him his rent accounts to copy, which he did first of all for the pleasure of obliging the gentleman, and would take nothing at all for his trouble, but was always proud to serve the family.—By and by, a good farm bounding us to the east fell into his honour's hands, and my son put in a proposal for it; why shouldn't he as well as another?—The proposals all went over to the master at the Bath, who knowing no more of the land than the child unborn, only having once been out a grousing on it before he went to England; and the value of lands, as the agent informed him, falling every year in Ireland, his honour wrote over in all haste a bit of a letter, saying he left it all to the agent, and that he must set it as well as he could to the best bidder, to be sure, and send him over £200. by return of post: with this the agent gave me a hint, and I spoke a good word for my son, and gave out in the country, that nobody need bid against us.—So his proposal was just the thing, and he a good tenant; and he got a promise of an abatement in the rent, after the first year, for advancing the half year's rent at signing the lease, which was wanting to compleat the agent's £200, by the return of the post, with all which my master wrote back he was well satisfied.— About this time we learned from the agent, as a great secret, how the money went so fast, and the reason of the thick coming of the master's drafts: he was a little too fond of play, and Bath, they say, was no place for a young man of his fortune, where there were so many of his own countrymen too haunting him up and down, day and night, who had nothing to lose—at last, at Christmas, the agent wrote over to stop the drafts, for he could raise no more money on bond or mortgage, or from the tenants, or any how, nor had he any more to lend himself, and desired at same time to decline the agency for the future, wishing Sir Kit his health and happiness, and the compliments of the season—for I saw the letter before ever it was sealed, when my son copied it.—When the answer came, there was a new turn in affairs, and the agent was turned out; and my son Jason, who had corresponded privately with his honor occasionally on business, was forthwith desired by his honor to take the accounts into his own hands, and look them over till further orders—It was a very spirited letter, to be sure: Sir Kit sent his service, and the compliments of the season, in return to the agent, and he would fight him with pleasure to-morrow, or any day, for sending him such a letter, if he was born a gentleman, which he was sorry (for both their sakes) to find (too late) he was not.—Then, in a private postscript, he condescended to tell us that all would be speedily settled to his satisfaction, and we should turn over a new leaf, for he was going to be married in a fortnight to the grandest heiress in England, and had only immediate occasion at present for £200, as he would not choose to touch his lady's fortune for travelling expences home to Castle Rackrent, where he intended to be, wind and weather permitting, early in the next month, and desired fires, and the house to be painted, and the new building to go on as fast as possible, for the reception of him and his lady before that time—with several words besides in the letter, which we could not make out, because, God bless him! he wrote in such a flurry—My heart warmed to my new lady when I read this; I was almost afraid it was too good news to be true—but the girls fell to scouring, and it was well they did, for we soon saw his marriage in the paper to a lady with I don't know how many tens of thousand pounds to her fortune—then I watched the post-office for his landing, and the news came to my son of his and the bride being in Dublin, and on the way home to Rackrent Gap—We had bonfires all over the country, expecting him down the next day, and we had his coming of age still to celebrate, which he had not time to do properly before he left the country; therefore a great ball was expected, and great doings upon his coming, as it were, fresh to take possession of his ancestors' estate.— I never shall forget the day he came home—we had waited and waited all day long till eleven o'clock at night, and I was thinking of sending the boy to lock the gates, and giving them up for that night, when there come the carriages thundering up to the great hall door—I got the first sight of the bride; for when the carriage door opened, just as she had her foot on the steps, I·held the flam^g full in her face to light her, at which she shuts her eyes, but I had a full view of the rest of her, and greatly shocked I was, for by that light she was little better than a blackamoor, and seemed crippled, but that was only sitting so long in the chariot—'You're kindly welcome to Castle Rackrent, my lady,' says I, (recollecting who she was)—'Did your honor hear of the bonfires?' His honor spoke never a word, nor so much as handed her up the steps;[26] he looked to me no more like himself than nothing at all; I know I took him for the skeleton of his honor—I was not sure what to say next to one or t'other, but seeing she was a stranger in a foreign country, I thought it but right to speak chearful to her, so I went back again to the bonfires—'My lady (says I, as she crossed the hall) there would have been fifty times as many, but for fear of the horses and frightening your ladyship—Jason and I forbid them, please your honor.' —With that she looked at me a little bewildered—'Will I have a fire lighted in the state room to-night?' was the next question I put to her—but never a word she answered, so I concluded she could not speak a word of English, and was from foreign parts—The short and the long of it was, I couldn't tell what to make of her, so I left her to herself, and went straight down to the servants' hall to learn something for certain about her. Sir Kit's own man was tired, but the groom set him a talking at last, and we had it all out before ever I closed my eyes that night. The bride might well be a great fortune—she was a *Jewish* by all accounts, who are famous for their great riches. I had never seen any of that tribe or nation before, and could only gather that she spoke a strange kind of English of her own, that she could not abide pork or sausages, and went neither to church nor mass.—Mercy upon his honor's poor soul, thought I, what will become of him and his, and all of us, with this heretic Blackamore[27] at the head of the Castle Rackrent estate. I never slept a wink all night for thinking of it, but before the servants I put my pipe in my mouth and kept my mind to myself; for I had a great regard for the family, and after this when strange gentlemen's servants came to the house, and would begin to talk about the bride, I took care to put the best foot foremost, and passed her for a Nabob, in the kitchen, which accounted for her dark complexion, and every thing.

The very morning after they came home, however, I saw how things were, plain enough, between Sir Kit and my lady, though they were walking together arm in arm after breakfast, looking at the new buildings and the improvements. 'Old Thady, (said my master, just as he used to do) how do you do?'—'Very well, I thank your honor's honor,' said I, but I saw he was not well pleased, and my heart was in my mouth as I walked along after him—'Is the large room damp, Thady?' said his honor—'Oh, damp, your honor! how should it but be as dry as a bone, (says I) after all the fires we have kept in it day and night—It's the barrack room[g] your honor's talking on'—'And what is a barrack room, pray, my dear'—were the first words I ever heard out of my lady's lips—'No matter, my dear,' said he, and went on talking to me, ashamed like I should witness her ignorance.—To be sure to hear her talk, one might have taken her for an innocent,[g] for it was 'what's this, Sir Kit? and what's that, Sir Kit?' all the way we went—To be sure, Sir Kit had enough to do to answer her—'And what do you call that, Sir Kit? (said she) that, that looks like a pile of black bricks, pray Sir Kit?' 'My turf stack, my dear,' said my master, and bit his lip—Where have you lived, my lady, all your life, not to know a turf stack when you see it, thought I, but I said nothing. Then, by-and-by, she takes out her glass and begins spying over the country—'And what's all that black swamp out yonder, Sir Kit?' says she—'My bog, my dear,' says he, and went on whistling—'It's a very ugly prospect, my dear,' says she—'You don't see it, my dear, (says he) for we've planted it out, when the trees grow up, in summer time,' says he—'Where are the trees, (said she) my dear,' still looking through her glass—'You are blind, my dear, (says he) what are these under your eyes?'—'These shrubs?' said she—'Trees,' said he—'May be they are what you call trees in Ireland, my dear, (says she) but they are not a yard high, are they?'—'They were planted out but last year, my lady' says I, to soften matters between them, for I saw she was going the way to make his honor mad with her—'they are very well grown for their age, and you'll not see the bog of Allyballycarricko'shaughlin at all at all

through the skreen, when once the leaves come out—
But, my lady, you must not quarrel with any part or parcel of Allyballycarricko'shaughlin, for you don't know
how many hundred years that same bit of bog has been in
the family, we would not part with the bog of Allyballycarricko'shaughlin upon no account at all; it cost the late
Sir Murtagh two hundred good pounds to defend his
title to it, and boundaries, against the O'Learys, who cut
a road through it.'—Now one would have thought this
would have been hint enough for my lady, but she fell
to laughing like one out of their right mind, and made
me say the name of the bog over for her to get it by heart
a dozen times—then she must ask me how to spell it, and
what was the meaning of it in English—Sir Kit standing
by whistling all the while—I verily believe she laid the
corner stone of all her future misfortunes at that very
instant—but I said no more, only looked at Sir Kit.

  There were no balls, no dinners, no doings, the
country was all disappointed—Sir Kit's gentleman said,
in a whisper to me, it was all my lady's own fault, because
she was so obstinate about the cross—'What cross?
(says I) is it about her being a heretic?'—'Oh, no such
matter, (says he) my master does not mind her heresies,
but her diamond cross, it's worth I can't tell you how
much, and she has thousands of English pounds concealed in diamonds about her, which she as good as
promised to give up to my master before he married,
but now she won't part with any of them, and she must
take the consequences.'

Her honey-moon, at least her Irish honey-moon, was scarcely well over, when his honour one morning said to me—'Thady, buy me a pig!'—and then the sausages were ordered, and here was the first open breaking out of my lady's troubles—my lady came down herself into the kitchen to speak to the cook about the sausages, and desired never to see them more at her table.—Now my master had ordered them, and my lady knew that—the cook took my lady's part, because she never came down into the kitchen, and was young and innocent in house-keeping, which raised her pity; besides, said she, at her own table, surely, my lady should order and disorder what she pleases—but the cook soon changed her note, for my master made it a principle to have the sausages, and swore at her for a Jew herself, till he drove her fairly out of the kitchen—then for fear of her place, and be-cause he threatened that my lady should give her no discharge without the sausages, she gave up, and from that day forward always sausages or bacon, or pig meat, in some shape or other, went up to table; upon which my lady shut herself up in her own room, and my master said she might stay there, with an oath; and to make sure of her, he turned the key in the door, and kept it ever after in his pocket—We none of us ever saw or heard her speak for seven years after that*—he carried her dinner

* This part of the history of the Rackrent family can scarcely be thought credible; but in justice to honest Thady, it is hoped the reader will recollect the history of the celebrated Lady Cathcart's conjugal imprisonment.[28]—The Editor was acquainted with Colonel M'Guire, Lady Cathcart's husband; he has lately seen and questioned the maid-servant who lived with Colonel

himself—then his honour had a great deal of company to dine with him, and balls in the house, and was as gay and gallant, and as much himself as before he was married—and at dinner he always drank my lady Rackrent's good health, and so did the company, and he sent out always a servant, with his compliments to my Lady Rackrent, and the company was drinking her

M'Guire during the time of Lady Cathcart's imprisonment.—Her Ladyship was locked up in her own house for many years; during which period her husband was visited by the neighbouring gentry, and it was his regular custom at dinner to send his compliments to Lady Cathcart, informing her that the company had the honor to drink her ladyship's health, and begging to know whether there was any thing at table that she would like to eat? the answer was always—'Lady Cathcart's compliments, and she has every thing she wants'—An instance of honesty in a poor Irishwoman deserves to be recorded.—Lady Cathcart had some remarkably fine diamonds, which she had concealed from her husband, and which she was anxious to get out of the house, lest he should discover them: she had neither servant nor friend to whom she could entrust them; but she had observed a poor beggar-woman who used to come to the house—she spoke to her from the window of the room in which she was confined—the woman promised to do what she desired, and Lady Cathcart threw a parcel, containing the jewels, to her.—The poor woman carried them to the person to whom they were directed; and several years afterwards, when Lady Cathcart recovered her liberty, she received her diamonds safely.

At Colonel M'Guire's death, her ladyship was released.—The Editor, within this year, saw the gentleman who accompanied her to England after her husband's death.—When she first was told of his death, she imagined that the news was not true, and that it was told only with an intention of deceiving her.—At his death she had scarcely cloaths sufficient to cover her; she wore a red wig, looked scared, and her understanding seemed stupified; she said that she scarcely knew one human creature from another: her imprisonment lasted above twenty years.—These circumstances may appear strange to an English reader; but there is no danger in the present times, that any individual should exercise such tyranny as Colonel M'Guire's with impunity, the power being now all in the hands of government, and there being no possibility of obtaining from Parliament an act of indemnity for any cruelties.

ladyship's health, and begged to know if there was any thing at table he might send her; and the man came back, after the sham errand, with my lady Rackrent's compliments, and she was very much obliged to Sir Kit—she did not wish for any thing, but drank the company's health.—The country, to be sure, talked and wondered at my lady's being shut up, but nobody chose to interfere or ask any impertinent questions, for they knew my master was a man very apt to give a short answer himself, and likely to call a man out for it afterwards—he was a famous shot—had killed his man before he came of age, and nobody scarce dare look at him whilst at Bath.—Sir Kit's character was so well known in the county, that he lived in peace and quietness ever after, and was a great favorite with the ladies, especially when in process of time, in the fifth year of her confinement, my lady Stopgap fell ill, and took entirely to her bed, and he gave out that she was now skin and bone, and could not last through the winter.—In this he had two physicians' opinions to back him (for now he called in two physicians for her), and tried all his arts to get the diamond cross from her on her death bed, and to get her to make a will in his favour of her separate possessions—but she was there too tough for him—He used to swear at her behind her back, after kneeling to her to her face, and call her, in the presence of his gentleman, his stiff-necked Israelite, though before he married her, that same gentleman told me he used to call her (how he could bring it out I don't know!) 'my pretty Jessica'[29]—To be sure, it must have been hard for her to guess what sort of a husband he reckoned to make her—when she was lying, to all expectation, on her death-bed, of a broken heart, I could not but pity her, though she was a Jewish; and considering too it was no fault of her's to be taken with my master so young as she was at the Bath, and so fine a gentleman as Sir Kit was when he courted her—and considering too, after all they had heard and seen of him as a husband, there were now no less than three ladies in our county talked of for his second wife, all at daggers drawing with each other, as his gentleman swore, at the balls, for Sir Kit for their partner—I could not but think them bewitched, but they all reasoned with themselves, that Sir Kit would make a good husband to any Christian, but a Jewish, I suppose, and especially as he was now a reformed rake; and it was not known how my lady's fortune was settled in her will, nor how the Castle Rackrent estate was all mortgaged, and bonds out against him, for he was never cured of his gaming tricks—but that was the only fault he had, God bless him!

My lady had a sort of fit, and it was given out she was dead, by mistake; this brought things to a sad crisis for my poor master—one of the three ladies shewed his letters to her brother, and claimed his promises, whilst another did the same. I don't mention names—Sir Kit, in his defence, said he would meet any man who dared question his conduct, and as to the ladies, they must settle it amongst them who was to be his second, and his third, and his fourth, whilst his first was still alive, to his mortification and theirs. Upon this, as upon all former occasions, he had the voice of the country with him, on account of the great spirit and propriety he acted with.—He met and shot the first lady's brother—the next day he called out the second, who had a wooden leg, and their place of meeting by appointment being in a new ploughed field, the wooden leg man stuck fast in it. —Sir Kit seeing his situation, with great candour fired his pistol over his head, upon which the seconds interposed, and convinced the parties there had been a slight misunderstanding between them; thereupon they shook hands cordially, and went home to dinner together.— This gentleman, to shew the world how they stood together, and by the advice of the friends of both parties to re-establish his sister's injured reputation, went out with Sir Kit as his second, and carried his message next day to the last of his adversaries.—I never saw him in such fine spirits as that day he went out—sure enough he was within aims-ace[30] of getting quit handsomely of all his enemies; but unluckily, after hitting the toothpick out of his adversary's finger and thumb, he received a ball in a vital part, and was brought home, in little better than an hour after the affair, speechless, on a hand-barrow, to my lady; we got the key out of his pocket the first thing we did, and my son Jason ran to unlock the barrack-room, where my lady had been shut up for seven years, to acquaint her with the fatal accident. —The surprize bereaved her of her senses at first, nor would she believe but we were putting some new trick upon her, to entrap her out of her jewels, for a great while, till Jason bethought himself of taking her to the window, and shewed her the men bringing Sir Kit up the avenue upon the hand-barrow, which had immediately the desired effect; for directly she burst into tears, and pulling her cross from her bosom, she kissed it with as great devotion as ever I witnessed, and lifting up her eyes to Heaven, uttered some ejaculation, which none present heard—but I take the sense of it to be, she returned thanks for this unexpected interposition in her favour, when she had least reason to expect it.—My master was greatly lamented—there was no life in him when we lifted him off the barrow, so he was laid out immediately, and *waked* the same night.—The country was all in an uproar about him, and not a soul but cried shame upon his murderer, who would have been hanged surely, if he could have been brought to his trial whilst the gentlemen in the county were up about it, but he very prudently withdrew himself to the continent before the affair was made public.—As for the young lady who was the immediate cause of the fatal accident, however innocently, she could never shew her head after at the balls in the county or any place, and by the advice of her friends and physicians she was ordered soon after to Bath, where it was expected, if any where on this side of the grave, she would meet with the recovery of her health and lost peace of mind.—As a proof of his great popularity, I need only add, that there was a song made upon my master's untimely death in the newspapers, which was in every body's mouth, singing up and down through the country, even down to the mountains, only three days after his unhappy exit.—He was also greatly bemoaned at the Curragh,^{g} where his cattle were well known, and all who had taken up his bets formerly were particularly inconsolable for his loss to society.—His stud sold at the cant^g at the greatest price ever known in the country; his favourite horses were chiefly disposed of amongst his particular friends, who would give any price for them for his sake; but no ready money was required by the new heir, who wished not to displease any of the gentlemen of the neighbourhood just upon his coming to settle amongst them; so a long credit was given where requisite, and the cash has never been gathered in from that day to this.

But to return to my lady.—She got surprisingly well after my master's decease. No sooner was it known for certain that he was dead, than all the gentlemen within twenty miles of us came in a body as it were, to set my lady at liberty, and to protest against her confinement, which they now for the first time understood was against her own consent. The ladies too were as attentive as possible, striving who should be foremost with their morning visits; and they that saw the diamonds spoke very handsomely of them, but thought it a pity they were not bestowed, if it had so pleased God, upon a lady who would have become them better. All these civilities wrought little with my lady, for she had taken an unaccountable prejudice against the country and every thing belonging to it, and was so partial to her native land, that after parting with the cook, which she did immediately upon my master's decease, I never knew her easy one instant, night or day, but when she was packing up to leave us. Had she meant to make any stay in Ireland, I stood a great chance of being a great favorite with her, for when she found I understood the weather-cock, she was always finding some pretence to be talking to me, and asking me which way the wind blew, and was it likely, did I think, to continue fair for England.—But when I saw she had made up her mind to spend the rest of her days upon her own income and jewels in England, I considered her quite as a foreigner, and not at all any longer as part of the family.—She gave no vails[31] to the servants at Castle Rackrent at parting, notwithstanding the old proverb of '*as rich as a Jew*,' which, she being a Jewish, they built upon with reason— But from first to last she brought nothing but misfortunes amongst us; and if it had not been all along with her, his honor Sir Kit would have been now alive in all appearance.—Her diamond cross was, they say, at the bottom of it all; and it was a shame for her, being his wife, not to show more duty, and to have given it up when he condescended to ask so often for such a bit of a trifle in his distresses, especially when he all along made it no secret he married for money.—But we will not bestow another thought upon her—This much I thought it lay upon my conscience to say, in justice to my poor master's memory.

'Tis an ill wind that blows nobody no good—the same wind that took the Jew Lady Rackrent over to England brought over the new heir to Castle Rackrent.

Here let me pause for breath in my story, for though I had a great regard for every member of the family, yet without compare Sir Conolly, commonly called for short amongst his friends Sir Condy Rackrent, was ever my great favorite, and indeed the most universally beloved man I had ever seen or heard of, not excepting his great ancestor Sir Patrick, to whose memory he, amongst other instances of generosity, erected a handsome marble stone in the church of Castle Rackrent, setting forth in large letters his age, birth, parentage, and many other virtues, concluding with the compliment so justly due, that 'Sir Patrick Rackrent lived and died a monument of old Irish hospitality.'

CONTINUATION[32] OF THE MEMOIRS

OF THE

RACKRENT FAMILY

HISTORY OF
SIR CONOLLY RACKRENT

Sir Condy Rackrent, by the grace of God heir at law
to the Castle Rackrent estate, was a remote branch of the
family: born to little or no fortune of his own, he was
bred to the bar, at which having many friends to push
him, and no mean natural abilities of his own, he doubtless would in process of time, if he could have borne the
drudgery of that study, have been rapidly made king's
counsel at the least—But things were disposed of otherwise, and he never went circuit but twice, and then made
no figure for want of a fee, and being unable to speak in
public. He received his education chiefly in the college
of Dublin; but before he came to years of discretion,
lived in the country in a small but slated house, within
view of the end of the avenue. I remember him bare-
footed and headed, running through the street of
O'Shaughlin's town, and playing at pitch and toss, ball,
marbles, and what not, with the boys of the town,

amongst whom my son Jason was a great favorite with him. As for me, he was ever my white-headed boy*— often's the time when I would call in at his father's, where I was always made welcome, he would slip down to me in the kitchen, and love to sit on my knee whilst I told him stories of the family and the blood from which he was sprung, and how he might look forward, if the *then* present man should die without childer, to being at the head of the Castle Rackrent estate.—This was then spoke quite and clear at random to please the child, but it pleased Heaven to accomplish my prophecy afterwards, which gave him a great opinion of my judgment in business. He went to a little grammar school with many others, and my son amongst the rest, who was in his class, and not a little useful to him in his book learning, which he acknowledged with gratitude ever after. These rudiments of his education thus completed, he got a horse-back, to which exercise he was ever addicted, and used to gallop over the country whilst yet but a slip of a boy, under the care of Sir Kit's huntsman, who was very fond of him, and often lent him his gun and took him out a shooting under his own eye. By these means he became well acquainted and popular amongst the poor in the neighbourhood early, for there was not a cabin at which he had not stopped some morning or other along with the huntsman, to drink a glass of burnt whiskey out of an egg-shell, to do him good, and warm

* *White-headed boy*—is used by the Irish as an expression of fondness.— It is upon a par with the English term *crony*.—We are at a loss for the derivation of this term.[33]

his heart, and drive the cold out of his stomach.—The old people always told him he was a great likeness of Sir Patrick, which made him first have an ambition to take after him, as far as his fortune should allow. He left us when of an age to enter the college, and there completed his education and nineteenth year; for as he was not born to an estate, his friends thought it incumbent on them to give him the best education which could be had for love or money, and a great deal of money consequently was spent upon him at college and Temple— He was very little altered for the worse, by what he saw there of the great world, for when he came down into the country to pay us a visit we thought him just the same man as ever, hand and glove with every one, and as far from high, though not without his own proper share of family pride, as any man ever you see. Latterly, seeing how Sir Kit and the *Jewish* lived together, and that there was no one between him and the Castle Rackrent estate, he neglected to apply to the law as much as was expected of him, and secretly many of the tenants, and others, advanced him cash upon his note of hand value received, promising bargains of leases and lawful interest should he ever come into the estate.—All this was kept a great secret, for fear the present man hearing of it should take it into his head to take it ill of poor Condy, and so should cut him off for ever by levying a fine, and suffering a recovery to dock the entail^g—Sir Murtagh would have been the man for that, but Sir Kit was too much taken up philandering to consider the law in this case—or any other.—These practices I have mentioned account for the state of his affairs, I mean Sir Condy's, upon his coming into the Castle Rackrent estate.—He could not command a penny of his first year's income, which, and keeping no accounts, and the great sight of company he did, with many other causes too numerous to mention, was the origin of his distresses.—My son Jason, who was now established agent, and knew every thing, explained matters out of the face to Sir Conolly, and made him sensible of his embarrassed situation. With a great nominal rent-roll, it was almost all paid away in interest, which being for convenience suffered to run on, soon doubled the principal, and Sir Condy was obligated to pass new bonds for the interest, now grown principal, and so on. Whilst this was going on, my son requiring to be paid for his trouble, and many years service in the family gratis, and Sir Condy not willing to take his affairs into his own hands, or to look them even in the face, he gave my son a bargain of some acres which fell out of lease at a reasonable rent; Jason set the land as soon as his lease was sealed to under-tenants, to make the rent, and got two hundred a year profit rent, which was little enough, considering his long agency.—He bought the land at twelve years purchase two years afterwards, when Sir Condy was pushed for money on an execution, and was at the same time allowed for his improvements thereon. There was a sort of hunting lodge upon the estate convenient to my son Jason's land, which he had his eye upon about this time; and he was a little jealous of Sir Condy, who talked of setting it to a stranger, who was just come into the country—Captain Moneygawl was the man; he was son and heir to the Moneygawls of Mount Juliet's town, who had a great estate in the next county to ours, and my master was loth to disoblige the young gentleman, whose heart was set upon the lodge; so he wrote him back that the lodge was at his service, and if he would honor him with his company at Castle Rackrent, they could ride over together some morning and look at it before signing the lease.— Accordingly the Captain came over to us, and he and Sir Condy grew the greatest friends ever you see, and were for ever out a shooting or a hunting together, and were very merry in the evenings, and Sir Condy was invited of course to Mount Juliet's town, and the family intimacy that had been in Sir Patrick's time was now recollected, and nothing would serve Sir Condy but he must be three times a week at the least with his new friends—which grieved me, who knew by the Captain's groom and gentleman how they talked of him at Mount Juliet's town, making him quite, as one may say, a laughing stock and a butt for the whole company: but they were soon cured of *that* by an accident that surprised 'em not a little, as it did me.—There was a bit of a scrawl found upon the waiting maid of old Mr. Moneygawl's youngest daughter Miss Isabella, that laid open the whole; and her father, they say, was like one out of his right mind, and swore it was the last thing he ever should have thought of when he invited my master to his house, that his daughter should think of such a match.—But their talk signified not a straw; for as Miss Isabella's maid reported, her young mistress was fallen over head and ears in love with Sir Condy, from the first time that ever her brother brought him into the house to dinner: the servant who waited that day behind my master's chair was the first who knew it, as he says; though it's hard to believe him, for he did not tell till a great while afterwards; but however, it's likely enough as the thing turned out that he was not far out of the way; for towards the middle of dinner, as he says, they were talking of stage plays, having a play-house, and being great play actors at Mount Juliet's town, and Miss Isabella turns short to my master and says—'Have you seen the play-bill, Sir Condy?'—'No, I have not,' said he.—'Then more shame for you, (said the Captain her brother) not to know that my sister is to play Juliet to-night, who plays it better than any woman on or off the stage in all Ireland.'—'I am very happy to hear it,' said Sir Condy, and there the matter dropped for the present; but Sir Condy all this time, and a great while afterwards, was at a terrible nonplus, for he had no liking not he to stage plays, nor to Miss Isabella either; to his mind, as it came out over a bowl of whiskey punch at home, his little Judy M'Quirk, who was daughter to a sister's son of mine, was worth twenty of Miss Isabella —He had seen her often when he stopped at her father's cabin to drink whiskey out of the egg-shell, out of hunting, before he came to the estate, and as she gave out

was under something like a promise of marriage to her—
Any how I could not but pity my poor master, who was
so bothered between them, and he an easy-hearted man
that could not disoblige nobody, God bless him. To be
sure it was not his place to behave ungenerous to Miss
Isabella, who had disobliged all her relations for his
sake, as he remarked; and then she was locked up in her
chamber and forbid to think of him any more, which
raised his spirit, because his family was, as he observed,
as good as theirs at any rate, and the Rackrents a suitable
match for the Moneygawls any day in the year; all which
was true enough; but it grieved me to see that upon the
strength of all this Sir Condy was growing more in the
mind to carry off Miss Isabella to Scotland, in spite of
her relations, as she desired.

'It's all over with our poor Judy!' said I, with a heavy
sigh, making bold to speak to him one night when he was
a little cheerful, and standing in the servant's hall all
alone with me, as was often his custom—'Not at all (said
he) I never was fonder of Judy than at this present speaking, and to prove it to you, (said he, and he took from my
hand a halfpenny, change that I had just got along with
my tobacco); and to prove it to you, Thady, says he,
it's a toss up with me which I shall marry this minute,
her or Mr. Moneygawl of Mount Juliet's Town's daughter—so it is'—'Oh, boo! boo*! (says I, making light of
it, to see what he would go on to next)—your honor's
joking, to be sure, there's no compare between our poor

* *Boo! Boo!* an exclamation equivalent to *Pshaw!* or *Nonsense*.

Judy and Miss Isabella, who has a great fortune, they
say.'—'I'm not a man to mind a fortune, nor never was,
(said Sir Condy proudly,) whatever her friends may say;
and to make short of it, (says he) I'm come to a determination upon the spot;' with that he swore such a terrible
oath, as made me cross myself*—'and by this book,
(said he, snatching up my ballad book, mistaking it for
my prayer-book, which lay in the window)—and by this
book, (said he) and by all the books that ever were shut
and opened—it's come to a toss up with me, and I'll
stand or fall by the toss, and so, Thady, hand me over
that *pin*† out of the ink-horn,' and he makes a cross on
the smooth side of the halfpenny[34]—'Judy M'Quirk,
(said he) her mark,‡' God bless him! his hand was a little
unsteadied by all the whiskey punch he had taken, but
it was plain to see his heart was for poor Judy.—My
heart was all as one as in my mouth, when I saw the
halfpenny up in the air, but I said nothing at all, and
when it came down, I was glad I had kept myself to
myself, for to be sure now it was all over with poor

* *As made me cross myself*—The Roman Catholics. [35]
† *Pin* read *pen*—it formerly was vulgarly pronounced *pin* in Ireland.
‡ *Her mark*—It *was* the custom in Ireland for those who could not write,
to make a cross to stand for their signature, as was formerly the practice of
our English monarchs.—The Editor inserts the facsimile of an Irish *mark*,
which may hereafter be valuable to a judicious antiquary—

Her
Judy   ×   M'Quirk
Mark.

In bonds or notes, signed in this manner, a witness is requisite, as the name
is frequently written by him or her.

Judy.—'Judy's out a luck,' said I, striving to laugh—
'I'm out a luck,' said he, and I never saw a man look so
cast down; he took up the halfpenny off the flag, and
walked away quite sobered like by the shock.—Now
though as easy a man you would think as any in the wide
world, there was no such thing as making him unsay
one of these sort of vows,* which he had learned to
reverence when young, as I well remember teaching
him to toss up for bog berries on my knee.—So I saw
the affair was as good as settled between him and Miss
Isabella, and I had no more to say but to wish her joy,
which I did the week afterwards upon her return from
Scotland with my poor master.

My new lady was young, as might be supposed of a
lady that had been carried off by her own consent to
Scotland, but I could only see her at the first through
her veil, which, from bashfulness or fashion, she kept
over her face—'And am I to walk through all this crowd
of people, my dearest love?' said she to Sir Condy, meaning us servants and tenants, who had gathered at the
back gate—'My dear (said Sir Condy) there's nothing
for it but to walk, or to let me carry you as far as the

* *Vows*—It has been maliciously and unjustly hinted, that the lower classes
of the people in Ireland pay but little regard to oaths; yet it is certain that
some oaths or vows have great power over their minds.—Sometimes they
swear they will be revenged on some of their neighbours; this is an oath they
never are known to break.—But what is infinitely more extraordinary and
unaccountable, they sometimes make a vow against whiskey; these vows are
usually limited to a short time.—A woman who has a drunken husband is
most fortunate if she can prevail upon him to go to the priest, and make a vow
against whiskey for a year, or a month, or a week, or a day.

house, for you see the back road's too narrow for a carriage, and the great piers have tumbled down across the front approach, so there's no driving the right way by reason of the ruins'—'Plato, thou reasonest well!'[36] said she, or words to that effect, which I could no ways understand; and again, when her foot stumbled against a broken bit of a car wheel, she cried out—'Angels and ministers of grace, defend us!'[37]—Well, thought I, to be sure if she's no Jewish like the last, she is a mad woman for certain, which is as bad: it would have been as well for my poor master to have taken up with poor Judy, who is in her right mind any how.

She was dressed like a mad woman, moreover, more than like any one I ever saw afore or since, and I could not take my eyes off her, but still followed behind her, and her feathers on the top of her hat were broke going in at the low back door, and she pulled out her little bottle out of her pocket to smell to when she found herself in the kitchen, and said, 'I shall faint with the heat of this odious, odious place'—'My dear, it's only three steps across the kitchen, and there's a fine air if your veil was up,' said Sir Condy, and with that threw back her veil, so that I had then a full sight of her face; she had not at all the colour of one going to faint, but a fine complexion of her own, as I then took it to be, though her maid told me after it was all put on; but even complexion and all taken in, she was no way, in point of good looks, to compare to poor Judy; and with all she had a quality toss with her; but may be it was my over partiality to

Judy, into whose place I may say she stept, that made me notice all this.—To do her justice, however, she was, when we came to know her better, very liberal in her house-keeping, nothing at all of the Skin-flint in her; she left every thing to the housekeeper, and her own maid, Mrs. Jane, who went with her to Scotland, gave her the best of characters for generosity; she seldom or ever wore a thing twice the same way, Mrs. Jane told us, and was always pulling her things to pieces, and giving them away, never being used in her father's house to think of expence in any thing—and she reckoned, to be sure, to go on the same way at Castle Rackrent; but when I came to enquire, I learned that her father was so mad with her for running off after his locking her up, and forbidding her to think any more of Sir Condy, that he would not give her a farthing; and it was lucky for her she had a few thousands of her own, which had been left to her by a good grandmother, and these were very convenient to begin with. My master and my lady set out in great stile; they had the finest coach and chariot, and horses and liveries, and cut the greatest dash in the county, returning their wedding visits!—and it was immediately reported that her father had undertaken to pay all my master's debts, and of course all his tradesmen gave him a new credit, and every thing went on smack smooth, and I could not but admire my lady's spirit, and was proud to see Castle Rackrent again in all its glory.—My lady had a fine taste for building and furniture, and play-houses, and she turned every thing topsy-turvy, and made the barrack-room into a theatre, as she called it, and she went on as if she had a mint of money at her elbow; and to be sure I thought she knew best, especially as Sir Condy said nothing to it one way or the other. All he asked, God bless him! was to live in peace and quietness, and have his bottle, or his whiskey punch at night to himself.—Now this was little enough, to be sure, for any gentleman, but my lady couldn't abide the smell of the whiskey punch.—'My dear, (says he) you liked it well enough before we were married, and why not now?'—'My dear, (said she) I never smelt it, or I assure you I should never have prevailed upon myself to marry you.'—'My dear, I am sorry you did not smell it, but we can't help that now, (returned my master, without putting himself in a passion, or going out of his way, but just fair and easy helped himself to another glass, and drank it off to her good health). All this the butler told me, who was going backwards and forwards unnoticed with the jug, and hot water, and sugar, and all he thought wanting.—Upon my master's swallowing the last glass of whiskey punch, my lady burst into tears, calling him an ungrateful, base, barbarous wretch! and went off into a fit of hysterics, as I think Mrs. Jane called it, and my poor master was greatly frighted, this being the first thing of the kind he had seen; and he fell straight on his knees before her, and, like a good-hearted cratur as he was, ordered the whiskey punch out of the room, and bid 'em throw open all the windows, and cursed himself, and then my lady came to herself again, and

when she saw him kneeling there, bid him get up, and
not forswear himself any more, for that she was sure
he did not love her, nor never had: this we learnt
from Mrs. Jane, who was the only person left present
at all this—'My dear, (returns my master, thinking to
be sure of Judy, as well he might) whoever told you so
is an incendiary, and I'll have 'em turned out of the
house this minute, if you'll only let me know which of
them it was.'—'Told me what?' says my lady, starting
upright in her chair.—'Nothing, nothing at all, (said
my master, seeing he had overshot himself, and that my
lady spoke at random) but what you said just now that
I did not love you, Bella, who told you that?'—'My own
sense,' said she, and she put her handkerchief to her face,
and leant back upon Mrs. Jane, and fell to sobbing as
if her heart would break.—'Why now Bella, this is very
strange of you, (said my poor master) if nobody has
told you nothing, what is it you are taking on for at this
rate,[38] and exposing yourself and me for this way?'—'Oh
say no more, say no more, every word you say kills me,
(cried my lady, and she ran on like one, as Mrs. Jane says,
raving)—Oh Sir Condy, Sir Condy! I that had hoped to
find in you "my father, brother, husband, friend".'[39]—
'Why now faith this is a little too much; do Bella, try to
recollect yourself, my dear; am not I your husband, and
of your own chusing, and is not that enough?'—'Oh
too much! too much!' cried my lady, wringing her
hands.—'Why, my dear, come to your right senses for
the love of heaven—see is not the whiskey punch, jug

and bowl and all, gone out of the room long ago? what is it in the wide world you have to complain of?'—But still my lady sobbed and sobbed, and called herself the most wretched of women; and among other out of the way provoking things, asked my master, was he fit company for her, and he drinking all night.—This nettling him, which it was hard to do, he replied, that as to drinking all night, he was then as sober as she was herself, and that it was no matter how much a man drank, provided it did no ways affect or stagger him—that as to being fit company for her, he thought himself of a family to be fit company for any lord or lady in the land, but that he never prevented her from seeing and keeping what company she pleased, and that he had done his best to make Castle Rackrent pleasing to her since her marriage, having always had the house full of visitors, and if her own relations were not amongst them, he said, that was their own fault and their pride's fault, of which he was sorry to find her ladyship had so unbecoming a share—So concluding, he took his candle and walked off to his room, and my lady was in her tantarums for three days after, and would have been so much longer, no doubt, but some of her friends, young ladies and cousins and second cousins, came to Castle Rackrent, by my poor master's express invitation, to see her, and she was in a hurry to get up, as Mrs. Jane called it, a play for them, and so got well, and was as finely dressed and as happy to look at as ever, and all the young ladies who used to be in her room dressing of her said in

Mrs. Jane's hearing, that my lady was the happiest bride ever they had seen, and that to be sure a love match was the only thing for happiness, where the parties could any way afford it.

As to affording it, God knows it was little they knew of the matter; my lady's few thousands could not last for ever, especially the way she went on with them, and letters from tradesfolk came every post thick and three-fold, with bills as long as my arm of years and years standing; my son Jason had 'em all handed over to him, and the pressing letters were all unread by Sir Condy, who hated trouble and could never be brought to hear talk of business, but still put it off and put it off, saying— settle it any how, or bid 'em call again to-morrow, or speak to me about it some other time.—Now it was hard to find the right time to speak, for in the mornings he was a-bed and in the evenings over his bottle, where no gentleman chuses to be disturbed.—Things in a twelve-month or so came to such a pass, there was no making a shift to go on any longer, though we were all of us well enough used to live from hand to mouth at Castle Rack-rent. One day, I remember, when there was a power of company, all sitting after dinner in the dusk, not to say dark, in the drawing-room, my lady having rung five times for candles and none to go up, the housekeeper sent up the footman, who went to my mistress and whispered behind her chair how it was.—'My lady, (says he) there are no candles in the house.'—'Bless me, (says she) then take a horse, and gallop off as fast as you can to Carrick O'Fungus and get some.'—'And in the mean time tell them to step into the play-house, and try if there are not some bits left,' added Sir Condy, who happened to be within hearing. The man was sent up again to my lady, to let her know there was no horse to go but one that wanted a shoe.—'Go to Sir Condy, then, I know nothing at all about the horses, (said my lady) why do you plague me with these things?'—How it was settled I really forget, but to the best of my remembrance, the boy was sent down to my son Jason's to borrow candles for the night. Another time in the winter, and on a desperate cold day, there was no turf in for the parlour and above stairs, and scarce enough for the cook in the kitchen, the little *gossoon** was sent off to the neighbours to see and beg or borrow some, but none could he bring back with him for love or money; so as needs must we were forced to trouble Sir Condy—'Well, and if there's no turf to be had in the town or country, why what signifies talking any more about it, can't ye go and cut down a tree?'[40]—'Which tree, please your honor?' I made bold to say.—'Any tree at all that's good to burn, (said Sir Condy); send off smart, and get one down and the fires lighted before my lady gets up to breakfast, or the house will be too hot to hold us.'—He was always

---

* *Gossoon*—a little boy—from the French word *Garçon*.—In most Irish families there *used* to be a bare-footed Gossoon, who was slave to the cook and the butler, and who in fact, without wages, did all the hard work of the house.—Gossoons were always employed as messengers.—The Editor has known a gossoon to go on foot, without shoes or stockings, fifty-one English miles between sun-rise and sun-set.

very considerate in all things about my lady, and she
wanted for nothing whilst he had it to give.—Well,
when things were tight with them about this time, my
son Jason put in a word again about the lodge, and made
a genteel offer to lay down the purchase money to relieve
Sir Condy's distresses.—Now Sir Condy had it from
the best authority, that there were two writs come down
to the Sheriff [41] against his person, and the Sheriff, as
ill luck would have it, was no friend of his, and talked
how he must do his duty, and how he would do it, if it
was against the first man in the county, or even his own
brother, let alone one who had voted against him at the
last election, as Sir Condy had done.—So Sir Condy
was fain to take the purchase money of the lodge from
my son Jason to settle matters; and sure enough it was
a good bargain for both parties, for my son bought the
fee simple of a good house for him and his heirs for ever
for little or nothing, and by selling of it for that same my
master saved himself from a gaol. Every way it turned
out fortunate for Sir Condy; for before the money was
all gone there came a general election, and he being so
well beloved in the county, and one of the oldest families,
no one had a better right to stand candidate for the
vacancy; and he was called upon by all his friends, and
the whole county I may say, to declare himself against
the old member, who had little thought of a contest.
My master did not relish the thoughts of a troublesome
canvas, and all the ill will he might bring upon himself
by disturbing the peace of the county, besides the

expence, which was no trifle; but all his friends called
upon one another to subscribe, and formed themselves
into a committee, and wrote all his circular letters for
him, and engaged all his agents, and did all the business
unknown to him, and he was well pleased that it should
be so at last, and my lady herself was very sanguine
about the election, and there was open house kept night
and day at Castle Rackrent, and I thought I never saw
my lady look so well in her life as she did at that time;
there were grand dinners, and all the gentlemen drinking success to Sir Condy till they were carried off; and
then dances and balls, and the ladies all finishing with
a raking pot of tea^g in the morning. Indeed it was well
the company made it their choice to sit up all nights, for
there was not half beds enough[42] for the sights of people
that were in it, though there were shake downs in the
drawing-room always made up before sun-rise, for those
that liked it. For my part, when I saw the doings that
were going on, and the loads of claret that went down
the throats of them that had no right to be asking for it,
and the sights of meat that went up to table and never
came down, besides what was carried off to one or
t'other below stairs, I couldn't but pity my poor master
who was to pay for all, but I said nothing for fear of
gaining myself ill will. The day of election will come
some time or other, says I to myself, and all will be
over—and so it did, and a glorious day it was as any
I ever had the happiness to see; huzza! huzza! Sir Condy
Rackrent for ever, was the first thing I hears in the

morning, and the same and nothing else all day, and not a soul sober only just when polling, enough to give their votes as became 'em, and to stand the brow-beating of the lawyers who came tight enough upon us; and many of our freeholders were knocked off, having never a free-hold that they could safely swear to, and Sir Condy was not willing to have any man perjure himself for his sake, as was done on the other side, God knows, but no matter for that.—Some of our friends were dumb-founded, by the lawyers asking them—had they ever been upon the ground where their freeholds lay?—Now Sir Condy being tender of the consciences of them that had not been on the ground, and so could not swear to a freehold when cross-examined by them lawyers, sent out for a couple of cleaves-full of the sods of his farm of Gultee-shinnagh:[43] and as soon as the sods came into town he set each man upon his sod, and so then ever after, you know, they could fairly swear they had been upon the ground*.—We gained the day by this piece of honesty.[44] I thought I should have died in the streets for joy when I seed my poor master chaired, and he bare-headed and it raining as hard as it could pour; but all the crowds following him up and down, and he bowing and shaking hands with the whole town.—'Is that Sir Condy Rack-rent in the chair?' says a stranger man in the crowd—'The same,' says I—who else should it be? God bless him!'—'And I take it then you belong to him,' says he.—'Not at all,' (says I) 'but I live under him, and have done

* This was actually done at an election in Ireland.

so these two hundred years and upwards, me and mine.'
—'It's lucky for you, then,' rejoins he, 'that he is where
he is, for was he any where else but in the chair this
minute he'd be in a worse place, for I was sent down on
purpose to put him up*, and here's my order for so
doing in my pocket.'—It was a writ that villain the wine
merchant had marked against my poor master, for some
hundreds of an old debt which it was a shame to be
talking of at such a time as this.—'Put it in your pocket
again, and think no more of it any ways for seven years
to come, my honest friend, (says I), he's a member a
Parliament now, praised be God, and such as you can't
touch him; and if you'll take a fool's advice, I'd have ye
keep out of the way this day, or you'll run a good chance
of getting your deserts amongst my master's friends,
unless you chuse to drink his health like every body
else.'—'I've no objection to that in life,' said he; so we
went into one of the public houses kept open for my
master, and we had a great deal of talk about this thing
and that, and 'how is it (says he) your master keeps on so
well upon his legs; I heard say he was off Holantide
twelve-month past.'—'Never was better or heartier in
his life,' said I.—'It's not that I'm after speaking of,
(said he) but there was a great report of his being ruined.'
—'No matter, (says I) the Sheriffs two years running
were his particular friends, and the Sub-sheriffs were
both of them gentlemen, and were properly spoken to;
and so the writs lay snug with them, and they, as I

* *To put him up*—to put him in gaol.

understand by my son Jason the custom in them cases is, returned the writs as they came to them to those that sent 'em, much good may it do them, with word in Latin that no such person as Sir Condy Rackrent, Bart. was to be found in those parts.'—'Oh, I understand all those ways better, no offence, than you,' says he, laughing, and at the same time filling his glass to my master's good health, which convinced me he was a warm friend in his heart after all, though appearances were a little suspicious or so at first.—'To be sure, (says he, still cutting his joke) when a man's over head and shoulders in debt, he may live the faster for it and the better if he goes the right way about it—or else how is it so many live on so well, as we see every day, after they are ruined?'— 'How is it, (says I, being a little merry at the time) how is it but just as you see the ducks in the kitchen yard just after their heads are cut off by the cook, running round and round faster than when alive.'—At which conceit he fell a laughing, and remarked he had never had the happiness yet to see the chicken yard at Castle Rackrent.—'It won't be long so, I hope, (says I) you'll be kindly welcome there, as every body is made by my master; there is not a freer spoken gentleman or a better beloved, high or low, in all Ireland.'—And of what passed after this I'm not sensible, for we drank Sir Condy's good health and the downfall of his enemies till we could stand no longer ourselves—And little did I think at the time, or till long after, how I was harbouring my poor master's greatest of enemies myself. This fellow had the impudence, after coming to see the chicken-yard, to get me to introduce him to my son Jason—little more than the man that never was born did I guess at his meaning by this visit; he gets him a correct list fairly drawn out from my son Jason of all my master's debts, and goes straight round to the creditors and buys them all up, which he did easy enough, seeing the half of them never expected to see their money out of Sir Condy's hands. Then when this base-minded limb of the law, as I afterwards detected him in being, grew to be sole creditor over all, he takes him out a custodiam[45] on all the denominations and sub-denominations, and every carton and half carton[g] upon the estate—and not content with that, must have an execution against the master's goods and down to the furniture, though little worth, of Castle Rackrent itself.—But this is a part of my story I'm not come to yet, and it's bad to be fore-stalling—ill news flies fast enough all the world over. To go back to the day of the election, which I never think of but with pleasure and tears of gratitude for those good times; after the election was quite and clean over, there comes shoals of people from all parts, claiming to have obliged my master with their votes, and putting him in mind of promises which he could never remember himself to have made—one was to have a freehold for each of his four sons—another was to have a renewal of a lease—another an abatement—one came to be paid ten guineas for a pair of silver buckles sold my master on the hustings, which turned out to be no better than copper gilt—another had a long bill for oats, the half of which never went into the granary to my certain knowledge, and the other half were not fit for the cattle to touch; but the bargain was made the week before the election, and the coach and saddle horses were got into order for the day, besides a vote fairly got by them oats—so no more reasoning on that head—but then there was no end to them that were telling Sir Condy he had engaged to make their sons excisemen, or high constables, or the like; and as for them that had bills to give in for liquor, and beds, and straw, and ribbons, and horses, and post-chaises for the gentlemen freeholders that came from all parts and other counties to vote for my master, and were not, to be sure, to be at any charges, there was no standing against all these; and worse than all the gentlemen of my master's committee, who managed all for him, and talked how they'd bring him in without costing him a penny, and subscribed by hundreds very genteelly, forgot to pay their subscriptions, and had laid out in agents and lawyers, fees and secret service money, the Lord knows how much, and my master could never ask one of them for their subscription, you are sensible, nor for the price of a fine horse he had sold one of them, so it all was left at his door. He could never, God bless him again, I say, bring himself to ask a gentleman for money, despising such sort of conversation himself; but others, who were not gentlemen born, behaved very uncivil in pressing him at this very time, and all he could do to content 'em all was to take himself out of the way as fast as possible to Dublin, where my lady had taken a house as fitting for him, a Member of Parliament, to attend his duty in there all the winters.— I was very lonely when the whole family was gone, and all the things they had ordered to go and forgot sent after them by the stage. There was then a great silence in Castle Rackrent, and I went moping from room to room, hearing the doors clap for want of right locks, and the wind through the broken windows that the glazier never would come to mend, and the rain coming through the roof and best ceilings all over the house, for want of the slater whose bill was not paid; besides our having no slates or shingles for that part of the old building which was shingled, and burnt when the chimney took fire, and had been open to the weather ever since. I took myself to the servants' hall in the evening to smoke my pipe as usual, but missed the bit of talk we used to have there sadly, and ever after was content to stay in the kitchen and boil my little potatoes*, and put up my bed there; and every post day I looked in the newspaper, but no news of my master in the house.—He never spoke good or bad—but, as the butler wrote down word to my son Jason, was very ill used by the government about a place that was promised him and never given, after his supporting them against his conscience very honorably, and being greatly abused for it, which hurt him greatly,

---

* *My little potatoes*—Thady does not mean by this expression that his potatoes were less than other people's, or less than the usual size—*little* is here used only as an Italian diminutive, expressive of fondness.

he having the name of a great patriot in the country before. The house and living in Dublin too was not to be had for nothing, and my son Jason said Sir Condy must soon be looking out for a new agent, for I've done my part and can do no more—if my lady had the bank of Ireland to spend, it would go all in one winter, and Sir Condy would never gainsay her, though he does not care the rind of a lemon for her all the while.

Now I could not bear to hear Jason giving out after this manner against the family, and twenty people standing by in the street. Ever since he had lived at the Lodge of his own he looked down, howsomever, upon poor old Thady, and was grown quite a great gentleman, and had none of his relations near him—no wonder he was no kinder to poor Sir Condy than to his own kith and kin*. —In the spring it was the villain that got the list of the debts from him brought down the custodiam, Sir Condy still attending his duty in Parliament; and I could scarcely believe my own old eyes, or the spectacles with which I read it, when I was shewn my son Jason's name joined in the custodiam; but he told me it was only for form's sake, and to make things easier, than if all the land was under the power of a total stranger.—Well, I did not know what to think—it was hard to be talking ill of my own, and I could not but grieve for my poor master's fine estate, all torn by these vultures of the law; so I said nothing, but just looked on to see how it would all end.

* *Kith and kin*—family or relations—*Kin* from *kind*—*Kith* from—— we know not what.

It was not till the month of June that he and my lady came down to the country.—My master was pleased to take me aside with him to the brewhouse that same evening, to complain to me of my son and other matters, in which he said he was confident I had neither art nor part: he said a great deal more to me, to whom he had been fond to talk ever since he was my white-headed boy before he came to the estate, and all that he said about poor Judy I can never forget, but scorn to repeat. —He did not say an unkind word of my lady, but wondered, as well he might, her relations would do nothing for him or her, and they in all this great distress.—He did not take any thing long to heart, let it be as it would, and had no more malice or thought of the like in him than the child that can't speak; this night it was all out of his head before he went to his bed.—He took his jug of whiskey punch—My lady was grown quite easy about the whiskey punch by this time, and so I did suppose all was going on right betwixt them, till I learnt the truth through Mrs. Jane, who talked over their affairs to the housekeeper, and I within hearing. The night my master came home, thinking of nothing at all, but just making merry, he drank his bumper toast 'to the deserts of that old curmudgeon my father-in-law, and all enemies at Mount Juliet's town.'—Now my lady was no longer in the mind she formerly was, and did no ways relish hearing her own friends abused in her presence, she said.—'Then why don't they shew themselves your friends, (said my master,) and oblige me with the loan of the money I condescended, by your advice, my dear, to ask?—It's now three posts since I sent off my letter, desiring in the postscript a speedy answer by the return of the post, and no account at all from them yet.'— 'I expect they'll write to *me* next post,' says my lady, and that was all that passed then; but it was easy from this to guess there was a coolness betwixt them, and with good cause.

The next morning being post day, I sent off the gossoon early to the post-office to see was there any letter likely to set matters to rights, and he brought back one with the proper post-mark upon it, sure enough, and I had no time to examine, or make any conjecture more about it, for into the servants' hall pops Mrs. Jane with a blue bandbox in her hand, quite entirely mad.— 'Dear Ma'am, and what's the matter?' says I.—'Matter enough, (says she) don't you see my band-box is wet through, and my best bonnet here spoiled, besides my lady's, and all by the rain coming in through that gallery window, that you might have got mended if you'd had any sense, Thady, all the time we were in town in the winter.'—'Sure I could not get the glazier, Ma'am,' says I.—'You might have stopped it up any how,' says she.—'So I did, Ma'am, to the best of my ability, one of the panes with the old pillow-case, and the other with a piece of the old stage green curtain—sure I was as careful as possible all the time you were away, and not a drop of rain came in at that window of all the windows in the house, all winter, Ma'am, when under my care;

and now the family's come home, and it's summer time, I never thought no more about it to be sure—but dear, it's a pity to think of your bonnet, Ma'am—but here's what will please you, Ma'am, a letter from Mount Juliet's town for my lady.' With that she snatches it from me without a word more, and runs up the back stairs to my mistress; I follows with a slate to make up the window—this window was in the long passage, or gallery, as my lady gave out orders to have it called, in the gallery leading to my master's bed-chamber and her's, and when I went up with the slate, the door having no lock, and the bolt spoilt, was a-jar after Mrs. Jane, and as I was busy with the window, I heard all that was saying within.

'Well, what's in your letter, Bella, my dear? (says he) you're a long time spelling it over.'—'Won't you shave this morning, Sir Condy,' says she, and put the letter in her pocket.—'I shaved the day before yesterday, (says he) my dear,[46] and that's not what I'm thinking of now—but any thing to oblige you, and to have peace and quietness, my dear'—and presently I had a glimpse of him at the cracked glass over the chimney-piece, standing up shaving himself to please my lady.—But she took no notice, but went on reading her book, and Mrs. Jane doing her hair behind.—'What is it you're reading there, my dear?—phoo, I've cut myself with this razor; the man's a cheat that sold it me, but I have not paid him for it yet—What is it you're reading there? did you hear me asking you, my dear?' 'The sorrows of Werter,'[47] replies my lady, as well as I could hear.—'I think more of the sorrows of Sir Condy, (says my master, joking like).—What news from Mount Juliet's town?'—'No news, (says she) but the old story over again; my friends all reproaching me still for what I can't help now.'—'Is it for marrying me, (said my master, still shaving); what signifies, as you say, talking of that when it can't be helped now.'

With that she heaved a great sigh, that I heard plain enough in the passage.—'And did not you use me basely, Sir Condy, (says she) not to tell me you were ruined before I married you?'—'Tell you, my dear, (said he) did you ever ask me one word about it? and had not you friends enough of your own, that were telling you nothing else from morning to night, if you'd have listened to them slanders.'—'No slanders, nor are my friends slanderers; and I can't bear to hear them treated with disrespect as I do, (says my lady, and took out her pocket handkerchief)—they are the best of friends, and if I had taken their advice—But my father was wrong to lock me up, I own; that was the only unkind thing I can charge him with; for if he had not locked me up, I should never have had a serious thought of running away as I did.'—'Well, my dear, (said my master) don't cry and make yourself uneasy about it now, when it's all over, and you have the man of your own choice in spite of 'em all.'—'I was too young, I know, to make a choice at the time you ran away with me, I'm sure,' says my lady, and another sigh, which made my master, half

shaved as he was, turn round upon her in surprise—
'Why Bella, (says he) you can't deny what you know as
well as I do, that it was at your own particular desire,
and that twice under your own hand and seal expressed,
that I should carry you off as I did to Scotland, and
marry you there.'—'Well, say no more about it, Sir
Condy, (said my lady, pettish like)—I was a child then,
you know.'—'And as far as I know, you're little better
now, my dear Bella, to be talking in this manner to your
husband's *face*; but I won't take it ill of you, for I know
it's something in that letter you put in your pocket just
now, that has set you against me all on a sudden, and
imposed upon your understanding.'—'It is not so very
easy as you think it, Sir Condy, to impose upon *my*
understanding', (said my lady)—'My dear, (says he)
I have, and with reason, the best opinion of your understanding of any man now breathing, and you know I
have never set my own in competition with it; till now,
my dear Bella, (says he, taking her hand from her book
as kind as could be,) till now—when I have the great
advantage of being quite cool, and you not; so don't
believe one word your friends say against your own Sir
Condy, and lend me the letter out of your pocket, till
I see what it is they can have to say.'—'Take it then,
(says she,) and as you are quite cool, I hope it is a proper
time to request you'll allow me to comply with the wishes
of all my own friends, and return to live with my father
and family, during the remainder of my wretched
existence, at Mount Juliet's Town.'

At this my poor master fell back a few paces, like one that had been shot—'You're not serious, Bella, (says he) and could you find it in your heart to leave me this way in the very middle of my distresses, all alone?'—But recollecting himself after his first surprise, and a moment's time for reflection, he said, with a great deal of consideration for my lady—'Well, Bella, my dear, I believe you are right; for what could you do at Castle Rackrent, and an execution against the goods coming down, and the furniture to be canted, and an auction in the house all next week—so you have my full consent to go, since that is your desire, only you must not think of my accompanying you, which I could not in honour do upon the terms I always have been since our marriage with your friends; besides I have business to transact at home—so in the mean time, if we are to have any breakfast this morning, let us go down and have it for the last time in peace and comfort, Bella.'

Then as I heard my master coming to the passage door, I finished fastening up my slate against the broken pane, and when he came out, I wiped down the window seat with my wig*, bade him a good morrow as kindly

* Wigs were formerly used instead of brooms in Ireland, for sweeping or dusting tables, stairs, &c. The Editor doubted the fact, till he saw a labourer of the old school sweep down a flight of stairs with his wig; he afterwards put it on his head again with the utmost composure, and said, 'Oh please your honour, it's never a bit the worse.'

It must be acknowledged that these men are not in any danger of catching cold by taking off their wigs occasionally, because they usually have fine crops of hair growing under their wigs.—The wigs are often yellow, and the hair which appears from beneath them black; the wigs are usually too small, and are raised up by the hair beneath, or by the ears of the wearers.

as I could, seeing he was in trouble, though he strove and thought to hide it from me.—'This window is all racked and tattered, (says I,) and it's what I'm striving to mend.' 'It *is* all racked and tattered plain enough, (says he) and never mind mending it, honest old Thady, says he, it will do well enough for you and I, and that's all the company we shall have left in the house by-and-bye.'—'I'm sorry to see your honour so low this morning, (says I,) but you'll be better after taking your breakfast.'—'Step down to the servants' hall, (says he) and bring me up the pen and ink into the parlour, and get a sheet of paper from Mrs. Jane, for I have business that can't brook to be delayed, and come into the parlour with the pen and ink yourself, Thady, for I must have you to witness my signing a paper I have to execute in a hurry.'—Well, while I was getting of the pen and ink-horn, and the sheet of paper, I ransacked my brains to think what could be the papers my poor master could have to execute in such a hurry, he that never thought of such a thing as doing business afore breakfast in the whole course of his life for any man living—but this was for my lady, as I afterwards found, and the more genteel of him after all her treatment.

I was just witnessing the paper that he had scrawled over, and was shaking the ink out of my pen upon the carpet, when my lady came in to breakfast, and she started as if it had been a ghost, as well she might, when she saw Sir Condy writing at this unseasonable hour.— 'That will do very well, Thady,' says he to me, and took

the paper I had signed to, without knowing what upon
the earth it might be, out of my hands, and walked,
folding it up, to my lady—

'You are concerned in this, my lady Rackrent, (says
he, putting it into her hands,) and I beg you'll keep this
memorandum safe, and shew it to your friends the first
thing you do when you get home, but put it in your
pocket now, my dear, and let us eat our breakfast, in
God's name.'—'What is all this?' said my lady, opening
the paper in great curiosity—'It's only a bit of a memorandum of what I think becomes me to do whenever I am
able, (says my master); you know my situation, tied
hand and foot at the present time being, but that can't
last always, and when I'm dead and gone, the land will
be to the good, Thady, you know; and take notice it's
my intention your lady should have a clear five hundred
a year jointure off the estate, afore any of my debts are
paid.'—'Oh, please your honour, says I, I can't expect
to live to see that time, being now upwards of fourscore
and ten years of age, and you a young man, and likely to
continue so, by the help of God.'—I was vexed to see
my lady so insensible too, for all she said was—'This is
very genteel of you, Sir Condy—You need not wait any
longer, Thady'—so I just picked up the pen and ink
that had tumbled on the floor, and heard my master
finish with saying—'You behaved very genteel to me,
my dear, when you threw all the little you had in your
own power, along with yourself, into my hands; and as
I don't deny but what you may have had some things

to complain of, (to be sure he was thinking then of Judy, or of the whiskey punch, one or t'other, or both); and as I don't deny but you may have had something to complain of, my dear, it is but fair you should have something in the form of compensation to look forward too agreeably in future; besides it's an act of justice to myself, that none of your friends, my dear, may ever have it to say against me I married for money, and not for love.'—'That is the last thing I should ever have thought of saying of you, Sir Condy,' said my lady, looking very gracious.—'Then, my dear, (said Sir Condy) we shall part as good friends as we met, so, all's right.'

I was greatly rejoiced to hear this, and went out of the parlour to report it all to the kitchen.—The next morning my lady and Mrs. Jane set out for Mount Juliet's town in the jaunting car; many wondered at my lady's chusing to go away, considering all things, upon the jaunting car, as if it was only a party of pleasure; but they did not know till I told them, that the coach was all broke in the journey down, and no other vehicle but the car to be had; besides, my lady's friends were to send their coach to meet her at the cross roads—so it was all done very proper.

My poor master was in great trouble after my lady left us.—The execution came down, and every thing at Castle Rackrent was seized by the gripers,[48] and my son Jason, to his shame be it spoken, amongst them—I wondered, for the life of me, how he could harden himself to do it, but then he had been studying the law, and had made himself attorney Quirk; so he brought down at once a heap of accounts upon my master's head—To Cash lent, and to ditto, and to ditto, and to ditto, and oats, and bills paid at the milliner's and linen-draper's, and many dresses for the fancy balls in Dublin for my lady, and all the bills to the workmen and tradesmen for the scenery of the theatre, and the chandler's and grocer's bills, and taylor's, besides butcher's and baker's, and worse than all, the old one of that base wine-merchant's, that wanted to arrest my poor master for the amount on the election day, for which amount Sir Condy afterwards passed his note of hand, bearing lawful interest from the date thereof; and the interest and compound interest was now mounted to a terrible deal on many other notes and bonds for money borrowed, and there was besides hush-money to the sub-sheriffs, and sheets upon sheets of old and new attornies' bills, with heavy balances, *as per former account furnished*, brought forward with interest thereon; then there was a powerful deal due to the Crown for sixteen years arrear of quit-rent[49] of the town lands of Carrickshaughlin, with drivers' fees, and a compliment to the receiver every year for letting the quit-rent run on, to oblige Sir Condy and Sir Kit afore him.—Then there was bills for spirits, and ribbons at the election time, and the gentlemen of the Committee's accounts unsettled, and their subscriptions never gathered; and there was cows to be paid for, with the smith and farrier's bills to be set against the rent of the demesne, with calf and hay-money: then there was all the servants' wages, since I don't know when, coming due to them, and sums advanced for them by my son Jason for clothes, and boots, and whips, and odd monies for sundries expended by them in journies to town and elsewhere, and pocket-money for the master continually, and messengers and postage before his being a parliament man— I can't myself tell you what besides; but this I know, that when the evening came on the which Sir Condy had appointed to settle all with my son Jason; and when he comes into the parlour, and sees the sight of bills and load of papers all gathered on the great dining table for him, he puts his hands before both his eyes, and cries out—'Merciful Jasus! what is it I see before me!'— Then I sets an arm chair at the table for him, and with a deal of difficulty he sits him down, and my son Jason hands him over the pen and ink to sign to this man's bill and t'other man's bill, all which he did without making the least objections; indeed, to give him his due, I never seen a man more fair, and honest, and easy in all his dealings, from first to last, as Sir Condy, or more willing to pay every man his own as far as he was able, which is as much as any one can do.—'Well, (says he, joking like with Jason) I wish we could settle it all with a stroke of my grey-goose-quill.—What signifies making me wade through all this ocean of papers here; can't you now, who understand drawing out an account, Debtor and Creditor, just sit down here at the corner of the table, and get it done out for me, that I may have a clear view of the balance, which is all I need be talking about, you know?'—'Very true, Sir Condy, nobody understands business better than yourself,' says Jason.—'So I've a right to do, being born and bred to the bar, (says Sir Condy)—Thady, do step out and see are they bringing in the tings[50] for the punch, for we've just done all we have to do this evening.'—I goes out accordingly, and when I came back, Jason was pointing to the balance, which was a terrible sight to my poor master.—'Pooh! pooh! pooh! (says he) here's so many noughts they dazzle my eyes, so they do, and put me in mind of all I suffered, larning of my numeration table, when I was a boy, at the day-school along with you, Jason—Units, tens, hundreds, tens of hundreds.—Is the punch ready, Thady?' says he, seeing me—'Immediately, the boy has the jug in his hand; it's coming up stairs, please your honour, as fast as possible,' says I, for I saw his honour was tired out of his life, but Jason, very short and cruel, cuts me off with—'Don't be talking of punch yet a while, it's no time for punch yet a bit—Units, tens, hundreds, goes he on, counting over the master's shoulder—units, tens, hundreds, thousands'—'A-a-agh! hold your hand, (cries my master,) where in this wide world am I to find hundreds, or units itself, let alone thousands?' —'The balance has been running on too long, (says Jason, sticking to him as I could not have done at the time if you'd have given both the Indies and Cork to boot); the balance has been running on too long, and I'm distressed myself on your account, Sir Condy, for money, and the thing must be settled now on the spot, and the balance cleared off,' says Jason. 'I'll thank you, if you'll only shew me how,' says Sir Condy.—'There's but one way, (says Jason) and that's ready enough; when there's no cash, what can a gentleman do but go to the land?'—'How can you go to the land, and it under custodiam to yourself already, (says Sir Condy) and another custodiam hanging over it? and no one at all can touch it, you know, but the custodees.'—'Sure can't you sell, though at a loss?—sure you can sell, and I've a purchaser ready for you,' says Jason.—'Have ye so? (said Sir Condy) that's a great point gained; but there's a thing now beyond all, that perhaps you don't know yet, barring Thady has let you into the secret.'—'Sarrah[51] bit of a sacret, or any thing at all of the kind has he learned from me these fifteen weeks come St. John's eve, (says I) for we have scarce been upon speaking terms of late— but what is it your honor means of a secret?'—'Why the secret of the little keepsake I gave my lady Rackrent the morning she left us, that she might not go back empty-handed to her friends.'—'My lady Rackrent, I'm sure, has baubles and keepsakes enough, as those bills on the table will shew, (says Jason); but whatever it is, (says he, taking up his pen) we must add it to the balance, for to be sure it can't be paid for.'—'No, nor can't till after my decease, (said Sir Condy) that's one good thing.'—Then coloring up a good deal, he tells Jason of the memorandum of the five hundred a year jointure he had settled upon my lady; at which Jason was indeed mad, and said

a great deal in very high words, that it was using a gentleman who had the management of his affairs, and was
moreover his principal creditor, extremely ill, to do such
a thing without consulting him, and against his knowledge and consent. To all which Sir Condy had nothing
to reply, but that, upon his conscience, it was in a hurry,
and without a moment's thought on his part, and he was
very sorry for it, but if it was to do over again he would
do the same; and he appealed to me, and I was ready to
give my evidence, if that would do, to the truth of all
he said.

So Jason with much ado was brought to agree to a
compromise.—'The purchaser that I have ready (says
he) will be much displeased to be sure at the incumbrance
on the land, but I must see and manage him—here's
a deed ready drawn up—we have nothing to do but to
put in the consideration money and our names to it.—
And how much am I going to sell?—the lands of
O'Shaughlin's-town, and the lands of Gruneaghoola-
ghan, and the lands of Crookaghnawaturgh, (says he,
just reading to himself)—and—'Oh, murder, Jason!—
sure you won't put this in'—the castle, stable, and appurtenances of Castle Rackrent—Oh, murder! (says I,
clapping my hands) this is too bad, Jason.'—'Why so?
(said Jason) when it's all, and a great deal more to the
back of it, lawfully mine was I to push for it.' 'Look at
him (says I, pointing to Sir Condy, who was just leaning
back in his arm chair, with his arms falling beside him
like one stupified) is it you, Jason, that can stand in his

presence and recollect all he has been to us, and all we have been to him, and yet use him so at the last?'—'Who will he find to use him better, I ask you? (said Jason)— If he can get a better purchaser, I'm content; I only offer to purchase to make things easy and oblige him—though I don't see what compliment I am under, if you come to that; I have never had, asked, or charged more than sixpence in the pound receiver's fees, and where would he have got an agent for a penny less?' 'Oh Jason! Jason! how will you stand to this in the face of the county, and all who know you, (says I); and what will people tink[52] and say, when they see you living here in Castle Rackrent, and the lawful owner turned out of the seat of his ancestors, without a cabin to put his head into, or so much as a potatoe to cat?'—Jason, whilst I was saying this and a great deal more, made me signs, and winks, and frowns; but I took no heed, for I was grieved and sick at heart for my poor master, and couldn't but speak.

'Here's the punch! (says Jason, for the door opened) —here's the punch!'—Hearing that, my master starts up in his chair and recollects himself, and Jason uncorks the whiskey—'Set down the jug here,' says he, making room for it beside the papers opposite to Sir Condy, but still not stirring the deed that was to make over all. Well, I was in great hopes he had some touch of mercy about him, when I saw him making the punch, and my master took a glass; but Jason put it back as he was going to fill again, saying, 'No, Sir Condy, it shan't be said of me, I got your signature to this deed when you were half-seas over; you know, your name and hand-writing in that condition would not, if brought before the courts, benefit me a straw, wherefore let us settle all before we go deeper in the punch-bowl.'—'Settle all as you will, (said Sir Condy, clapping his hands to his ears) but let me hear no more, I'm bothered to death this night.'— 'You've only to sign,' said Jason, putting the pen to him. —'Take all and be content,' said my master—So he signed—and the man who brought in the punch witnessed it, for I was not able, but crying like a child; and besides, Jason said, which I was glad of, that I was no fit witness, being so old and doating. It was so bad with me, I could not taste a drop of the punch itself, though my master himself, God bless him! in the midst of his trouble, poured out a glass for me and brought it up to my lips.—'Not a drop, I thank your honor's honor as much as if I took it though,' and I just set down the glass as it was and went out; and when I got to the street door, the neighbour's childer who were playing at marbles there, seeing me in great trouble, left their play, and gathered about me to know what ailed me; and I told them all, for it was a great relief to me to speak to these poor childer, that seemed to have some natural feeling left in them: and when they were made sensible that Sir Condy was going to leave Castle Rackrent for good and all, they set up a whillalu that could be heard to the farthest end of the street; and one fine boy he was, that my master had given an apple to that morning, cried the loudest, but they all were the same sorry, for Sir Condy was greatly beloved amongst the childer* for letting them go a nutting in the demesne without saying a word to them, though my lady objected to them.—The people in the town who were the most of them standing at their doors, hearing the childer cry, would know the reason of it; and when the report was made known, the people one and all gathered in great anger against my son Jason, and terror at the notion of his coming to be landlord over them, and they cried, No Jason! No Jason!—Sir Condy! Sir Condy! Sir Condy Rackrent for ever! and the mob grew so great and so loud I was frighted, and made my way back to the house to warn my son to make his escape, or hide himself for fear of the consequences.—Jason would not believe me, till they came all round the house and to the windows with great shouts—then he grew quite pale, and asked Sir Condy what had he best do ?— 'I'll tell you what you'd best do, (said Sir Condy, who was laughing to see his fright) finish your glass first, then let's go to the window and shew ourselves, and I'll tell 'em, or you shall if you please, that I'm going to the Lodge for change of air for my health, and by my own desire, for the rest of my days.'—'Do so,' said Jason, who never meant it should have been so, but could not refuse him the Lodge at this unseasonable time. Accordingly Sir Condy threw up the sash and explained matters, and thanked all his friends, and bid 'em look in at the punch bowl, and observe that Jason and he had been sitting over it very good friends; so the mob was

* This is the invariable pronunciation of the lower Irish.53

content, and he sent 'em out some whiskey to drink his health, and that was the last time his honor's health was ever drank at Castle Rackrent.

The very next day, being too proud, as he said to me, to stay an hour longer in a house that did not belong to him, he sets off to the Lodge, and I along with him not many hours after. And there was great bemoaning through all O'Shaughlin's town, which I stayed to witness, and gave my poor master a full account of when I got to the Lodge. —He was very low and in his bed when I got there, and complained of a great pain about his heart, but I guessed it was only trouble, and all the business, let alone vexation, he had gone through of late; and knowing the nature of him from a boy, I took my pipe, and while smoking it by the chimney, began telling him how he was beloved and regretted in the county, and it did him a deal of good to hear it.—'Your honor has a great many friends yet that you don't know of, rich and poor, in the county (says I); for as I was coming along on the road I met two gentlemen in their own carriages, who asked after you, knowing me, and wanted to know where you was, and all about you, and even how old I was—think of that.'—Then he wakened out of his doze, and began questioning me who the gentlemen were. And the next morning it came into my head to go, unknown to any body, with my master's compliments round to many of the gentlemen's houses where he and my lady used to visit, and people that I knew were his great friends, and would go to Cork to serve him any day in the year, and

I made bold to try to borrow a trifle of cash from them.—
They all treated me very civil for the most part, and asked
a great many questions very kind about my lady and Sir
Condy and all the family, and were greatly surprised to
learn from me Castle Rackrent was sold, and my master
at the Lodge for his health; and they all pitied him greatly,
and he had their good wishes if that would do, but money
was a thing they unfortunately had not any of them at this
time to spare. I had my journey for my pains, and I, not
used to walking, nor supple as formerly, was greatly tired,
but had the satisfaction of telling my master when I got to
the Lodge all the civil things said by high and low.

'Thady, (says he) all you've been telling me brings a
strange thought into my head; I've a notion I shall not be
long for this world any how, and I've a great fancy to see
my own funeral afore I die.' I was greatly shocked at the
first speaking to hear him speak so light about his funeral,
and he to all appearance in good health, but recollecting
myself, answered—'To be sure it would be a fine sight
as one could see, I dared to say, and one I should be
proud to witness, and I did not doubt his honor's would
be as great a funeral as ever Sir Patrick O'Shaughlin's
was, and such a one as that had never been known in the
county afore or since.' But I never thought he was in
earnest about seeing his own funeral himself, till the
next day he returns to it again.—'Thady, (says he) as far
as the wake* goes, sure I might without any great trouble

* A wake^g in England is a meeting avowedly for merriment—in Ireland, it
is a nocturnal meeting avowedly for the purpose of watching and bewailing
the dead; but in reality for gossipping and debauchery.

have the satisfaction of seeing a bit of my own funeral.'—
'Well, since your honor's honor's so bent upon it, (says
I, not willing to cross him, and he in trouble) we must
see what we can do.'—So he fell into a sort of a sham disorder, which was easy done, as he kept his bed and no
one to see him; and I got my shister, who was an old
woman very handy about the sick, and very skilful, to
come up to the Lodge to nurse him; and we gave out,
she knowing no better, that he was just at his latter end,
and it answered beyond any thing; and there was a great
throng of people, men, women and childer, and there
being only two rooms at the Lodge, except what was
locked up full of Jason's furniture and things, the house
was soon as full and fuller than it could hold, and the
heat, and smoke, and noise wonderful great; and standing
amongst them that were near the bed, but not thinking
at all of the dead, I was started by the sound of my
master's voice from under the great coats that had been
thrown all at top, and I went close up, no one noticing.—
'Thady, (says he) I've had enough of this, I'm smother-
ing, and I can't hear a word of all they're saying of the
deceased.'—'God bless you, and lie still quiet (says I)
a bit longer, for my shister's afraid of ghosts, and would
die on the spot with the fright, was she to see you come to
life all on a sudden this way without the least prepara-
tion.'—So he lays him still, though well nigh stifled, and
I made all haste to tell the secret of the joke, whispering
to one and t'other, and there was a great surprise, but not
so great as we had laid out it would.—'And aren't we to

have the pipes and tobacco, after coming so far to-night?'
says some; but they were all well enough pleased when
his honor got up to drink with them, and sent for more
spirits from a shebean-house*, where they very civilly
let him have it upon credit—so the night passed off very
merrily, but to my mind Sir Condy was rather upon the
sad order in the midst of it all, not finding there had been
such a great talk about himself after his death as he had
always expected to hear.

The next morning when the house was cleared of
them, and none but my shister and myself left in the
kitchen with Sir Condy, one opens the door and walks in,
and who should it be but Judy M'Quirk herself.—I forgot to notice that she had been married long since, whilst
young Captain Moneygawl lived at the Lodge, to the
Captain's huntsman, who after a while listed and left
her, and was killed in the wars. Poor Judy fell off greatly
in her good looks after her being married a year or two,
and being smoke-dried in the cabin and neglecting herself like, it was hard for Sir Condy himself to know her
again till she spoke; but when she says, 'It's Judy
M'Quirk, please your honor, don't you remember her?'
—'Oh, Judy, is it you? (says his honor)—yes, sure I
remember you very well—but you're greatly altered,
Judy.'—'Sure it's time for me, (says she) and I think
your honor since I *seen* you last, but that's a great while
ago, is altered too.'—'And with reason, Judy, (says Sir

* *Shebean-house*, a hedge alehouse.—Shebean properly means weak small-
beer, taplash.[54]

Condy, fetching a sort of sigh)—but how's this, Judy, (he goes on) I take it a little amiss of you that you were not at my wake last night?' 'Ah, don't be being jealous of that, (says she) I didn't hear a sentence of your honor's wake till it was all over, or it would have gone hard with me but I would have been at it sure—but I was forced to go ten miles up the country three days ago to a wedding of a relation of my own's, and didn't get home till after the wake was over; but (says she) it won't be so, I hope, the next time*, please your honor.'—'That we shall see, Judy, (says his honor) and may be sooner than you think for, for I've been very unwell this while past, and don't reckon any way I'm long for this world.' At this Judy takes up the corner of her apron, and puts it first to one eye and then to t'other, being to all appearance in great trouble; and my shister put in her word, and bid his honor have a good heart, for she was sure it was only the gout that Sir Patrick used to have flying about him, and that he ought to drink a glass or a bottle extraordinary to keep it out of his stomach, and he promised to take her advice, and sent out for more spirits immediately; and Judy made a sign to me, and I went over to the door to her, and she said—'I wonder to see Sir Condy so low!—Has he heard the news?' 'What news?' says I. —'Didn't ye hear it, then? (says she) my lady Rackrent that was is kilt ^{g} and lying for dead, and I don't doubt but it's all over with her by this time.'—'Mercy on us all,

* At the coronation of one of our monarchs, the king complained of the confusion which happened in the procession—The great officer who presided told his majesty, 'That it should not be so next time.'

(says I) how was it?'—'The jaunting car it was that that ran away with her, (says Judy).—I was coming home that same time from Biddy M'Guggin's marriage, and a great crowd of people too upon the road coming from the fair of Crookaghnawatur, and I sees a jaunting car standing in the middle of the road, and with the two wheels off and all tattered.—What's this? says I.'— 'Didn't ye hear of it? (says they that were looking on) it's my lady Rackrent's car that was running away from her husband, and the horse took fright at a carrion that lay across the road, and so ran away with the jaunting car, and my lady Rackrent and her maid screaming, and the horse ran with them against a car that was coming from the fair, with the boy asleep on it, and the lady's petticoat hanging out of the jaunting car caught, and she was dragged I can't tell you how far upon the road, and it all broken up with the stones just going to be pounded, and one of the road makers with his sledge hammer in his hand stops the horse at the last; but my lady Rackrent was all kilt* and smashed, and they lifted her into a cabin hard by, and the maid was found after, where she had been thrown, in the gripe of the ditch, her cap and bonnet all full of bog water—and they say

---

* *Kilt and smashed*—Our author is not here guilty of an anticlimax.—The mere English reader, from a similarity of sound between the words *kilt* and *killed*, might be induced to suppose that their meanings are similar, yet they are not by any means in Ireland synonymous terms. Thus you may hear a man exclaim—'I'm kilt and murdered!'—but he frequently means only that he has received a black eye, or a slight contusion.—*I'm kilt all over*—means that he is in a worse state than being simply *kilt*—Thus—*I'm kilt with the cold*— is nothing to—*I'm kilt all over with the rheumatism.*ᵍ

my lady can't live any way. Thady, pray now is it true what I'm told for sartain, that Sir Condy has made over all to your son Jason?'—'All,' says I.—'All entirely,' says she again.—'All entirely,' says I.—'Then (says she) that's a great shame, but don't be telling Jason what I say.'—'And what is it you say? (cries Sir Condy, leaning over betwixt us, which made Judy start greatly)—I know the time when Judy M'Quirk would never have stayed so long talking at the door, and I in the house.' 'Oh, (says Judy) for shame, Sir Condy, times are altered since then, and it's my lady Rackrent you ought to be thinking of.'—'And why should I be thinking of her, that's not thinking of me now?' says Sir Condy.—'No matter for that, (says Judy, very properly) it's time you should be thinking of her if ever you mean to do it at all, for don't you know she's lying for death?'—'My lady Rackrent! (says Sir Condy in a surprise) why it's but two days since we parted, as you very well know, Thady, in her full health and spirits, and she and her maid along with her going to Mount Juliet's town on her jaunting car.'— 'She'll never ride no more on her jaunting car, (said Judy) for it has been the death of her sure enough.'— 'And is she dead then?' says his honor.—'As good as dead, I hear, (says Judy) but there's Thady here has just learnt the whole truth of the story as I had it, and it is fitter he or any body else should be telling it you than I, Sir Condy—I must be going home to the childer.'—But he stops her, but rather from civility in him, as I could see very plainly, than any thing else, for Judy was, as his honor remarked, at her first coming in, greatly changed, and little likely, as far as I could see—though she did not seem to be clear of it herself—little likely to be my lady Rackrent now, should there be a second toss-up to be made.—But I told him the whole story out of the face, just as Judy had told it to me, and he sent off a messenger with his compliments to Mount Juliet's town that evening to learn the truth of the report, and Judy bid the boy that was going call in at Tim M'Enerney's shop in O'Shaughlin's town and buy her a new shawl.—'Do so, (says Sir Condy) and tell Tim to take no money from you, for I must pay him for the shawl myself.'—At this my shister throws me over a look, and I says nothing, but turned the tobacco in my mouth, whilst Judy began making a many words about it, and saying how she could not be beholden for shawls to[55] any gentleman. I left her there to consult with my shister, did she think there was any thing in it, and my shister thought I was blind to be asking her the question, and I thought my shister must see more into it than I did, and recollecting all past times and every thing, I changed my mind, and came over to her way of thinking, and we settled it that Judy was very like to be my lady Rackrent after all, if a vacancy should have happened.

The next day, before his honor was up, somebody comes with a double knock at the door, and I was greatly surprised to see it was my son Jason.—'Jason, is it you? (says I) what brings you to the Lodge? (says I) is it my lady Rackrent? we know that already since yesterday.'

'May be so, (says he) but I must see Sir Condy about it.'
—'You can't see him yet, (says I) sure he is not awake.'
'What then, (says he) can't he be wakened? and I standing at the door.'—'I'll not be disturbing his honor for
you, Jason (says I); many's the hour you've waited in
your time, and been proud to do it, till his honor was at
leisure to speak to you.—His honor,' says I, raising my
voice—at which his honor wakens of his own accord,
and calls to me from the room to know who it was I was
speaking to. Jason made no more ceremony, but follows
me into the room.—'How are you, Sir Condy, (says he)
I'm happy to see you looking so well; I came up to know
how you did to-day, and to see did you want for any
thing at the Lodge.'—'Nothing at all, Mr. Jason, I thank
you, (says he, for his honor had his own share of pride,
and did not chuse, after all that had passed, to be beholden, I suppose, to my son)—but pray take a chair
and be seated, Mr. Jason.'—Jason sat him down upon
the chest, for chair there was none, and after he had sat
there some time, and a silence on all sides—'What news
is there stirring in the country, Mr. Jason M'Quirk?'
says Sir Condy, very easy, yet high like.—'None that's
news to you, Sir Condy, I hear (says Jason) I am sorry
to hear of my lady Rackrent's accident.'—'I am much
obliged to you, and so is her ladyship, I'm sure,' answers
Sir Condy, still stiff; and there was another sort of a
silence, which seemed to lie the heaviest on my son
Jason.

'Sir Condy, (says he at last, seeing Sir Condy disposing

himself to go to sleep again) Sir Condy, I dare say you recollect mentioning to me the little memorandum you gave to lady Rackrent about the £500 a year jointure.'— 'Very true, (said Sir Condy) it is all in my recollection.' —'But if my lady Rackrent dies there's an end of all jointure,' says Jason. 'Of course,' says Sir Condy.— 'But it's not a matter of certainty that my lady Rackrent won't recover,' says Jason.—'Very true, Sir,' says my master.—'It's a fair speculation then, for you to consider what the chance of the jointure on those lands when out of custodiam will be to you.'—'Just five hundred a year, I take it, without any speculation at all,' said Sir Condy. —'That's supposing the life dropt and the custodiam off, you know, begging your pardon, Sir Condy, who understand business, that is a wrong calculation.'— 'Very likely so, (said Sir Condy) but Mr. Jason, if you have any thing to say to me this morning about it, I'd be obliged to you to say it, for I had an indifferent night's rest last night, and wouldn't be sorry to sleep a little this morning.'—'I have only three words to say, and those more of consequence to you, Sir Condy, than me. You are a little cool, I observe, but I hope you will not be offended at what I have brought here in my pocket,'— and he pulls out two long rolls, and showers down golden guineas upon the bed. 'What's this? (said Sir Condy) it's long since'—but his pride stops him—'All these are your lawful property this minute, Sir Condy, if you please,' said Jason.—'Not for nothing, I'm sure, (said Sir Condy, and laughs a little)—nothing for nothing, or

I'm under a mistake with you, Jason.'—'Oh, Sir Condy,
we'll not be indulging ourselves in any unpleasant retro-
spects, (says Jason) it's my present intention to behave,
as I'm sure you will, like a gentleman in this affair.—
Here's two hundred guineas, and a third I mean to add,
if you should think proper to make over to me all your
right and title to those lands that you know of.'—'I'll
consider of it,' said my master; and a great deal more,
that I was tired listening to, was said by Jason, and all
that, and the sight of the ready cash upon the bed worked
with his honor; and the short and the long of it was, Sir
Condy gathered up the golden guineas and tied up in
a handkerchief, and signed some paper Jason brought
with him as usual, and there was an end of the business;
Jason took himself away, and my master turned himself
round and fell asleep again.

I soon found what had put Jason in such a hurry to
conclude this business. The little gossoon we had sent
off the day before with my master's compliments to
Mount Juliet's town, and to know how my lady did after
her accident, was stopped early this morning, coming
back with his answer through O'Shaughlin's town, at
Castle Rackrent by my son Jason, and questioned of all
he knew of my lady from the servants at Mount Juliet's
town; and the gossoon told him my lady Rackrent was
not expected to live over night, so Jason thought it high
time to be moving to the Lodge, to make his bargain with
my master about the jointure afore it should be too late,
and afore the little gossoon should reach us with the

news. My master was greatly vexed, that is, I may say, as much as ever I seen him, when he found how he had been taken in; but it was some comfort to have the ready cash for immediate consumption in the house any way.

And when Judy came up that evening, and brought the childer to see his honor, he unties the handkerchief, and God bless him! whether it was little or much he had, 'twas all the same with him, he gives 'em all round guineas a-piece.—'Hold up your head, (says my shister[56] to Judy, as Sir Condy was busy filling out a glass of punch for her eldest boy)—Hold up your head, Judy, for who knows but we may live to see you yet at the head of the Castle Rackrent estate.'—'May be so, (says she) but not the way you are thinking of.'—I did not rightly understand which way Judy was looking when she makes this speech, till a while after.—'Why Thady, you were telling me yesterday that Sir Condy had sold all entirely to Jason, and where then does all them guineas in the handkerchief come from?' 'They are the purchase money of my lady's jointure,' says I.—Judy looks a little bit puzzled at this.—'A penny for your thoughts, Judy, (says my shister)—hark, sure Sir Condy is drinking her health.'—He was at the table in *the room*,* drinking with the exciseman and the gauger,[57] who came up to see his honor, and we were standing over the fire in the kitchen.—'I don't much care is he drinking my health or not (says Judy), and it is not Sir Condy I'm thinking of, with all your jokes, whatever he is of me.' 'Sure you

* *The room*—the principal room in the house.

wouldn't refuse to be my lady Rackrent, Judy, if you had the offer?' says I.—'But if I could do better?' says she. 'How better?' says I and my shister both at once.— 'How better! (says she) why what signifies it to be my lady Rackrent and no Castle? sure what good is the car and no horse to draw it?'—'And where will ye get the horse, Judy?' says I.—'Never you mind that, (says she) —may be it is your own son Jason might find that.'— 'Jason! (says I) don't be trusting to him, Judy. Sir Condy, as I have good reason to know, spoke well of you, when Jason spoke very indifferently of you, Judy.' —'No matter (says Judy), it's often men speak the contrary just to what they think of us.'—'And you the same way of them, no doubt, (answers I).—Nay don't be denying it, Judy, for I think the better of ye for it, and shouldn't be proud to call ye the daughter of a shister's son of mine, if I was to hear ye talk ungrateful, and any way disrespectful of his honor.'—'What disrespect, (says she) to say I'd rather, if it was my luck, be the wife of another man?' 'You'll have no luck, mind my words, Judy,' says I; and all I remembered about my poor master's goodness in tossing up for her afore he married at all came across me, and I had a choaking in my throat that hindered me to say more.—'Better luck, any how, Thady, (says she) than to be like some folk, following the fortunes of them that have none left.' 'Oh King of Glory! (says I) hear the pride and ungratitude of her, and he giving his last guineas but a minute ago to her childer, and she with the fine shawl on her he made her a present of but yesterday!'—'Oh troth, Judy, you're wrong now,' says my shister, looking at the shawl.—'And was not he wrong yesterday then, (says she) to be telling me I was greatly altered, to affront me?'—'But Judy, (says I) what is it brings you here then at all in the mind you are in—is it to make Jason think the better of you?'—'I'll tell you no more of my secrets, Thady, (says she) nor would have told you this much, had I taken you for such an unnatural fader as I find you are, not to wish your own son prefarred to another.'— 'Oh troth, *you* are wrong, now, Thady,' says my shister. —Well, I was never so put to it in my life between these womens, and my son and my master, and all I felt and thought just now, I could not upon my conscience tell which was the wrong from the right.—So I said not a word more, but was only glad his honor had not the luck to hear all Judy had been saying of him, for I reckoned it would have gone nigh to break his heart, not that I was of opinion he cared for her as much as she and my shister fancied, but the ungratitude of the whole from Judy might not plase him, and he could never stand the notion of not being well spoken of or beloved like behind his back. Fortunately for all parties concerned, he was so much elevated at this time, there was no danger of his understanding any thing, even if it had reached his ears. There was a great horn at the Lodge, ever since my master and Captain Moneygawl was in together, that used to belong originally to the celebrated Sir Patrick, his ancestor, and his honor was fond often of telling the story that he larned from me when a child, how Sir Patrick drank the full of this horn without stopping, and this was what no other man afore or since could without drawing breath.—Now Sir Condy challenged the gauger, who seemed to think little of the horn, to swallow the contents, and it filled to the brim, with punch; and the gauger said it was what he could not do for nothing, but he'd hold Sir Condy a hundred guineas he'd do it.—'Done, (says my master) I'll lay you a hundred golden guineas to a tester* you don't.'—'Done,' says the gauger, and done and done's enough between two gentlemen. The gauger was cast, and my master won the bet, and thought he'd won a hundred guineas, but by the wording it was adjudged to be only a tester that was his due, by the exciseman. It was all one to him, he was as well pleased, and I was glad to see him in such spirits again.

The gauger, bad luck to him! was the man that next proposed to my master to try ! 'mself could he take at a draught the contents of the great horn.—'Sir Patrick's horn! (said his honor) hand it to me—I'll hold you your own bet over again I'll swallow it.'—'Done, (says the gauger) I'll lay ye any thing at all you do no such thing.' —'A hundred guineas to sixpence I do, (says he) bring me the handkerchief.'—I was loth, knowing he meant the handkerchief with the gold in it, to bring it out

* *Tester*—Sixpence—from the French word tête, a head. A piece of silver stamped with a head, which in old French was called, 'un testion,' and which was about the value of an old English sixpence.—Tester is used in Shakspeare.[58]

in such company, and his honor not very well able to
reckon it. 'Bring me the handkerchief then, Thady,' says
he, and stamps with his foot; so with that I pulls it out
of my great coat pocket, where I had put it for safety.—
Oh, how it grieved me to see the guineas counting upon
the table, and they the last my master had. Says Sir
Condy to me—'Your hand is steadier than mine to-night,
Old Thady, and that's a wonder; fill you the horn for
me.'—And so wishing his honor success, I did—but I
filled it, little thinking of what would befall him.—He
swallows it down, and drops like one shot.—We lifts
him up, and he was speechless and quite black in the face.
We put him to bed, and in a short time he wakened
raving with a fever on his brain. He was shocking either
to see or hear.—'Judy! Judy! have ye no touch of feeling? won't you stay to help us nurse him?' says I to her,
and she putting on her shawl to go out of the house.—
'I'm frighted to see him, (says she) and wouldn't, nor
couldn't stay in it—and what use?—he can't last till the
morning.' With that she ran off.—There was none but
my shister and myself left near him of all the many
friends he had. The fever came and went, and came and
went, and lasted five days, and the sixth he was sensible
for a few minutes, and said to me, knowing me very well
 —'I'm in burning pain all within side of me, Thady,'—
I could not speak, but my shister asked him, would he
have this thing or t'other to do him good?—'No, (says
he) nothing will do me good no more'—and he gave a
terrible screech with the torture he was in—then again

a minute's ease—'brought to this by drink (says he)—where are all the friends?—where's Judy?—Gone, hey?—Aye, Sir Condy has been a fool all his days'—said he, and there was the last word he spoke, and died. He had but a very poor funeral, after all.

If you want to know any more, I'm not very well able to tell you; but my lady Rackrent did not die as was expected of her, but was only disfigured in the face ever after by the fall and bruises she got; and she and Jason, immediately after my poor master's death, set about going to law about that jointure; the memorandum not being on stamped paper, some say it is worth nothing, others again it may do; others say, Jason won't have the lands at any rate—many wishes it so—for my part, I'm tired wishing for any thing in this world, after all I've seen in it—but I'll say nothing; it would be a folly to be getting myself ill will in my old age. Jason did not marry, nor think of marrying Judy, as I prophesied, and I am not sorry for it—who is?—As for all I have here set down from memory and hearsay of the family, there's nothing but truth in it from beginning to end, that you may depend upon, for where's the use of telling lies about the things which every body knows as well as I do?

The Editor could have readily made the catastrophe of Sir Condy's history more dramatic and more pathetic, if he thought it allowable to varnish the plain round tale of faithful Thady. He lays it before the English reader as a specimen of manners and characters, which are perhaps unknown in England. Indeed the domestic habits of no nation in Europe were less known to the English than those of their sister country, till within these few years.

Mr. Young's picture of Ireland,[59] in his tour through that country, was the first faithful portrait of its inhabitants. All the features in the foregoing sketch were taken from the life, and they are characteristic of that mixture of quickness, simplicity, cunning, carelessness, dissipation, disinterestedness, shrewdness and blunder, which in different forms, and with various success, has been brought upon the stage or delineated in novels.

It is a problem of difficult solution to determine, whether an Union[60] will hasten or retard the amelioration of this country. The few gentlemen of education who now reside in this country will resort to England: they are few, but they are in nothing inferior to men of the same rank in Great Britain. The best that can happen will be the introduction of British manufacturers in their places.

Did the Warwickshire militia,[61] who were chiefly artisans, teach the Irish to drink beer, or did they learn from the Irish to drink whiskey?[62]

ADVERTISEMENT
TO THE
ENGLISH READER

───────

SOME friends who have seen Thady's history since it has been printed[63] have suggested to the Editor, that many of the terms and idiomatic phrases with which it abounds could not be intelligible to the English reader without farther explanation. The Editor has therefore furnished the following Glossary.

GLOSSARY[64]

Page 7. *Monday morning*] Thady begins his Memoirs of the Rack-rent Family by dating *Monday morning*, because no great under-taking can be auspiciously commenced in Ireland on any morning but *Monday morning*.—'Oh, please God we live till Monday morning, we'll set the slater to mend the roof of the house—On Monday morning we'll fall to and cut the turf—On Monday morn-ing we'll see and begin mowing—On Monday morning, please your honor, we'll begin and dig the potatoes,' &c.

All the intermediate days between the making of such speeches and the ensuing Monday are wasted, and when Monday morning comes it is ten to one that the business is deferred to *the next* Monday morning. The Editor knew a gentleman who, to counteract this prejudice, made his workmen and laborers begin all new pieces of work upon a Saturday.

Page 9. Let alone the three kingdoms itself] *Let alone*, in this sen-tence, means *put out of the consideration*. This phrase *let alone*, which is now used as the imperative of a verb, may in time become a conjunction, and may exercise the ingenuity of some future etymologist. The celebrated Horne Tooke has proved most satis-factorily, that the conjunction *but* comes from the imperative of the Anglo-Saxon verb (*beonutan*) *to be out*; also that *if* comes from *gif*, the imperative of the Anglo-Saxon verb which signifies *to give*, &c. &c.

Page 11. Whillaluh] Ullaloo, Gol, or lamentation over the dead—

'Magnoque ululante tumultu.' VIRGIL.
'Ululatibus omne
Implevere nemus.' OVID.

A full account of the Irish Gol or Ullaloo, and of the Caoinan or
Irish funeral song, with its first semichorus, second semichorus, full
chorus of sighs and groans, together with the Irish words and music,
may be found in the fourth volume of the Transactions of the
Royal Irish Academy. For the advantage of *lazy* readers, who would
rather read a page than walk a yard, and from compassion, not to
say sympathy with their infirmity, the Editor transcribes the following passages.

'The Irish have been always remarkable for their funeral lamentations, and this peculiarity has been noticed by almost every traveller
who visited them. And it seems derived from their Celtic ancestors,
the primæval inhabitants of this isle. . . .'

'It has been affirmed of the Irish, that to cry was more natural to
them than to any other nation, and at length the Irish cry became
proverbial. . . .'

'Cambrensis in the twelfth century says, the Irish then musically
expressed their griefs; that is, they applied the musical art, in which
they excelled all others, to the orderly celebration of funeral
obsequies, by dividing the mourners into two bodies, each alternately singing their part, and the whole at times joining in full
chorus. . . . The body of the deceased, dressed in grave clothes and
ornamented with flowers, was placed on a bier or some elevated spot.
The relations and Keeners (*singing mourners*) ranged themselves in
two divisions, one at the head and the other at the feet of the corpse.
The bards and croteries had before prepared the funeral Caoinan.
The chief bard of the head chorus began by singing the first stanza
in a low, doleful tone, which was softly accompanied by the harp:
at the conclusion the foot semichorus began the lamentation, or
Ullaloo, from the final note of the preceding stanza, in which they
were answered by the head semichorus; then both united in one
general chorus. The chorus of the first stanza being ended, the chief
bard of the foot semichorus began the second Gol or lamentation,
in which they were answered by that of the head;[64a] and then as
before both united in the general full chorus. Thus alternately were
the song and chorusses performed during the night. The genealogy,
rank, possessions, the virtues and vices of the dead were rehearsed,
and a number of interrogations were addressed to the deceased: as,

Why did he die? If married, whether his wife was faithful to him, his sons dutiful, or good hunters or warriors? If a woman, whether her daughters were fair or chaste? If a young man, whether he had been crossed in love? or if the blue-eyed maids of Erin treated him with scorn?'

We are told that formerly the feet (the metrical feet) of the Caoinan were much attended to, but on the decline of the Irish bards these feet were gradually neglected, the Caoinan fell into a sort of slip-shod metre amongst women. Each province had differ-ent Caoinans, or at least different imitations of the original. There was the Munster cry, the Ulster cry, &c. It became an extempore performance, and every set of Keeners varied the melody according to their own fancy.

It is curious to observe how customs and ceremonies degenerate. The present Irish cry or howl cannot boast of much melody, nor is the funeral procession conducted with much dignity. The crowd of people who assemble at these funerals sometimes amounts to a thousand, often to four or five hundred. They gather as the bearers of the hearse proceed on their way, and when they pass through any village, or when they come near any houses, they begin to cry— Oh! Oh! Oh! Oh! Oh! Agh! Agh! raising their notes from the first *Oh!* to the last *Agh!* in a kind of mournful howl. This gives notice to the inhabitants of the village that a *funeral is passing*, and immedi-ately they flock out to follow it. In the province of Munster it is a common thing for the women to follow a funeral, to join in the universal cry with all their might and main for some time, and then to turn and ask—'Arrah! who is it that's dead?—who is it we're crying for?'—Even the poorest people have their own burying-places, that is, spots of ground in the church-yards, where they say that their ancestors have been buried ever since the wars of Ireland: and if these burial-places are ten miles from the place where a man dies, his friends and neighbours take care to carry his corpse thither. Always one priest, often five or six priests, attend these funerals; each priest repeats a mass, for which he is paid sometimes a shilling, sometimes half a crown, sometimes half a guinea, or a guinea, according to the circumstances, or as they say, according to the *ability* of the deceased. After the burial of any very poor man

who has left a widow or children, the priest makes what is called
a collection for the widow; he goes round to every person present,
and each contributes sixpence or a shilling, or what they please.
The reader will find in the note upon the word *Wake* more parti-
culars respecting the conclusion of the Irish funerals.

Certain old women, who cry particularly loud and well, are in
great request, and, as a man said to the Editor, 'Every one would
wish and be proud to have such at his funeral, or at that of his
friends.' The lower Irish are wonderfully eager to attend the funerals
of their friends and relations, and they make their relationships
branch out to a great extent. The proof that a poor man has been well
beloved during his life, is his having a crowded funeral. To attend
a neighbour's funeral is a cheap proof of humanity, but it does not,
as some imagine, cost nothing. The time spent in attending funerals
may be safely valued at half a million to the Irish nation: the Editor
thinks that double that sum would not be too high an estimate. The
habits of profligacy and drunkenness which are acquired at *wakes*
are here put out of the question. When a labourer, a carpenter, or a
smith is not at his work, which frequently happens, ask where he is
gone, and ten to one the answer is—'Oh faith, please your honor, he
couldn't do a stroke to-day, for he's gone to *the* funeral.'

Even beggars, when they grow old, go about begging *for their own
funerals*; that is, begging for money to buy a coffin, candles, pipes
and tobacco.—For the use of the candles, pipes and tobacco, see
Wake.

Those who value customs in proportion to their antiquity, and
nations in proportion to their adherence to antient customs, will
doubtless admire the Irish *Ullaloo*, and the Irish nation, for per-
severing in this usage from time immemorial. The Editor, however,
has observed some alarming symptoms, which seem to prog-
nosticate the declining taste for the Ullaloo in Ireland. In a comic
theatrical entertainment represented not long since on the Dublin
stage, a chorus of old women was introduced, who set up the Irish
howl round the relics of a physician, who is supposed to have fallen
under the wooden sword of Harlequin. After the old women have
continued their Ullaloo for a decent time, with all the necessary
accompaniments of wringing their hands, wiping or rubbing their

eyes with the corners of their gowns or aprons, &c. one of the mourners suddenly suspends her lamentable cries, and turning to her neighbour, asks—'Arrah now, honey, who is it we're crying for?'

Page 12. The tenants were sent away without their whiskey] It is usual with some landlords to give their inferior tenants a glass of whiskey when they pay their rents. Thady calls it *their* whiskey; not that the whiskey is actually the property of the tenants, but that it becomes their *right*, after it has been often given to them. In this general mode of reasoning respecting *rights*, the lower Irish are not singular, but they are peculiarly quick and tenacious in claiming these rights.—'Last year your honor gave me some straw for the roof of my house, and I *expect* your honor will be after doing the same this year.'—In this manner gifts are frequently turned into tributes. The high and low are not always dissimilar in their habits. It is said that the Sublime Ottoman Porte is very apt to claim gifts as tributes: thus it is dangerous to send the Grand Seignor a fine horse on his birth-day one year, lest on his next birth-day he should expect a similar present, and should proceed to demonstrate the reasonableness of his expectations.

He demeaned himself greatly] Means, he lowered, or disgraced himself much.

Page 14. Duty fowls—and duty turkies—and duty geese] In many leases in Ireland, tenants were *formerly* bound to supply an inordinate quantity of poultry to their landlords. The Editor knew of sixty turkies[65] being reserved in one lease of a small farm.

English tenants] An English tenant does not mean a tenant who is an Englishman, but a tenant who pays his rent the day that it is due. It is a common prejudice in Ireland, amongst the poorer classes of people, to believe that all tenants in England pay their rents on the very day when they become due. An Irishman, when he goes to take a farm, if he wants to prove to his landlord that he is a substantial man, offers to become an *English tenant*. If a tenant disobliges his landlord by voting against him, or against his opinion, at an election, the tenant is immediately informed by the agent that he must become *an English tenant*. This threat does not imply that he is to change his language or his country, but that he must pay all the arrear of rent which he owes, and that he must thenceforward pay his rent on the day when it becomes due.

Canting] Does not mean talking or writing hypocritical nonsense, but selling substantially by auction.

Pages 14-15. Duty work] It was formerly common in Ireland to insert clauses in leases, binding tenants to furnish their landlords with laborers and horses for several days in the year. Much petty tyranny and oppression have resulted from this feudal custom. Whenever a poor man disobliged his landlord, the agent sent to him for his duty work, and Thady does not exaggerate when he says, that the tenants were often called from their own work to do that of their landlord. Thus the very means of earning their rent were taken from them: whilst they were getting home their landlord's harvest, their own was often ruined, and yet their rents were expected to be paid as punctually as if their time had been at their own disposal. This appears the height of absurd injustice.

In Esthonia, amongst the poor Sclavonian race of peasant slaves, they pay tributes to their lords, not under the name of duty work, duty geese, duty turkies, &c. but under the name of *righteousnesses*. The following ballad is a curious specimen of Estonian poetry:

> This is the cause that the country is ruined,
> And the straw of the thatch is eaten away,
> The gentry are come to live in the land—
> Chimneys between the village,
> And the proprietor upon the white floor!
> The sheep brings forth a lamb with a white forehead;
> This is paid to the lord for a *righteousness sheep*.
> The sow farrows pigs,
> They go to the spit of the lord.
> The hen lays eggs,
> They go into the lord's frying-pan.
> The cow drops a male calf,
> That goes into the lord's herd as a bull.
> The mare foals a horse foal,
> That must be for my lord's nag.
> The boor's wife has sons,
> They must go to look after my lord's poultry.

Page 15. Out of forty-nine suits which he had, he never lost one—
but seventeen] Thady's language in this instance is a specimen of
a mode of rhetoric common in Ireland. An astonishing assertion is
made in the beginning of a sentence, which ceases to be in the least
surprizing when you hear the qualifying explanation that follows.
Thus a man who is in the last stage of staggering drunkenness will,
if he can articulate, swear to you—'Upon his conscience now (and
may he never stir from the spot alive if he is telling a lie) upon his
conscience he has not tasted a drop of any thing, good or bad, since
morning at-all-at-all—but half a pint of whiskey, please your honor.'

Page 16. Fairy Mounts] Barrows. It is said that these high mounts
were of great service to the natives of Ireland, when Ireland was
invaded by the Danes. Watch was always kept on them, and upon the
approach of an enemy a fire was lighted to give notice to the next
watch, and thus the intelligence was quickly communicated through
the country. *Some years ago*, the common people believed that these
Barrows were inhabited by fairies, or as they call them, by the *good
people*.—'Oh troth, to the best of my belief, and to the best of my
judgment and opinion, (said an elderly man to the Editor) it was
only the old people that had nothing to do, and got together and
were telling stories about them fairies, but to the best of my judgment there's nothing in it.—Only this I heard myself not very many
years back, from a decent kind of a man, a grazier, that as he was
coming just *fair and easy* (*quietly*) from the fair, with some cattle and
sheep that he had not sold, just at the church of ——, at an angle
of the road like, he was met by a good looking man, who asked him
where was he going? And he answered, "Oh, far enough, I must be
going all night."—"No, that you mustn't nor won't (says the man),
you'll sleep with me the night, and you'll want for nothing, nor
your cattle nor sheep neither, nor your *beast* (*horse*); so come along
with me."—With that the grazier *lit* (alighted) from his horse, and it
was dark night; but presently he finds himself, he does not know in
the wide world how, in a fine house, and plenty of every thing to eat
and drink—nothing at all wanting that he could wish for or think
of—And he does not *mind* (*recollect*, or *know*) how at last he falls
asleep; and in the morning he finds himself lying, not in ever a bed

or a house at all, but just in the angle of the road where first he met the strange man: there he finds himself lying on his back on the grass, and all his sheep feeding as quiet as ever all round about him, and his horse the same way, and the bridle of the beast over his wrist. And I asked him what he thought of it, and from first to last he could think of nothing but for certain sure it must have been the fairies that entertained him so well. For there was no house to see any where nigh hand, or any building, or barn, or place at all, but only the church and the *mote* (*barrow*). There's another odd thing enough that they tell about this same church, that if any person's corpse, that had not a right to be buried in that church-yard, went to be burying there in it, no not all the men, women, or childer in all Ireland could get the corpse any way into the church-yard; but as they would be trying to go into the church-yard, their feet would seem to be going backwards instead of forwards; aye, continually backwards the whole funeral would seem to go; and they would never set foot with the corpse in the church-yard. Now they say, that it is the fairies do all this; but it is my opinion it is all idle talk, and people are after being wiser now.'

The country people in Ireland certainly *had* great admiration mixed with reverence, if not dread of fairies. They believed, that beneath these fairy mounts were spacious subterraneous palaces inhabited by *the good people*, who must not on any account be disturbed. When the wind raises a little eddy of dust upon the road, the poor people believe that it is raised by the fairies, that it is a sign that they are journeying from one of the fairy mounts to another, and they say to the fairies, or to the dust as it passes—'God speed ye, gentlemen, God speed ye.' This averts any evil that *the good people* might be inclined to do them. There are innumerable stories told of the friendly and unfriendly feats of these busy fairies; some of these tales are ludicrous, and some romantic enough for poetry. It is a pity that poets should lose such convenient, though diminutive machinery.—By the by, Parnell, who shewed himself so deeply 'skilled of faerie lore,' was an Irishman; and though he has presented his faeries to the world in the ancient English dress of 'Britain's Isle, and Arthur's days,' it is probable that his first acquaintance with them began in his native country.

Some remote origin for the most superstitious or romantic popular illusions or vulgar errors may often be discovered. In Ireland, the old churches and church-yards have been usually fixed upon as the scenes of wonders. Now the antiquarians tell us, that near the ancient churches in that kingdom caves of various constructions have from time to time been discovered, which were formerly used as granaries or magazines by the ancient inhabitants, and as places to which they retreated in time of danger. There is (p. 84 of the R. I. A. Transactions for 1789) a particular account of a number of these artificial caves at the West end of the church of Killossy, in the county of Kildare. Under a rising ground, in a dry sandy soil, these subterraneous dwellings were found: they have pediment roofs, and they communicate with each other by small apertures. In the Brehon laws these are mentioned, and there are fines inflicted by those laws upon persons who steal from the subterraneous granaries. All these things shew, that there was a real foundation for the stories which were told of the appearance of lights and of the sounds of voices near these places. The persons who had property concealed there very willingly countenanced every wonderful relation that tended to make these places objects of sacred awe or superstitious terror.

Page 17. Weed-ashes] By antient usage in Ireland, all the weeds on a farm belonged to the farmer's wife, or to the wife of the squire who holds the ground in his own hands. The great demand for alkaline salts in bleaching rendered these ashes no inconsiderable perquisite.

Sealing-money] Formerly it was the custom in Ireland for tenants to give the squire's lady from two to fifty guineas as a perquisite upon the sealing of their leases. The Editor not very long since knew of a baronet's lady accepting fifty guineas as sealing money, upon closing a bargain for a considerable farm.

Page 18. Sir Murtagh grew mad] Sir Murtagh grew angry.

The whole kitchen was out on the stairs] Means that all the inhabitants of the kitchen came out of the kitchen and stood upon the stairs. These, and similar expressions, shew how much the Irish are disposed to metaphor and amplification.

Page 21. Fining down the yearly rent] When an Irish gentleman, like Sir Kit Rackrent, has lived beyond his income, and finds himself distressed for want of ready money,[66] tenants obligingly offer to take his land at a rent far below the value, and to pay him a small sum of money in hand, which they call fining down the yearly rent. The temptation of this ready cash often blinds the landlord to his future interest.

Driver] A man who is employed to drive tenants for rent; that is, to drive the cattle belonging to tenants to pound. The office of driver is by no means a sinecure.

Page 22. I thought to make him a priest] It was customary amongst those of Thady's rank, in Ireland, whenever they could get a little money, to send their sons abroad to St. Omer's, or to Spain, to be educated as priests. Now they are educated at Maynooth.[67] The Editor has lately known a young lad, who began by being a post-boy, afterwards turn into a carpenter; then quit his plane and work-bench to study his *Humanities*, as he said, at the college of Maynooth: but after he had gone through his course of Humanities, he determined to be a soldier instead of a priest.

Page 25. Flam] Short for flambeau.

Page 26. Barrack room] Formerly it was customary, in gentlemen's houses in Ireland, to fit up one large bedchamber with a number of beds for the reception of occasional visitors. These rooms were called Barrack rooms.

Page 27. An innocent] in Ireland, means a simpleton, an idiot.

Page 35. The Curragh] is the Newmarket of Ireland.
   The Cant] The auction.

Page 40. And so should cut him off for ever, by levying a fine, and suffering a recovery to dock the entail][68] The English reader may perhaps be surprised at the extent of Thady's legal knowledge, and at the fluency with which he pours forth law terms; but almost every poor man in Ireland, be he farmer, weaver, shopkeeper, or steward, is, beside his other occupations, occasionally a lawyer. The nature of processes, ejectments, custodiams, injunctions, replevins, &c. &c. are perfectly known to them, and the terms are as familiar to them as to any attorney. They all love law. It is a kind of lottery, in which every man, staking his own wit or cunning against his richer neighbour's[69] property, feels that he has little to lose and much to gain.

'I'll have the law of you, so I will!'—is the saying of an Englishman who expects justice. 'I'll have you before his honor'—is the threat of an Irishman who hopes for partiality. Miserable is the life of a justice of the peace in Ireland the day after a fair, especially if he resides near a small town. The multitude of the *kilt* (*kilt* does not mean *killed*, but hurt) and wounded who come before his honor with black eyes or bloody heads is astonishing, but more astonishing is the number of those, who, though they are scarcely able by daily labour to procure daily food, will nevertheless, without the least reluctance, waste six or seven hours of the day lounging in the yard or hall of a justice of the peace, waiting to make some complaint about—nothing. It is impossible to convince them that *time is money*. They do not set any value upon their own time, and they think that others estimate theirs at less than nothing. Hence they make no scruple of telling a justice of the peace a story of an hour long about a *tester* (sixpence): and if he grow impatient, they attribute it to some secret prejudice which he entertains against them.

Their method is to get a story completely by heart, and to tell it, as they call it, *out of the face*, that is, from the beginning to the end, without interruption.

'Well, my good friend, I have seen you lounging about these three hours in the yard; what is your business?'

'Please your honor, it is what I want to speak one word to your honor.'

'Speak then, but be quick—What is the matter?'

'Nothing strange—The matter,[70] please your honor, is nothing at-all-at-all, only just about the grazing of a horse, please your honor, that this man here sold me at the fair of Gurtishannon last Shrove fair, which lay down three times with myself, please your honor, and *kilt* me; not to be telling your honor of how, no later back than yesterday night, he lay down in the house there within, and all the childer standing round, and it was God's mercy he did not fall a'-top of them, or into the fire to burn himself. So please your honor, to-day I took him back to this man, which owned him, and after a great deal to do I got the mare again I *swopped* (*exchanged*) him for; but he wont't pay the grazing of the horse for the time I had him, though he promised to pay the grazing in case the horse didn't answer; and he never did a day's work, good or bad, please your honor, all the time he was with me, and I had the doctor to him five times, any how. And so, please your honor, it is what I expect your honor will stand my friend, for I'd sooner come to your honor for justice than to any other in all Ireland. And so I brought him here before your honor, and expect your honor will make him pay me the grazing, or tell me, can I process him for it at the next assizes, please your honor?'

The defendant now, turning a quid of tobacco with his tongue into some secret cavern in his mouth, begins his defence with—

'Please your honor, under favor, and saving your honor's presence, there's not a word of truth in all this man has been saying from beginning to end, upon my conscience, and I wouldn't for the value of the horse itself, grazing and all, be after telling your honor a lie. For please your honor, I have a dependance upon your honor that you'll do me justice, and not be listening to him or the like of him. Please your honor, it's what he has brought me before your honor, because he had a spite against me about some oats I sold your honor, which he was jealous of, and a shawl his wife got at my shister's shop there without, and never paid for; so I offered to set the shawl against the grazing, and give him a receipt in full of all demands, but he wouldn't out of spite, please your honor; so he brought me before your honor, expecting your honor was mad with me for cutting down the tree in the horse park, which was none of my doing, please your honor—ill luck to them that went and belied me to your honor behind my back!—So if your honor is pleasing, I'll tell you the whole truth about the horse that he swopped against my mare, out of the face.—Last Shrove fair I met this man, Jemmy Duffy, please your honor, just at the corner of the road where the bridge is broke down that your honor is to have the presentment for this year—long life to you for it!—And he was at that time coming from the fair of Gurtishannon, and I the same way. 'How are you, Jemmy?' says I.—'Very well, I thank ye kindly,

Bryan,' says he; 'shall we turn back to Paddy Salmon's, and take a
naggin of whiskey to our better acquaintance?'—'I don't care if
I did, Jemmy,' says I; 'only it is what I can't take the whiskey,
because I'm under an oath against it for a month.' Ever since, please
your honor, the day your honor met me on the road, and observed
to me I could hardly stand I had taken so much—though upon my
conscience your honor wronged me greatly that same time—ill luck
to them that belied me behind my back to your honor!—Well,
please your honor, as I was telling you, as he was taking the whiskey,
and we talking of one thing or t'other, he makes me an offer to swop
his mare that he couldn't sell at the fair of Gurtishannon, because
nobody would be troubled with the beast, please your honor, against
my horse, and to oblige him I took the mare—sorrow take her! and
him along with her!—She kicked me a new car, that was worth
three pounds ten, to tatters the first time ever I put her into it, and
I expect your honor will make him pay me the price of the car, any
how, before I pay the grazing, which I've no right to pay at-all-at-all,
only to oblige him.—But I leave it all to your honor—and the whole
grazing he ought to be charging for the beast is but two and eight-
pence half-penny, any how, please your honor. So I'll abide by what
your honor says, good or bad. I'll leave it all to your honor.'

   I'll leave *it* all to your honor—literally means, I'll leave all the
trouble to your honor.

   The Editor knew a justice of the peace in Ireland, who had such
a dread of *having it all left to his honor*, that he frequently gave the
complainants the sum about which they were disputing to make
peace between them, and to get rid of the trouble of hearing their
stories *out of the face*. But he was soon cured of this method of
buying off disputes, by the increasing multitude of those who, out
of pure regard to his honor, came 'to get justice from him, because
they would sooner come before him than before any man in all
Ireland.'

Page 55. A raking pot of tea] We should observe, that this custom[71]
has long since been banished from the higher orders of Irish gentry.
The mysteries of a raking pot of tea, like those of the Bona Dea, are
supposed to be sacred to females, but now and then it has happened

that some of the male species, who were either more audacious or
more highly favored than the rest of their sex, have been admitted
by stealth to these orgies. The time when the festive ceremony
begins varies according to circumstances, but it is never earlier
than twelve o'clock at night; the joys of a raking pot of tea depending
on its being made in secret, and at an unseasonable hour. After a
ball, when the more discreet part of the company had departed to
rest, a few chosen female spirits, who have footed it till they can
foot it no longer, and till the sleepy notes expire under the slurring
hand of the musician, retire to a bed-chamber, call the favorite
maid, who alone is admitted, bid her *put down the kettle*, lock the
door, and amidst as much giggling and scrambling as possible, they
get round a tea-table, on which all manner of things are huddled
together. Then begin mutual railleries and mutual confidences
amongst the young ladies, and the faint scream and the loud laugh
is heard, and the romping for letters and pocket-books begins, and
gentlemen are called by their surnames, or by the general name of
fellows—pleasant fellows! charming fellows! odious fellows!
abominable fellows!—and then all prudish decorums are forgotten,
and then we might be convinced how much the satyrical poet was
mistaken when he said,

'There is no woman where there's no reserve.'

The merit of the original idea of a raking pot of tea evidently
belongs to the washerwoman and the laundry-maid. But why
should not we have *Low life above stairs*, as well as *High life below
stairs*?

Page 59. Carton, or half Carton] Thady means cartron or half
cartron. 'According to the old record in the black book of Dublin,
a *cantred* is said to contain 30 *villatas terras*, which are also called
quarters of land (quarterons, *cartrons*); every one of which quarters
must contain so much ground as will pasture 400 cows and 17
plough-lands. A knight's fee was composed of 8 hydes, which
amount to 160 acres, and that is generally deemed about a *plough-
land*.'

The Editor was favored by a learned friend with the above
Extract, from a MS. of Lord Totness's in the Lambeth library.

Page 81. Wake] A wake, in England, means a festival held upon the anniversary of the Saint of the parish. At these wakes rustic games, rustic conviviality, and rustic courtship, are pursued with all the ardour and all the appetite, which accompany such pleasures as occur but seldom.—In Ireland a wake is a midnight meeting, held professedly for the indulgence of holy sorrow, but usually it is converted into orgies of unholy joy. When an Irish man or woman of the lower order dies, the straw which composed his bed, whether it has been contained in a bag to form a mattress, or simply spread upon the earthen floor, is immediately taken out of the house, and burned before the cabin door, the family at the same time setting up the death howl. The ears and eyes of the neighbours being thus alarmed, they flock to the house of the deceased, and by their vociferous sympathy excite and at the same time sooth the sorrows of the family.

It is curious to observe how good and bad are mingled in human institutions. In countries which were thinly inhabited, this custom prevented private attempts against the lives of individuals, and formed a kind of Coroner's inquest upon the body which had recently expired, and burning the straw upon which the sick man lay became a simple preservative against infection. At night the dead body is waked, that is to say, all the friends and neighbours of the deceased collect in a barn or stable, where the corpse is laid upon some boards, or an unhinged door supported upon stools, the face exposed, the rest of the body covered with a white sheet. Round the body are stuck in brass candlesticks, which have been borrowed perhaps at five miles distance, as many candles as the poor person can beg or borrow, observing always to have an odd number. Pipes and tobacco are first distributed, and then according to the *ability* of the deceased, cakes and ale, and sometimes whiskey, are *dealt* to the company.

> 'Deal on, deal on, my merry men all,
>   Deal on your cakes and your wine,
>   For whatever is dealt at her funeral to-day
>   Shall be dealt to-morrow at mine.'

After a fit of universal sorrow, and the comfort of a universal dram, the scandal of the neighbourhood, as in higher circles, occupy the company. The young lads and lasses romp with one another, and when the fathers and mothers are at last overcome with sleep and whiskey, (*vino & somno*) the youth become more enterprizing and are frequently successful. It is said that more matches are made at wakes than at weddings.

Page 84. Kilt] This word frequently occurs in the following pages, where it means not *killed*, but much *hurt*. In Ireland, not only cowards, but the brave 'die many times before their death'. There *Killing is no murder*.[72]

APPENDIX

MARIA EDGEWORTH AND TURGENEV

SCOTT's influence upon Ivan Turgenev (1818–83) is well attested. It has long been believed, in addition, that the Russian novelist was influenced by Scott's own source, the Irish novels of Maria Edgeworth. This would be a momentous fact of literary history, if true, especially since the influence is said to date from Turgenev's first book, *A Sportsman's Sketches*, written partly in Paris in 1847–50 and first collected in 1852—the book which, as Turgenev believed in later life, had led Tsar Alexander II to free the serfs in 1861.

The source of this legend of Irish influence is unique and scarcely known—an anonymous obituary of Turgenev in the *Daily News* of 7 September 1883, four days after the novelist's death near Paris. Though now forgotten, the article passed into the currency of literary history by being quoted in part by Thackeray's eldest daughter, Anne Ritchie, in her study of women novelists, *A Book of Sibyls* (1883), where a quotation from it was added in the proofs of the book as a footnote (p. 140 n.). The obituary, which is ignored by Turgenev's biographers, is entitled 'Turguéneff: By One Who Knew Him', and offers a number of intimate details about the novelist's appearance and conversation. The following passage on his literary sources has not been reprinted since 1883:

Turguéneff was the youngest of three very distinguished brothers. Were the eldest of the trio now living he would be almost a centenarian. He remembered Bonaparte, Bernardin [de] St. Pierre, Talleyrand, Sir Walter Scott, of whom he was for some weeks a guest at Abbotsford, Miss Edgeworth when she was in the zenith of her fame; visited Madame de Staël at Coppet, and fell in with Byron as he was making a tour on the Rhine. The eldest Turguéneff was a many-sided man, though not a professional author. He had great literary qualities. . . . When he grew up he made wide incursions into English literature, and came to the conclusion that Maria Edgeworth had struck on a vein which most of the great novelists of the future would exclusively work. She took the world as she found it and selected from it the materials that she thought would be interesting to write about, in a clear and natural style. It was Ivan Turguéneff himself who told me this, and he modestly said that he was an unconscious disciple of Miss Edgeworth in setting out on his literary career. He had not the advantage of knowing English. But as a youth he used to hear his brother translate to visitors at his country house in the Uralian hills passages from 'Irish Tales and Sketches', which he thought superior to her three-volume novels. Turguéneff also said to me, 'It is possible, nay probable, that if Maria Edgeworth had not written about the poor Irish of the co. Longford and the squires and squirees, that it would not have occurred to me to give a literary form to my impressions about the classes parallel to him [them?] in Russia. My brother used, in pointing out the beauties of her unambitious works, to call attention to their extreme simplicity and to the distinction with which she treated the simple ones of the earth.'

The claim of literary influence is unsupported in Turgenev's published letters, where Maria Edgeworth is nowhere mentioned. Nor do Turgenev's novels offer any clear influence of a direct debt. It must be admitted, too, that the obituary is inaccurate on several points. Ivan Turgenev, the novelist, was in fact the *second* of three sons (Nikolai, Ivan, Sergei), and the third died young. 'Uralian' is presumably an error for 'Oryol' in central Russia, some two hundred miles south-west of Moscow, where the Turgenevs lived. But errors like these do not overturn the authority of the obituary, especially since the second of the two might well be a misprint. And the claim that the elder brother of Turgenev met Maria Edgeworth is perhaps confirmed in a reference to 'Mons Turgenief a Russian' in an unpublished letter from Maria to Sophy Ruxton dated 21 March 1831.

There seems no way now of discovering who the author of the article may have been. His account of Turgenev's character and conversation is deeply circumstantial, and its detail carries conviction in itself. One anonymous obituary is all the evidence we have of the most celebrated of all literary debts owed to Maria Edgeworth after that of Scott himself; but it is probably enough.

COMMENTARY

ABBREVIATIONS

Butler copy   copy of *Castle Rackrent* (1800), first London edition, with manuscript notes by Maria Edgeworth. See Appendix A in my Oxford English Novels edition, 1964.

ME   Maria Edgeworth (1767–1849).

Memoir (1867)   *A Memoir of Maria Edgeworth, with a Selection from her Letters*. By Mrs. [F. A.] Edgeworth, edited by her Children. 3 vols. (1867) (privately printed).

RLE   Richard Lovell Edgeworth (1744–1817), the novelist's father.

1800 A   *Castle Rackrent*—1st London edition.
1800 B   ,,   2nd   ,,
1801   ,,   3rd   ,,
1804   ,,   4th   ,,
1810   ,,   5th   ,,
1815   ,,   6th   ,,
1832   *Tales and Novels by Maria Edgeworth*, 18 vols. (1832–3)—2nd collected edition, revised. Volume i includes *Rackrent*.

(*Title*) (1) RACKRENT] Rackrent is extortionate rent; cf. *The Absentee* (1812): 'It is where there's no jantleman over these under-agents, as here, they do as they plase, and when they have set the land they get rasonable from the head landlords, to poor cratures at a rack-rent, that they can't live and pay the rent . . .' (ch. x).

(2) 1782] The year when ME, at the age of fifteen, settled in Ireland, and also the year of the new constitution establishing the Irish Independency.

Page 1. (3) PREFACE] Evidently written last, probably very late in 1799, and printed last, as the note to the Glossary suggests. The final reference to the Union of Great Britain and Ireland as a foregone conclusion is more difficult to interpret. The Act of Union was not approved by the Irish Parliament, of which RLE was a member, until the spring of 1800, months after *Rackrent* appeared; but it was raised as an immediate political issue in 1798 and actively canvassed throughout 1799. It received the Royal Assent on 2 July 1800, and the Irish Parliament was prorogued for the last time on 2 August. Cf. *Memoirs and Correspondence of Viscount Castlereagh*, vol. iii (1849), pp. 201 f.; and, for an eye-witness account of the last prorogation by a fifteen-year-old, Thomas De Quincey, *Autobiography*, Edinburgh (1853), ch. ix.

Page 2. (4) A plain unvarnished tale] 'I will a round unvarnish'd tale deliver,' *Othello*, I. iii. 90. Cf. p. 96.

Page 3. (5) pointing] pointing of *1801*, &c.

(6) the life of Savage] Samuel Johnson's *An Account of the Life of Mr. Richard Savage* (1744), later included in his *Lives of the English Poets*, had defended the reputation of his dissolute friend, 'a man whose writings entitle him to an eminent rank in the classes of learning'. Margaret Cavendish, Duchess of Newcastle (1624?–74) was the author of a eulogistic biography of her royalist husband, *The Life of William Cavendish* (1667).

(7) The author of the following memoirs] Old Thady, the character representing RLE's steward John Langan, and the only character in the novel who, according to ME's late account, was not imaginary. Cf. Introduction, p. vii and n., above. The transparent fiction that the novel is a 'memoir' edited by ME is maintained with fair consistency throughout, even to a note by the 'Editor' which terminates the novel.

Page 4. (8) Sir Kit] *1801*, &c.; Kitt *1800 A* and *B*. The name is misspelt throughout the 1800 Preface, and in both ways in the text of the novel itself.

Page 5. (9) Squire Western or Parson Trulliber] Western is the

hearty Tory squire in Fielding's *Tom Jones* (1749), Trulliber the
boorish curate in his *Joseph Andrews* (1742), II. xiv.

(10) of her former existence] *1832* adds '1800' to the end of the
Preface.

Page 7. (11) Spencer] Edmund Spenser (1552–99), *A Vewe of the
Present State of Ireland* (1596); *Prose Works*, edited by Rudolf
Gottfried, Baltimore (1949), lines 1561 f.; for the confusions in
Spenser's scholarly references in this passage, cf. ibid., pp. 329 f.
Spenser's *Vewe* is later praised in *The Absentee*, where a sensible
middle-aged English officer in Dublin recommends to the hero,
Lord Colambre, 'the works [on Ireland] which had afforded him
most satisfaction; and with discriminative, not superficial celerity,
touched on all ancient and modern authors, from Spenser and
Davies, to Young and Beaufort' (ch. vi). There is an unexplained
note on Spenser on the first fly-leaf of the Butler copy: 'Shooling—
law against v. Spenser'.

Page 8, note. (12) in this war] in his warr   Spenser, op. cit.

Note. (13) (this should be black bogs)] ME's interpolation.

(14) true and loyal to the family] Butler copy has a note on the first
fly-leaf quoting this phrase, with 'write a note on Loyal High
Constable'.

Page 9. (15) Moneygawls] Butler copy, *1832*; Castle-moneygawls
1800-15. The change conforms to p. 42, below.

Page 11. (16) He that goes to bed] The song, which is of unknown
authorship, is in its various forms at least as old as the early seven-
teenth century. Cf. *Rollo : or the Bloody Brother* (1639), a play of the
early 1620's by John Fletcher and others:

> And he that will to bed goe sober,
> Falls with the leafe still in October . . . (II. ii);

and Thomas Fuller (1654–1734), *Gnomologia : Adagies and Proverbs*
(1732), no. 6219:

> Often drunk, and seldom sober,
> Falls like the Leaves in October.

(17) flocked!] Butler copy; flocked *1800 A*, &c.

(18) it? Just] Butler copy; it, just *1800–15*; it? just *1832*.

(19) villains acted] villains who came to serve acted *1800 A*, &c.
The four words are deleted in the Butler copy.

Page 14. (20) herriot] heriot *1800 B*, &c. A payment, often consisting
of the best animal, made to the landlord on the death of a tenant.

Page 15. (21) 'learning is better than house or land'] Cf. Samuel
Foote (1720–77), *Taste* (1752), an unsuccessful comedy dedicated
to RLE's friend Sir Francis Delaval:

> '. . . as the old Saying is,
>
> When House and Land are gone and spent,
> Then Learning is most excellent' (I. i);

or David Garrick, in his prologue to Goldsmith's *She Stoops to
Conquer* (1733):

> When ign'rance enters, folly is at hand;
> Learning is better far than house and land.

Page 16, note. (22) Fairy Mounts] Two notes on the first fly-leaf of
the Butler copy may refer to this footnote, or to the next. See
Appendix A. In an unpublished letter of October 1802, written at
Sittingbourne on the way to Dover and Paris, ME wrote to her
brother Sneyd: 'Will you beg dear Aunt Mary to look in my bureau
for a note about *fairies* for Castle Rackrent. It is written in her own
hand—If she finds it she will be so kind to send it to Johnson   he is
going to publish a *4th Ed of Rackrent*.' The note does not survive.
The fourth edition (1804) did not appear for another two years, and
then without additional notes.

(23) loy] a narrow spade.

Page 17. (24) that my grandfather heard, before I was born long,
under] *1800–15*; that my grandfather heard under *1832*.

Page 20, note. (25) superiors, and tyranny] *1801* (third edition), &c.,
Butler copy; superiors, any tyranny *1800 A* and *B*.

Page 25. (26) handed her up the steps] *1800 B*, &c., Butler copy;
handed her the steps *1800 A*.

COMMENTARY

122

Page 26. (27) this heretic Blackamore] his heretic Blackamoor *1804*, &c.

Page 29, note. (28) Lady Cathcart's conjugal imprisonment] The story is told in detail in an obituary of Elizabeth Malyn, Lady Cathcart (1692?–1789) in *The Gentleman's Magazine*, lix (1789), pp. 766–7. She was the widow of the eighth Baron Cathcart (d. 1740), her third husband, when she married Col. Hugh Macguire, an Irish soldier-adventurer and fortune-hunter, in 1745. When she refused to give him her property and jewels he abducted her from their home in Hertfordshire to a castle in Co. Fermanagh, where he kept her confined till his death in 1764, when she returned to England, dying childless in 1789. Mrs. Thrale knew her, and Steele had described her in her nineteenth year in *Tatler*, no. 248 (9 Nov. 1710). Cf. Edward Ford, *Tewin-Water: or the Story of Lady Cathcart*, Enfield (1876). Ford, in an unpublished letter to ME's sister Harriet (Mrs. Richard Butler), suggests that ME may have heard the story from Lady Cathcart's bailiff, 'who had gone over to Ireland to bring her home—this must have been the very man who told Miss Edgeworth in 1800 the wretched state in which he found her'. An unpublished letter of 21 Jan. 1820 from ME to Mrs. Ruxton confirms this. But ME, in her letter to Mrs. Stark of 6 September 1834 (*Memoir* (1867), iii. 152–3), insisted that the resemblance was slight: 'There is a fact mentioned in a note, of Lady Cathcart having been shut up by her husband, Mr. McGuire, in a house in this neighbourhood [i.e. near Edgeworthstown]. So much I knew, but the characters are totally different from what I had heard. Indeed, the real people had been so long dead, that little was known of them. Mr. McGuire had no resemblance, at all events, to my Sir Kit; and I knew nothing of Lady Cathcart but that she was fond of money, and would not give up her diamonds.'

Page 31. (29) 'my pretty Jessica'] *Merchant of Venice*, v. i. 21.

Page 33. (30) aims-ace] ames-ace *1832*, i.e. ambs-ace, a double ace, the lowest possible throw at dice, or next to nothing.

Page 36. (31) vails] tips.

Page 38. (32) CONTINUATION] According to ME's letter to Mrs. Stark of 6 September 1834 (*Memoir* (1867), iii. 153), 'Sir Condy's history was added two years afterwards [i.e. after the composition of the first part of *Rackrent*]: it was not drawn from life, but the good-natured and indolent extravagance were suggested by a relation of mine long since dead.' See Introduction, p. vii, n.

Page 39, note. (33) white-headed boy] footnote omitted in *1810*, &c. The use of 'white' as a term of endearment is at least as old as the 15th century; cf. *OED white a* 9. As an Irish colloquialism it may have been influenced by Irish 'bán' (white), which is similarly used.

Page 45. (34) halfpenny] A note on the first fly-leaf of the Butler copy refers to this passage. See Appendix A.

Note. (35) as made me cross myself] Footnote omitted in *1810*, &c.

Page 47. (36) 'Plato, thou reasonest well!'] Addison, *Cato: a Tragedy* (1713), v. i. 1.

(37) 'Angels and ministers of grace, defend us!'] *Hamlet*, 1. iv. 39.

Page 50. (38) rate] *1800 B*, &c.; rent *1800 A*.

(39) hoped to find in you 'my father, brother, husband, friend'] hoped to find a—*1800 A*, &c. The addition, which is printed here for the first time, is from the margin of the Butler copy.

Page 53. (40) cut down a tree] A note on the first fly-leaf of the Butler copy probably refers to this passage: 'Tree—kitchen fire.' See Appendix A.

Page 54. (41) writs come down to the Sherriff] Years later, in an unpublished letter to her sister Harriet of 25 April 1825, ME congratulated herself on her picture of Irish judicial corruption: 'The state of our Sherriff-business will astonish the English—They will see that Castle Rackrent was no fable—It is impossible in some cases to color up to the truth—I shd not have dared to have represented Sir Condy or any of his tribe as paying £1500 per annum as hush money fees to the Sherriff or Sub.'

Page 55. (42) not half beds enough] A note on the first fly-leaf of the
Butler copy probably refers to this passage: 'No beds for servants—
they sleep in the day time.'

Page 56. (43) Gulteeshinnagh] *1810* adds the only new footnote
since 1800:

> At St. Patrick's meeting, London, March 1806, the Duke of Sussex said,
> he had the honour of bearing an Irish title, and, with the permission of the
> company, he should tell them an anecdote of what he had experienced on
> his travels. When he was at Rome, he went to visit an Irish Seminary, and
> when they heard who he was, and that he had an Irish title, some of them
> asked him, 'Please your Royal Highness, since you are an Irish peer, will you
> tell us if you ever trod upon Irish ground?' When he told them he had not,
> 'O! then,' said one of the Order, 'you shall soon do so.' They then spread
> some earth, which had been brought from Ireland, on a marble slab, and
> made him stand upon it.

(44) by this piece of honesty] The Glossary of *1810*, &c., adds
the only new item here:

> In a dispute which occurred some years ago in Ireland, between Mr. E.
> and Mr. M., about the boundaries of a farm, an old tenant of Mr. M.'s cut
> a *sod* from Mr. E.'s land, and inserted it in a spot prepared for its reception
> in Mr. M.'s land; so nicely was it inserted, that no eye could detect the
> junction of the grass. The old man who was to give his evidence as to the
> property, stood upon the inserted sod when the *viewers* came, and swore
> that the ground he *then stood upon* belonged to his landlord, Mr. M.

> The Editor had flattered himself that the ingenious contrivance which
> Thady records, and the similar subterfuge of this old Irishman, in the dispute
> concerning boundaries, were instances of '*cuteness* unparalleled in all but
> Irish story: an English friend, however, has just mortified the Editor's
> national vanity by an account of the following custom, which prevails in
> part of Shropshire. It is discreditable for women to appear abroad after the
> birth of their children till they have been *churched*. To avoid this reproach
> and at the same time to enjoy the pleasure of gadding, whenever a woman
> goes abroad before she has been to church, she takes a tile from the roof of her
> house, and puts it upon her head: wearing this panoply all the time she pays
> her visits, her conscience is perfectly at ease; for she can afterwards safely
> declare to the clergyman, that she 'has never been from under her own roof
> till she came to be churched'.

Page 59. (45) custodiam] a three-year grant of land made by the
Exchequer under Irish law to a lessee.

Page 65. (46) my dear] my *1800 A*, where 'dear' is accidentally printed only as a catchword; corrected *1800 B*, &c.

(47) 'The sorrows of Werter'] Goethe's *Werther* (1774) had been translated into English for the first time, incomplete, by Richard Graves (1779), a version often reprinted before 1800.

Page 71. (48) gripers] extortioners.

Page 72. (49) quit-rent] a rent paid by the occupier in lieu of services rendered.

Page 74. (50) tings] things *1804*, &c.

Page 75. (51) Sarrah] Sorrow, i.e. the Devil, a strong negation. Cf. John Galt, *The Provost*, Edinburgh (1822): 'Without a smith there was no egress, and sorrow a smith was to be had' (ch. v).

Page 77. (52) tink] think *1800 B*, &c.

Page 79, note. (53) childer] footnote omitted in *1832*.

Page 83, note. (54) taplash] washings of casks or glasses; dregs.

Page 87. (55) shawls to] shawls by *1800 A*, corrected by erratum, p. 182.

Page 91. (56) shister] *1832*; sister *1800–15*.

(57) gauger] exciseman, one who gauges the content of a cask.

Page 94, note. (58) tester] a silver coin, from French *teston*, derived from Italian *testa*, a head. Cf. Shakespeare, *2 Henry IV*, III. ii. 296; *Merry Wives*, I. iii. 96.

Page 97. (59) Mr. Young's picture of Ireland] Arthur Young (1741–1820), *A Tour in Ireland* (1780), had described conditions throughout Ireland in 1776–9, before ME settled there.

(60) Union] The Union was debated by the Irish Parliament throughout 1799, and finally approved by George III on 2 July 1800, some six months after the appearance of *Rackrent*.

(61) Warwickshire militia] A number of English militia served in Ireland in the 1790's during the French wars.

(62) to drink whiskey?] *1832* adds '1800' to the end of the post-script.

Page 98. (63) ADVERTISEMENT TO THE ENGLISH READER ... since it has been printed] The preliminary leaves, i.e. the half-title, title, table of contents, dedication, preface and the like, are normally printed last, so that ME may have shown the printed text of the novel to friends before writing the Preface and Glossary. Because of her hasty decision to add a Glossary at the last moment, and before the novel, the prelims of *1800* were swollen to the exceptional bulk of forty-five pages. The signatures are [ ]², a–b⁸, c⁶.

Page 99. (64) GLOSSARY] In fact a commentary and, as the preceding Advertisement explains, an afterthought, since Thady's narrative was already equipped with footnotes. For the printer's convenience it was printed before the novel in *1800 A* and in the first Irish edition (Dublin, 1800), and assumed its natural place after the novel in *1800 B*, &c.

In an unpublished letter to her cousin, Sophy Ruxton (7 May 1800), written a few months after the novel appeared, ME confessed that one of the notes was by her father: 'has Castle Rackrent ever reached you?—One of the notes in the Glossary is my father's writing.—Guess which it is—if you think it worth while'. Cf. Glossary, note to p. 40, above.

The device of a commentary is exceptional in the eighteenth-century English novel, but not without precedent: Beckford, for example, had furnished his *Vathek* (1787) with one. ME's example was later followed by Scott in some of the Waverley novels, where the commentary became a characteristic of the historical novel.

Page 100. (64a) he was answered by that of the head;] they were answered by that of the foot *1800 A*, corrected in *1800 B*.

Page 103. (65) sixty turkies] thirty turkies *1800*, &c., corrected in the margin of the Butler copy.

Page 108. (66) for want of ready money] for ready money *1800 A*, &c., corrected in the margin of the Butler copy.

(67) Maynooth] Minnouth *1800*, corrected in Butler copy and in *1832*. St. Patrick's College, Maynooth, in Co. Kildare, was founded in 1795 as the chief seminary for Irish priests, who had previously gone abroad to be trained. The chief benefactor was Edmund Burke.

(68) *to dock the entail*] This legal note was perhaps by RLE; cf. 129, above.

terms are] terms *1800 A*, &c., corrected in the margin of the Butler copy.

Page 109. (69) his richer neighbour's] his neighbour's *1800*, &c., corrected in the margin of the Butler copy.

(70) 'Nothing strange—The matter,] 'The matter, *1800 A*, &c., corrected in the margin of the Butler copy.

Page 111. (71) observe, that this custom] observe, this custom *1800 A*, &c., corrected in the margin of the Butler copy. Cf. *Memoirs* (1820), i. 70.

Page 114. (72) There *Killing is no murder*] There *killing is no murder*. *1800–15*, corrected in margin of Butler copy and in *1832*.

THE WORLD'S CLASSICS

A Select List

HANS ANDERSEN: Fairy Tales
Translated by L. W. Kingsland
Introduction by Naomi Lewis
Illustrated by Vilhelm Pedersen and Lorenz Frølich

LUDOVICO ARIOSTO: Orlando Furioso
Translated by Guido Waldman

ARISTOTLE: The Nicomachean Ethics
Translated by David Ross

JANE AUSTEN: Emma
Edited by James Kinsley and David Lodge

HONORÉ DE BALZAC: Père Goriot
Translated and Edited by A. J. Krailsheimer

CHARLES BAUDELAIRE: The Flowers of Evil
Translated by James McGowan
Introduction by Jonathan Culler

R. D. BLACKMORE: Lorna Doone
Edited by Sally Shuttleworth

MARY ELIZABETH BRADDON: Lady Audley's Secret
Edited by David Skilton

CHARLOTTE BRONTË: Jane Eyre
Edited by Margaret Smith

EMILY BRONTË: Wuthering Heights
Edited by Ian Jack

GEORG BÜCHNER:
Danton's Death, Leonce and Lena, Woyzeck
Translated by Victor Price

My Lady Ludlow and Other Stories
Edited by Edgar Wright

GEORGE GISSING: The Nether World
Edited by Stephen Gill

WILLIAM GODWIN: Caleb Williams
Edited by David McCracken

J. W. VON GOETHE: Faust, Part One
Translated by David Luke

H. RIDER HAGGARD: King Solomon's Mines
Edited by Dennis Butts

THOMAS HARDY: A Pair of Blue Eyes
Edited by Alan Manford

Tess of the D'Urbervilles
Edited by Juliet Grindle and Simon Gatrell

NATHANIEL HAWTHORNE:
Young Goodman Brown and Other Tales
Edited by Brian Harding

WILLIAM HAZLITT: Selected Writings
Edited by Jon Cook

HESIOD: Theogony *and* Works and Days
Translated by M. L. West

JAMES HOGG: The Private Memoirs and
Confessions of a Justified Sinner
Edited by John Carey

HOMER: The Iliad
Translated by Robert Fitzgerald
Introduction by G. S. Kirk

MOLIÈRE: Don Juan and Other Plays
Translated by George Graveley and Ian Maclean

GEORGE MOORE: Esther Waters
Edited by David Skilton

E. NESBIT: The Railway Children
Edited by Dennis Butts

ORIENTAL TALES
Edited by Robert L. Mack

OVID: Metamorphoses
Translated by A. D. Melville
Introduction and Notes by E. J. Kenney

EDGAR ALLAN POE: Selected Tales
Edited by Julian Symons

JEAN RACINE: Britannicus, Phaedra, Athaliah
Translated by C. H. Sisson

ANN RADCLIFFE: The Italian
Edited by Frederick Garber

THE MARQUIS DE SADE:
The Misfortune of Virtue and Other Early Tales
Translated and Edited by David Coward

PAUL SALZMAN (Ed.):
An Anthology of Elizabethan Prose Fiction

OLIVE SCHREINER: The Story of an African Farm
Edited by Joseph Bristow

SIR WALTER SCOTT: The Heart of Midlothian
Edited by Claire Lamont

MARY SHELLEY: Frankenstein
Edited by M. K. Joseph

ÉMILE ZOLA:
The Attack on the Mill and Other Stories
Translated by Douglas Parmée

Nana
Translated and Edited by Douglas Parmée

A complete list of Oxford Paperbacks, including The World's Classics,
OPUS, Past Masters, Oxford Authors, Oxford Shakespeare, and Oxford
Paperback Reference, is available in the UK from the Arts and Reference
Publicity Department (BH), Oxford University Press, Walton Street,
Oxford OX2 6DP.

In the USA, complete lists are available from the Paperbacks Marketing
Manager, Oxford University Press, 200 Madison Avenue, New York,
NY 10016.

Oxford Paperbacks are available from all good bookshops. In case of
difficulty, customers in the UK can order direct from Oxford University
Press Bookshop, Freepost, 116 High Street, Oxford, OX1 4BR, enclosing full
payment. Please add 10 per cent of published price for postage and
packing.